Government is a tangled mess that few people truly understand.
*How Our Government Really Works: Despite What They Say* discusses
how the United States Government works on many levels as
Daniel R. Rubin advises readers on how to understand
what's going on in the confusing jungle of power in America.
From checks and balances, the role of the three branches,
why government is as it is today, *How Our Government Really Works*
is a fine and insightful addition to political science
and history collections, much recommended.

**The Midwest Book Review**

By analyzing our nation's inception, the U.S. Constitution,
Supreme Court decisions, and the seemingly never-ending game
of politics that plays out in Washington every day, *How Our
Government Really Works* provides the reader with a more accurate
and insightful picture than what the politically-biased media
may want you to know. This book is a perfect educational tool
for understanding the complexity of our government.

**Brandon Stevens**
Student, New College of Florida
Sarasota, Florida

*How Our Government Really Works* isn't just a great read, it's a must-read
for every citizen of the United States. Daniel R. Rubin offers a clear,
non-partisan explanation of the U.S. government—its functions,
responsibilities and standards—with real life examples. In an age when
political parties and mainstream media spin seem to dictate the
information we receive, this book takes us back to the facts and reminds
us what we're all about and that we are all on the same side.

**Robyn Davis**
Radio host of "The Robyn Report"

I read the first edition of *How Our Government Really Works* in high school for my AP U.S. Government and Politics class and passed the AP exam because of it. Now that I am entering my second year in college, I still find myself referring to it to make sure I can see past the political rhetoric in the news.

**Dakota Whaley**
Student, University of South Florida
Tampa, Florida

I strongly recommend this book for everyone interested in learning more about American Government and Politics! My former professor's brilliant analysis of American Government is a must-read for every American.

**Zach Carroll**
Student, University of Florida
Gainesville, Florida

*How Our Government Really Works* brings Rubin's top-notch teaching to an easy to understand handbook on the inner workings of our country's government. With this book as a guide, I was able to score a 5 on the AP Government Exam!

**Dylan Chiodo**
Student, Georgia Institute of Technology
Atlanta, Georgia

In order for the longevity of a self-governing people to persevere, the People must be well educated enough to properly provide oversight over their government. *How Our Government Really Works* is a great read for anyone looking to understand the constitutional principles of our Government, and join the educated electorate.

**Dustin Ehling**
Student, University of Central Florida
Orlando, Florida

If students in my introductory classes were instructed to the level included in the book, time in these classes could be devoted to a more serious and complex examination of American government and politics than is now possible.

**Robert Crew**
Professor, Associate Dean and Director of the Master's
in Applied American Politics and Public Policy
Florida State University

This book will change the way you understand politics and allow you to see what really is going on in our government. It is not about ideology, it is about facts, reflecting a dedication to the truth, to the U.S. Constitution, and to our great country. Neither Republican nor Democratic, but all-inclusive, it is a must-read for students in a political science class, and for any American who wishes to be an informed voter.

**Andrew Micciche**
Student, University of South Florida
Tampa, Florida

In a time when "government" has been reduced to a political catch phrase, Daniel Rubin's book offers a thorough explanation of what the American government is and how it is supposed to function. His background as a lawyer enables him to present information clearly and concisely. His experience as a teacher gives him the ability to select which aspects of government are most frequently misunderstood. His savvy as a writer translates this knowledge to readers of any age from high school through adulthood. *How Our Government Really Works* carries particular importance this election year when sane voices are calling for an informed citizenry.

**Dr. Fern Tavalin**
Education Consultant
Sarasota, Florida

Instead of reveling in the bliss of ignorance or withdrawing
from politics altogether, we should take a look at Daniel R. Rubin's
book, *How Our Government Really Works.* Instead of staying home and
letting others rule over our system, Rubin recommends in his book
that we take the time to understand the puppet masters
and to find a constitutional way to cut the strings. I recommend
that you pick up Rubin's book to find out how to set things straight.

**John Louis Meeks, Jr.**
Florida Times-Union

An inspiring teacher, Daniel Rubin breaks down the concepts and
misconceptions regarding the role of government in our lives.
This book is a resource for students, teachers and anyone else
who wishes to explore how our government works
and how to engage as active citizens.

**Bernadette D. Bennett**
Educator, Sarasota, Florida

Sorry, Chris Matthews! Next year my A.P. United States Government
and American Politics students will be reading Daniel Rubin's
*How Our Government Really Works, Despite What They Say!*
This book provides an excellent analysis on how our government
actually is structured and provides clear definitions and examples
that make it perfect for anyone interested in learning how
the Framers put together our government and why so many
misunderstand how it is supposed to really work!

**Tom Fleming**
A.P. Government and American Politics Teacher
River Ridge High School
New Port Ritchey, Florida

*How Our Government Really Works, Despite What They Say* takes an in-depth look into politics. Daniel R. Rubin sheds light on the current state of bi-partisan affairs within our government system. The text stresses a need for informed citizens who participate in the process of civic responsibility while demanding the most from their elected officials. Political foundations and terms are explained and concise. This text is a comprehensive read into the critical analysis of how modern government was formed and is presently structured. Current political examples and the impact of modern day media are used to illustrate why the politics of today are failing us as a nation. Any and all citizens who would like to see a constructive change should read this for a better understanding of the status quo.

**Christine Braun**
Civics Instructor
Pine View School for the Gifted

*How Our Government Really Works, Despite What They Say* is an excellent resource for students, teachers or anyone who wants to understand the politics of today and how we got here as a society. It should be mandatory reading for any student of history or enlightened citizen. Do not listen to others explain your government to you. Learn for yourself!

**Michael Lamond**
Venice Florida
longtime co-host of "The Robyn Report"

A comprehensive look at the workings of our government, presenting complex ideas in an easy reading style, with up-to-date examples. It's a great reference and review for those teaching Civics and Government and for parents of students who want to know what their children are learning.

**Lynne Waller Remo**
Educator, Venice, Florida

Daniel Rubin provides an inviting, refreshing approach to understanding government in a growing complex political environment. This book is an excellent reference for my students. Perhaps it should be reading for our elected officials, as well— they could learn a thing or two!!

**Kristine Frailing**
AP Government and American Politics Instructor
Broward County Public Schools
Ft. Lauderdale, Florida

Clearly communicated with a causally written voice, Daniel Rubin succeeds in something most authors fail at: he presents complex material in an assessable manner. Direct and to-the-point, *How Our Government Really Works* offers a broad overview of its topic without getting buried in the minutia of obscure regulations, irrelevant court doctrine or burdensome vocabulary. This book should be required reading not just for the electorate, but also for politicians so they do not take for granted the office they hold. It is true, current, accurate and relevant.

**John Cornet**
AP United States Government and American Politics
Phoenix High School, Phoenix,Oregon

Daniel Rubin and his book gave me all the tools and confidence to discuss politics with my peers and to help others understand what is going on in our world. With most books you read in school, you don't remember them or use the information ever again, but I will use what I learned from *How Our Government Really Works* for the rest of my life.

**Heather Hoke**
Student, University of Alabama
Tuscaloosa, Alabama

# How Our Government
# REALLY WORKS
## Despite What They Say

### Daniel R. Rubin

Bardolf & Company
Sarasota, Florida

Bardolf & Company

HOW OUR GOVERNMENT REALLY WORKS
Despite What They Say

Third edition

ISBN 978-1-938842-19-1

Library of Congress Control Number: 2012945160.

Published by Bardolf & Company
5430 Colewood Pl.
Sarasota, FL 34232
941-232-0113
www.bardolfandcompany.com

Cover design by Shaw Creative
www.shawcreativegroup.com

Cover photo of author by Shellie Rubin

To Hashem,

my family,

my current and former students,

my fellow teachers at Venice High
and throughout America
who teach not for the money
but for the chance
to make a positive influence
on all students,

and to the founders and framers
that created the greatest nation
on the face of the Earth.

# ❧ Contents ❧

# ❀ Preface
## to the Third Edition ❀

With three national book awards under its belt, increasing numbers of students using it in AP U. S. Government and Politics classes
and college political science survey courses, *How Our Government Really
Works* is becoming a recognized work in the academic world. To make
it more user-friendly, I have expanded this new edition with appendices
of the Declaration of Independence, the Articles of Confederation and
the United States Constitution, as well as a more extensive index. While
it may appear that I have steered the book further towards academic interests, I am hopeful it remains popular with all Americans seeking an
overview of our democracy.

I recommend that readers frequently refer to the added documents.
By doing so, they will be less swayed by pundits proclaiming knowledge
of the Constitution when merely repeating talking points and narratives
that favor a particular political party or interest group. After all, when
is actual knowledge of the United States Constitution ever a bad thing?

Since the publication of the previous edition, events have continued
to shape American politics in remarkable, and often frustrating ways.
As we near another mid-term election, it is as important as ever for voters to understand the difference between facts, and rhetoric designed to
enflame passions solely for political gain. From a government shut-down
in October 2013 over the Affordable Health Care Act, to relentless Congressional investigations of the president, to revelations of domestic spy-
ing and encroachments on our personal privacy, much has happened;
yet remains the same. Public opinion towards a second-term president is

typically low, but the loss of faith in Congress to accomplish anything of significance is at an historic nadir; and the disgust with the dysfunction in Washington is matched only by a sense of powerlessness on the part of the electorate to effect positive change.

Our framers created a government with checks and balances in order to develop a vibrant democracy, capable of reaching multi-partisan solutions to the myriad of problems our great nation faces. Only through an understanding of our great system of government, why it was created and how it is currently being abused by political parties, interest groups and ideologically oriented, for-profit media, will we begin to appreciate the actual power we all still have as citizens—the power to change our government through the voting booth (and why it is critical that we protect every American's right to do so). As Thomas Jefferson once wrote, "Whenever the people are well-informed, they can be trusted with their own government."

I would be remiss if I did not thank my editor, Chris Angermann, for his continued support and splendid assistance in this on-going project. I also want to thank Barbara Farrar, who took on the task of creating and organizing a user-friendly index. In addition, I would like to mention that since the first edition came out, my wife Shellie and I were blessed with another grandchild. So, having a special reason for wanting the very best for America and our future, I want to recognize my grandsons, Moshe and Dovy, and granddaughter Hannah Rose. And finally, a heartfelt, sincere thank you to all of my colleagues and former students that have endorsed this work.

Daniel R. Rubin
August 2014
Venice, Florida

# ❧ ACKNOWLEDGMENTS ❧

This project can be best described as an adventure. What started out as an effort to update my lecture notes, became a mission to expand my audience to include concerned citizens interested in how our government is structured and how it really works, despite all of the political talking points and rhetoric that exists on the political street. Integrating all the material became a daunting task. Fortunately, I had plenty of help and encouragement to see me through the process, and I am grateful to all of the people who contributed to the journey.

I could not have completed this book without the able assistance of Chris Angermann, my tried and true editor and publisher. You have provided critical guidance, served as a sounding board for my ideas and helped to craft my manuscript to the point where it was capable of being read and understood without me in front of the reader explaining it further. Your assistance has been immeasurable, and without your help, this project would never have found its way to publication. Many thanks to you, Chris. You are the best!

My gratitude also goes to:

To Barbara Farrar and Bill Mowry. You took a chance and hired me to teach my first classes as an attorney turned educator. You both gave me enough leeway to develop my own style of teaching and offered me ample opportunities to shine in the classroom. I will always be thankful for your support, guidance and friendship.

To Joseph Newman. Your vast wealth of knowledge amassed while living in America for 100 years continues to astound me! You are the perfect person to discuss politics and American history. Your style of asking probing questions has encouraged me to sharpen my own opinions. I appreciate every moment I have with you.

To my parents, Jean and Phyllis Rubin, and my In-laws, Barbara and Marvin Goldstein. I appreciate your love and support, even though you could not begin to fathom why I would leave the everyday practice of law in order to become an educator. I know you are proud of me for this book.

To my sister, Ellyn. You are one of a kind. That is what makes you special.

To my daughter Aaryn, my son-in-law Dr. Ephraim Hollander and my son Nathan. Words cannot begin to measure the amount of love and pride I have for each of you! You are the "assets" in my life from which I reap dividends and benefits on a daily basis.

To my grandsons, Moshe and Dovy. I cannot help but smile whenever I see you or read about your recent exploits. One day I hope you will show this book to others with pride knowing that your Zayde wrote it!

To my current and former students at Venice High. You energize me and keep me on my toes. I eat and sleep curriculum because you let me know on a daily basis that I am having a positive influence upon you. When that stops happening, I will step aside. Until then, I will continue to dedicate my full efforts for you.

Last but not least, to my best friend, partner, companion and soul mate, Shellie Fay. We met when we were children, we fell in love as teens and we are growing older together. This is *your* project. Enjoy it to the fullest and remember that writing *can* be fun. I thank Hashem for giving you to share my life with.

# ❀ FOREWORD ❀

James Madison in the "Federalist Papers" said, "But what is government itself but the greatest of all reflections on human nature? If men were angels, no government would be necessary. If angels were to govern men, neither external nor internal controls on government would be necessary." But men are not angels. As Alexander Hamilton pointed out, "Men will pursue their own interests, it is as easy to change human nature as to oppose the strong current of selfish passions."

So try to imagine yourself listening in at the Constitutional Convention in Philadelphia in 1787, a gathering that included some of the greatest minds in the colonies. The Articles of Confederation, the original agreement between the states, was an abject failure; there was the threat of total disunity and even the fear of civil war between some of the states. The mercantile North had different views and needs than the agricultural, plantation-dominated South. There were even rumors that some states might seek to reunite with England.

Given that maelstrom of conflicting ideas, it is remarkable that the better nature of those great minds prevailed, leading to the proposal of a new form of government. Human nature wasn't changed, but humans chose to find a way to cooperate to carry on a common way of life to benefit everyone. Of course, it was only a proposal submitted to the people for ratification. It would be a year before nine states voted yes and it became the Constitution, but ratified it was, and the United States of America as we know it was born.

Much has changed in our country in the more than 200 years since its inception, and our view and practice of government has undergone considerable transformation. Just consider how the rights of women and minorities, virtually nonexistent in 1789, have grown. But the fundamental principles set forth by the framers of our Constitution not only remain intact, but have proven to be remarkably flexible in responding to those changes. At the same time, there have been, and continue to be, many misconceptions about the role and operation of our government.

That is where *How Our Government Really Works, Despite What They Say* comes in.

You will enjoy reading this book! In it, Daniel Rubin does what he likes to do most: teach. But fear not. His is not the kind of teaching that will bore you, but a narrative that will have you turning the page to read on. In a conversational style, Rubin describes for us the structure of our government as proposed in the Constitution. His approach is designed to promote increased interest and curiosity in the way our system works, and hopefully, lead to increased participation in it as well. In that effort he joins many others who seek to rekindle the spark of "We the people." Supreme Court Justices Sandra Day O'Connor and Daniel Souter in separate speeches have said that civic education has been sadly neglected and almost abandoned, and that, as a result, the realization of the responsibility to vote and participate in our government is also neglected. They both speak to how important those two activities are for the maintenance of good government. It has been asked, "If Washington is a city infected by fools and knaves, where did they come from and who sent them there?" Of course the answer is: We did, either by voting them in or by not voting and letting them get there by default.

*How Our Government Really Works, Despite What They Say* is an exciting story of the politics of our day that clarifies the issues and rhetoric surrounding them. There has never been a period in our history when people have not been affected to some degree by politics and government. Currently, we have two factions widely at odds with each other. One wants a small government and limited powers, the other calls for government to redress the maldistribution of wealth and to be big enough to do the things it believes need to be done. Each claims to represent "We the people."

While both are entitled to their points of view, they are not always right when they call on the founders and framers of the Constitution of our country in support of their causes. So we need books like this one to help us discern what is truth, ignorance and downright manipulation. As someone who has voted in more than one-third of our 56 presidential elections—I am betraying my age as a nonagenarian here—I have witnessed enough of our history to side with Thomas Jefferson, who once wrote, "When the principles of difference between the Republicans and Federalists (Democrats) is so pronounced, I hold it as honorable to take a firm and decided part and as immoral to take a middle line."

It behooves us to inform ourselves to understand the political process, participate in our democracy, take sides and make certain that our government is a government of the people, by the people and for the people.

Joseph Newman
Founder of The Nations Group of Sarasota
May 2012

...and that government of the people, by the people, for the people, shall not perish from the earth.

—Abraham Lincoln

I

# ❀ GOVERNMENT ❀
## Too Big or Just Right?

What is **government** and what role does it play in American society? How we answer that question depends primarily on our perspective. We can approach government with clear-eyed vision, through rose-colored lenses, or blinded by ideology and established, unquestioning beliefs. In practice, most of us like to think that our modern system operates as representative, democratic government—we elect people to *represent* us in making large-scale decisions that affect our lives. But what role does politics play in this equation? How do interest groups fit into this mechanism? We must appreciate these and other issues in order to properly understand and evaluate our government's actual function and its role in our society.

Many people feel that government is a *coercive force* and view it with skepticism and distrust. Some, who believe in anarchy or conspiracy theories, go even further. To them, government is an all-powerful usurper of personal freedom and liberty, and they worry that it can become an instrument of compulsion and destruction, stripping citizens of their basic natural rights and requiring them to conform to a set of rules, regulations and laws that are not in their best interests.

No doubt, the denial of basic fundamental rights *would* lead individuals to believe government is coercive—limiting free speech and freedom of religion, or favoring one religion over another, etc. Is American democracy a model that protects freedoms or limits them? From a comparative political science standpoint, other theories of governance, such as communism, socialism, and pure libertarianism, are inherently coercive. But democracy?

A historical perspective might give one pause. When the United States was first created, women were afforded no constitutional rights. A black slave was counted as three-fifths of a white man in the census. Native Americans had virtually no rights. Our history is replete with anti-democratic acts and practices, including fugitive slave laws, anti-Chinese acts, Jim Crow laws and racial segregation, poll taxes and literacy tests for voting, sedition acts, and the internment of Japanese-Americans during World War II. But as America grew more established, our society matured and recognized these measures as obsolete and unnecessary. Eventually, we may realize that the need for the Patriot Act, which curtails individual liberties, is also no longer necessary.

Not all coercion is necessarily bad. After all, the federal government has forced states to accept changes and reforms we consider positive when they likely would not embrace them on their own—for example, in elections, education and civil rights. So, while coercion is considered a bad word, perhaps *gentle persuasion* might be more acceptable. The latter suggests a view of government as *protector of individualism*. American democracy has had a powerful role as guardian of "Life, Liberty and the Pursuit of Happiness." Although inconsistent in the way they have applied these ideas, the three branches of government—legislative, executive and judicial—do provide safeguards for individual liberties (see the Bill of Rights and fundamental rights) through the passage and interpretation of laws.

By extension, government can also be viewed as the provider for "the greater good." Education initiatives assist the progress of reforms throughout the nation. The Environmental Protection Agency (EPA) enforces clean air and water requirements. Federal, state and local police agencies, including the FBI, work to prevent crime and ensure public safety.

Take it one step further, and government becomes the provider of basic needs in American society, from food for the needy (food stamps) to shelter (low-income housing, disaster relief) to medicine (Medicaid, prescription drug plans, and pure food and drug laws via the FDA and USDA). The reach of government extends to the workplace, where collective bargaining through the years has improved safety (through OSHA) and instituted minimum wage laws and 40-hour work weeks. Government also offers a basic safety net for retirees and the elderly (Social Security and Medicare).

Many of these policies and programs provoke controversy and lead to interesting questions. Does the government have the right to require people to get health care, as under the provisions of the Patient Protection and Affordable Health Care Reform Act, derogatorily referred to as "Obamacare"? And how does one define the role of government when it comes to promoting equality? What happens if the protection of basic freedoms differs from state to state? In the maintaining of order—by the National Guard and the Department of Homeland Security, for example—can the notion of freedom always be compatible with the need for social harmony and stability?

These are challenging questions, and how people answer them depends a great deal on their political points of view, whether they consider themselves liberals, conservatives, independents, or members of more modern political movements on the right (like the Tea Party), or on the left (like the "We are the 99%" Movement). Political ideologies determine with which lens we ultimately view the role of government.

We will discuss these issues and their implications in a later chapter. But to fully understand them and how they affect us, we also need to have a historical perspective. So let's begin with a look at how our government was formed and how its essential institutions evolved over time.

# 2

## ❋ ORIGINAL INTENT ❋

### WHY STATES' RIGHTS DID NOT WORK

We live in an age of instant information. Computers, televisions, Droids, iPhones and other marvels of communication connect us to people all over the world and give us access to knowledge at our fingertips. At the same time, we are subjected to a barrage of misinformation about our American political roots from many different sides. Political parties try to sway us into believing a version of our history most beneficial to their cause. Interest groups distort our origins as a nation to suit their purposes. The media sensationalize news in an effort to maximize profits. A frank and open discussion of what America stood for at its inception and during its development into a great nation is often "subject to interpretation."

It should come as no surprise, then, that many Americans are unaware of the real story of how our founders and the framers of the Constitution created our democratic republic.

Contrary to what many believe, especially revisionists and advocates of states' rights, our country was originally designed to operate under a governmental system called a "confederation" or combination of individual states with separate and distinct powers. So separate were the powers held by each state, that the notion of the United States essentially existed in name only.

## The Articles of Confederation

Following independence from England, our Founding Fathers, each maintaining loyalty to his former colony or "country"—which would later become his individual state—created a system under an agreement known as the **Articles of Confederation.** Reacting against absolute power of the British monarchy, they distrusted unilateral authority and opted for a decentralized government. Under the Articles, each state held powers exclusive of the other states and superior to the few laws that empowered a central government. Individual states maintained their own currencies, banking institutions, trade regulations, and militias. They had separate constitutions, whose provisions varied widely. The federal government of the infant nation had a congress that consisted of a single house, no chief executive and no central judiciary to handle disputes between states.

As a result, there was no coordinated policy to unite the country. Each state had the right to taxation, resulting in economies that were independent from one another. Trade barriers pitted stronger against weaker states, leading to further economic turmoil. Without a central government, each state was free to contract with foreign countries without regard to how it would affect America as a sovereign nation. If a dispute arose between states, there was no mechanism to resolve it, engendering lingering distrust, especially between states with geographic and military advantages.

These conditions festered for a period of 10 years. The confederation's weaknesses and deficiencies became painfully apparent when the debt incurred during the Revolutionary War had to be repaid to the nation's foreign benefactors. States like Virginia, which had a strong economy, were readily able to meet their war-related financial obligations, while weaker states, like Georgia, remained mired in debt. Recognizing the shortcomings of the Articles of Confederation was easy, but no efforts to replace them gained momentum because the stronger, wealthier states clung to their dominance and power.

It was not until **Shays' Rebellion,** an armed uprising in Massachusetts in 1786 protesting foreclosure laws, that the individual states realized the importance of a national defense. The revolt also drew attention to the glaring need for a set of uniform laws, provisions for their universal and equal enforcement, and a judiciary system that would provide proper remedies for disputes between states. When Shays' Rebellion was quelled, even the harshest critics of a strong central government had to admit that national institutions were needed in order to ensure the survival of the United States.

Ironically, after Shays and his followers laid down their arms, many of them ran for public office in an effort to change the foreclosure laws as members of the Massachusetts legislature, and they succeeded. This resulted in a general acceptance of the concept that armed rebellion is not necessary in America to change the rule of law and that elections would be a more suitable, bloodless alternative.

The movement to create the framework for a national government led to the assembly of the Constitutional Convention in Philadelphia in 1787. Its original purpose was to repair the deficiencies in the existing Articles of Confederation, but delegates soon learned upon arriving in Philadelphia that a move was afoot to fashion a new uniform and supreme government capable of launching and maintaining an army, providing for taxes, regulating and controlling interstate commerce and foreign trade, and arbitrating legal matters through a judiciary and a Supreme Court. The establishment of a uniform currency and founding of a national bank were also considered of paramount importance.

## FEDERALISM

The delegates met at Independence Hall in Philadelphia, Pennsylvania from May 14 to September 17, 1787 and created a new constitutional government for the United States. It was the first time in history that the concept of **federalism**, the sharing of governmental powers between a strong central government and its constituent parts, became embodied in a modern state.

From the beginning of the American Revolution, our Founding Fathers were students of theories regarding liberty and governance popular at the time. Especially influential was the "Second Treatise of Civil Government" (1689) by **John Locke**, the English political philosopher, which asserted that some individual liberty must be ceded to government in order to preserve the legitimacy of a community and its laws. Locke also believed that legitimate government must not only represent the people, it must also be *of* the people. Included in Locke's theory was the notion that juries should be comprised of citizens and that laws must be executed with the full participation of the community. Years after drafting the Declaration of Independence, Thomas Jefferson admitted that the ideas of liberty it contained originated with the theories in John Locke's treatise.

Another important 18th-century philosopher, **Baron de Montesquieu**, promoted the theory of a "separation of powers" between chambers of a central government in an effort to avoid concentrating too much authority in one political body. He also theorized that conflict between the two "houses" would lead to competition and result in the most effective, efficient and legitimate form of governance and legislation.

The genius of the conventioneers in Philadelphia was the appreciation of the views of Locke and Montesquieu, along with a healthy dose of a new American attitude towards governance, liberty and democracy. The framers of our Constitution embraced the notions of representative government and the relatively modern concept of checks and balances, along with the creation of a chief executive in the form of a president. The process was anything but smooth, however. In the sweltering summer heat, the delegates wrestled with a variety of ideas relating to the form of government needed to create a foundation on which a great nation would rise.

## THE TWO HOUSES

The first step was to create a legislature that would represent all of the people. Of course, "all" did not include everyone. Black slaves, indentured servants, newly arrived immigrants and women were not considered "people" at the time. Even whites that were not property owners did not originally merit full-fledged rights as far as "citizenship" was concerned. It was agreed, however, that the best way to establish a balanced, well represented government was to create a bicameral legislature. **Bicameralism** requires two distinct bodies of representatives with separate elections and obligations, each with powers to check and balance the other. Only with coordination and accommodation would the best legislation be created.

At least *that* was the theory. As any student of American history knows, three plans were considered at the convention: The Virginia Plan, the New Jersey Plan and the Connecticut Compromise. The last of the three, which ultimately was chosen, called for two houses of **Congress**: one would be a body of **representatives** consisting of members determined by the population of each state; the other would be the **Senate,** which would have two members from each state. Representatives from congressional districts would be directly elected by the **electorate,** and be responsible only to their constituents. Each representative would serve a two-year term.

Initially, senators were elected by state legislatures, but the passage of the **Seventeenth Amendment**, enacted in 1913 as a progressive reform, established their direct election by all the people of each state. Each term lasted six years, with one-third of the senators up for election every two years. The framers felt that staggering their elections, would result in a more cohesive chamber and provide legislative continuity. The convention delegates decided not to impose limits on the number of terms either members of the House or Senate could serve.

To emphasize how important the framers felt that the legislature be representative "of the people," the Constitution of the United States, after a brief introduction, immediately deals with the broad powers and principles of governance awarded to Congress. **Article I** sets forth the parameters for what we now take for granted as the role of the **legislative branch**.

The House of Representatives would have the exclusive authority to originate all revenue and tax bills. The Senate would, as with *all* proposed legislation, have the ability to shape and create its own version of a bill. Only upon the agreement of both chambers of government would a law be passed and then submitted to the executive branch for approval or rejection.

While the House was empowered to bring articles of impeachment against governmental officials, formally charging them with high crimes and misdemeanors, the Senate would act as the trial venue, holding the exclusive authority to decide on conviction or acquittal. The Senate would also enjoy the exclusive authority to **ratify** treaties and to **confirm** or reject presidential appointments to Cabinet and judicial positions.

Originally, the framers felt that Congress would be the most important institution of our government, with the House of Representatives closest to the people, checked and balanced by the intellectual and more prestigious members of the Senate. They reasoned that senators representing a statewide constituency with a term three times longer than a member of the House would naturally acquire a greater national image and profile. But the arguments of the proponents for a strong central government, particularly those found in the "Federalist Papers" (collectively authored under the name of "Publius"), left the door open for a clash of egos and wits among all three branches of government—legislative, executive and judicial—and the possibility that "power" was fluid, rising and falling based upon the times and personalities of those wielding it. Not surprisingly, the real names of the authors of the "Federalist Papers" were Alexander Hamilton, James Madison and to a lesser extent, John Jay, all framers who would play pivotal roles in the government of the new nation.

## THE EXECUTIVE AND JUDICIAL BRANCHES

**Article II** of the Constitution established the authority and responsibilities of the executive branch, led by a president. Determining the role of the president was a major sticking point at the Constitutional Convention, however. Still stinging from the injustices sustained at the hands of the British monarchy, many representatives felt uncomfortable granting one man the power necessary to fill the role as the nation's chief executive. It was only after considerable debate that their fears were allayed by the argument that the Constitution itself would provide adequate checks and balances by dividing governance between the executive and legislative branches. They were particularly pleased when Congress was granted the exclusive power to declare war. Requiring the president to face reelection every four years also dispelled some of the concerns that he would simply become another version of a king. The fact that the iconic George Washington became the first president helped ease such fears, as did Washington's determination to serve without wearing his military uniform, making it clear that he intended to be simply the first citizen among many.

**Article III** established the judicial branch, creating a superior or Supreme Court that would oversee a federal and state judiciary and become the ultimate arbiter in all legal disputes.

Perhaps the prime genius of the constitutional framers lay in their decision to create a government whose three branches not only provide a **separation of powers** within our government, but also have authority to exercise **checks and balances** for each other.

It is important to note that at its initial stage of creation the Constitution assigned each branch of government **explicit, delegated** or **enumerated** powers. Whether or not the original framers intended to leave it at that no one can tell with certainty. Yet, despite the fact that many modern political theorists and ideologues argue that this was the case, the courts have consistently ruled that there are additional powers embedded within the Constitution even though they are *not* explicitly stated. These are known as **inherent powers,** and it is important to be able to distinguish between them and those powers that are explicitly delegated.

## THE REST OF THE ARTICLES

Coming out of the Articles of Confederation era, the framers paid particular attention to regulating the interactions among states by incorporating federal control. In **Article IV** they set forth requirements that the states exercise full faith, credit, privileges and immunities among one another. The article also deals with the requirements for the admission of new states (the last time this provision came into play was in 1959 when Hawaii, the 50th state, entered the Union). Article IV further enumerates the powers of Congress to determine the fate of all public lands and territories and offers safeguards that insurrections within states or invasions of one or more states by another would require federal intervention.

**Article V** addresses the mechanisms of amending or changing the Constitution, either by Congress or the states. The only strict prohibition against amending relates to the composition of the U.S. Senate. In an effort to ensure compliance with the Connecticut Compromise, the Article insists that each state shall always have equal representation there and that the number of senators shall always remain fixed at two per state.

Because the Articles of Confederation failed to address the conflict between rich and poor states, the framers decided to put into **Article VI** a guarantee that all obligations and debts of the federal government be supreme to debts incurred by an individual state, and that all states would be collectively responsible to repay what the country owed for the Revolutionary War. This was a serious issue at the time because the wealthy states had already paid their share of that debt, while poorer states had not. To counter the fears of the latter that they would be controlled by their stronger economic fellow states, the framers asserted that the national debt would be everyone's responsibility, which leveled the playing field and assured all members of their equal footing under the new system.

The framers also posited the "supremacy" of all acts passed by the federal government regardless of current or future provisions to the contrary in state constitutions. Interestingly, following the passage of "Obamacare," many states led by GOP legislatures and governors proposed amendments to their state constitutions that would limit the impact of federal laws if the states disagreed with their application and interpretation. Once again, the framers anticipated this action and specifically stated in Article VI:

> This Constitution, and the Laws of the United States which shall be made in Pursuance thereof; and all Treaties made, or which shall be made, under the Authority of the United States, shall be the supreme Law of the Land; and the Judges in every State shall be bound thereby, any Thing in the Constitution or Laws of any State to the Contrary notwithstanding.

Article VI also addressed another issue important at the time. Many members of the Constitutional Convention referred to their home states as their "country" and maintained their allegiance to it accordingly. Because the framers worried that the new federal government needed uniformity and authority, Article VI requires all elected state legislators and governors, as well as federal officials, to swear an oath and affirmation to uphold the United States Constitution. Modern arguments, including those raised in incidents occurring in 2014 in support of state's rights pursuant to the Tenth Amendment seem to pale a bit when read in conjunction with Article VI of the Constitution. An example of a recent attempt to circumvent Federal Supremacy was the lawsuit by Florida Governor Rick Scott (R) seeking to allow his state Agency for Health Care Administration to oversee the often troubled Veterans Affairs hospitals and clinics in Florida. Despite such efforts, it has been law since the case of ***McCulloch v. Maryland*** (1819) that States have no authority to regulate or control Federal institutions.

## RATIFICATION

**Article VII** defines the requirements for accepting the new form of government. Nine of the 13 original states were needed to ratify the Constitution in their legislatures. But the process of getting there was anything but easy. Once the proposed Constitution had been completed, it came time to convince the nation that the creation of a new, powerful central government was essential for stability and prosperity. To do so, the framers promoted the theory of **federalism**, or the sharing of powers between a central government and the 13 original states. The idea of an all-powerful government capable of stripping states of their established power was a tough sell. That is why James Madison, Alexander Hamilton and John Jay wrote the series of 85 articles known as the "Federalist Papers" to argue for adoption. Still, it took the assurance that the new government's authority would not infringe upon the powers previously held by the states or the civil liberties of its citizens before state legislatures began to seriously consider voting for the new Constitution and a truly *national* federal government.

To accomplish this objective, a group of 10 amendments known as the Bill of Rights was drafted and appended to the Constitution, spelling out rights not fully articulated in the Connecticut Compromise document. Some of our most cherished American principles, including the guarantees of freedom of speech, religion and the press, and the right to speedy trials, were enshrined there. The concept of a Bill of Rights was already incorporated in some state constitutions, and many of the framers feared that without protecting these rights explicitly, the new national government would soon intrude irreversibly into the lives of citizens. Initially, a set of 12 amendments was proposed by a committee led by Gouverneur Morris of New York, but a re-worked 10 were approved and included in the Constitution that was presented for ratification to the 13 original states. As of this date, we have a total of 27 amendments, the last of which was passed by Congress in 1789 but not ratified by the states until 1992.

Although it took three years, by the time Rhode Island finally ratified the Constitution on May 29, 1790, every state had approved the document, and the *United* States of America was born.

# 3

# ✦ FEDERALISM ✦

## DOES "BIG BROTHER" PROTECT OR HURT US?

Politicians make a habit these days of accusing our federal government of being too big, out of control and purposely designed to constrain and steal the rights of states and individuals. These politicians also pander to their voter base by claiming that our civil liberties are better protected by each state rather than a "big brother" federal government. Most Americans are unaware, however, that the constitutional system designed by the framers *anticipated* having strong central government as the *only* way to ensure our civil rights and liberties. The tendency of individual states would be to operate solely in their own interests, returning us to the days of failure under the Articles of Confederation.

**Federalism** is actually a form of government where powers and resources are shared by a strong central government with the states and by extension with local government and related agencies. This allows for *unity without uniformity*—respecting the fact that one state's needs are not necessarily the same as another's, for example, snow removal in Vermont vs. beach restoration in Florida, etc.

## THE ROLE OF MANDATES

One of the ways the federal government accomplishes this is by creating programs that are directed and administered by the states according to

**mandates**—orders or requirements that force compliance by each state. But while mandates compel states to administer federal programs according to prescribed rules and regulations, they frequently allow for experimentation and modification to fit the unique needs of each state. They also encourage states to work together in cases of regional interests such as shared watersheds, evacuation routes, mass transit and economic concerns. Mandates may also help level the playing field between wealthy and poor states (via the interstate highway system or rural mail delivery, for example).

Mandates come in a variety of forms, and are either **funded** or **unfunded**. Obviously, mandates **funded** by the federal government include the benefits that come with **revenue sharing** when tax dollars collected throughout the nation are redistributed to individual states based upon need. Suffice it to say, they also often come with "strings attached." For example, the federal government might require a state to spend money on a local wastewater treatment plant in accordance with EPA guidelines or run the risk of losing other federal funds made available via revenue sharing.

**Unfunded mandates** impose federal requirements on states without providing financial support and incentives. They commonly occur in areas such as air and water pollution cleanup, services to illegal immigrants, services to the poor (education and medical care), inspections of nursing homes and hospitals, and auto emission inspections (in states with significant air pollution). Because unfunded mandates often put unwanted financial pressure on states, especially in light of balanced budget requirements, they are becoming a frequent source of irritation, as well as potentially divisive political issues. The recent efforts of states to curtail Medicare/Medicaid funding and related programs[1] and attempts to curb environmental protection regulations are just two examples.

Defining the role of mandates in the federal system clearly delineates the ideological differences between the major political parties. Republicans routinely urge restraint of the federal bureaucracy, viewing it as inefficient, wasteful and bloated. Democrats think that the federal system is necessary to even the playing field and to ensure that all states abide by national policy. While Republicans typically argue for less regulation, Democrats argue for more.

One of the favorite policies of Democrats has been air and water pollution regulation. Left to their own devices, many states would dispense with environmental protection laws in order to attract heavy industry. Many GOP governors and state houses have passed legislation to deregulate business as a stated goal, usually at the expense of clean water and air. If not for federal mandates, state efforts to seek economic advantages will always trump efforts to protect the environment—hence the push for a standardized environmental policy.[2]

When it comes to benefitting from the mandate system, states often act in inconsistent, some would say, hypocritical ways. Texas and Louisiana, for example, are two of the most conservative states in the nation, and they lead the fight against federal largess and excess, except when a natural disaster strikes. Then they jump to the head of the line and demand the full help and resources of the federal government they previously decried as wasteful and unnecessary.[3]

Shortly before Hurricane Katrina, then Republican Louisiana Congressman Piyush "Bobby" Jindal railed against the size and waste of the federal government. But as newly installed governor, when federal stimulus money became available for devastation relief, he was at the doorstep of the federal government begging for money. When federal stimulus money arrived in Louisiana, Jindal traveled around the state with large cardboard checks made out to needy programs, all the while taking credit for the economic handouts. He conveniently forgot that the money came directly from the federal government and the very stimulus fund he had vehemently protested.[4]

Although Mandates are a constant feature of federalism, most Americans cannot fathom the extent of federal revenue sharing and the role it plays in providing financial security for States. In fact, several States rely so heavily on federal revenue sharing, they would not be able to balance their own State budgets without assistance from the federal government. According to Tax Foundation.Org., 32.8% of all State general revenue comes from the federal Government. Mississippi alone receives 45.8% of its total revenue from the federal government, followed by South Dakota (41.5%), Tennessee (41.3%) and Missouri (40.8%).

So why all the political rhetoric about how revenue sharing is bad for America? Because like a fishing line tossed into open water, States needing revenue often bite the federal bait of needed cash and are reeled into complying with the mandates that come with "strings attached." And no State wants to admit to its citizens that it is controlled financially by the federal Government.

## FEDERALISM UNDER ATTACK

The very concept of **Federalism** has recently come under attack by opponents to the 2010 Patient Protection and Affordable Health Care Reform Act (Obamacare). In an effort to defeat President Obama's health care initiatives, 26 states filed federal lawsuits challenging the constitutionality of the act's mandate requiring Americans to purchase health care insurance. Republicans claimed that Congress cannot force Americans to buy something they may not want. They also asserted that under the Tenth Amendment, states have the right to be free of any undue influence by the federal government. Democrats disagreed. Lost in the debate was the fact that people who have no health insurance routinely use their local hospital's emergency room for basic health care needs without the ability to pay. Emergency room care is one of the most expensive types of care available, and in the case of the uninsured poor, taxpayers foot the bill through the administration of federal Medicaid funds by state.

This issue was finally resolved on June 28, 2012. In the matter of ***United States Department of Health and Human Services v. Florida***, (Docket No. 11-398), the Supreme Court in a 5 to 4 decision held that Congress has the constitutional authority to impose a public mandate to require citizens to purchase health care. Chief Justice John Roberts, writing for the majority, ruled that the mandate was really a form of a tax, and that Congress therefore has the express power to regulate it, regardless whether states approve or not.

The notion that the federal government should not have all of the powers it presently has is not new. States that claim they have a right to undo regulations made in Washington with which they disagree have their antecedents in previous centuries. In the early 1820s, proponents of states' rights followed the position of John C. Calhoun of South Carolina, who rejected the imposition of high tariffs on the states and believed in the right to nullify them. He and his followers even threatened to secede from the Union over the issue. The Nullifiers refused to acknowledge that the Constitution was the supreme law of the land and argued that the federal government had overreached when imposing the tariff. President Andrew Jackson convinced Congress to pass the Force Act, requiring reluctant states to pay the tariff invoking the **Supremacy Clause** (Article VI) of the Constitution. Jackson won that battle, but it took the Civil War—at a cost of over 600,000 American lives—to settle the issue of secession once and for all in favor of a union of united states.

Ignoring these historical precedents, modern Republicans have taken Ronald Reagan's slogan that the problems with our country reside in "Big Government" and made it their battle cry. Reagan wanted to create a **New Federalism**, wherein the federal government would establish funded criteria for needed social programs, but leave the details to the states. Ironically, as president, Reagan expanded the size of the federal government and increased our national debt (while raising taxes as well).

But because many of his supporters believe in the overall mystique created by him, some ideologues prefer to seek a system of **devolution**. In devolution Federalism is altered in a way that grants the states greater authority in their dealings with federal issues within their boundaries.

Many proponents of limiting the federal government insist that the language of the Tenth Amendment, which states, "The powers not delegated to the United States by the Constitution, nor prohibited by it to the States, are reserved to the States respectively, or to the people," supports their side of the argument. Yet, despite the language of this amendment, few Constitutional rights remain reserved to the states. The evolutionary expansion of the **Necessary and Proper Clause**, the **Commerce Clause** and the **Supremacy Clause** through acts of Congress and the president, along with decisions of the U.S. Supreme Court, leave little doubt where the actual authority lies in our system of government (see ***McCulloch v. Maryland***, for example). The narrow areas of power reserved for the states are confined to policies relating to education, drinking age, driving age, marriage laws, and state and local elections, and recent court rulings have begun to shrink those areas as well.

## OTHER ASPECTS OF FEDERALISM

There are some forms of **Cooperative Federalism** where state and federal functions overlap and the responsibilities for certain projects are split between the two. Examples include highway, school and hospital construction, taxation and police enforcement.

**Creative Federalism** allows States to experiment with social policies that may run counter to existing Federal law. Instead of maintaining laws and regulations that no longer are deemed necessary in an ever-changing society, Creative Federalism may be used to experiment or try out new options on a limited state-by-state basis. By granting States leeway to conduct such experiments, successes can then be adapted by other States and/or the federal Government, while the impact of failures can be contained and limited solely to the States conducting the social policy experiments. Examples include aspects of tort reform, expansion of Medicaid, and the creation of policies and regulations concerning medical and recreational marijuana.

There are also times when our federal and state governments operate two types of Federalism associated with baking metaphors. The **Marble Cake Theory of Federalism** refers to a mix of federal and state interests in one particular area of concern. Consider disaster relief, for example. Although the Federal Emergency Management Agency (FEMA) is in charge of disaster relief and coordination, state and local governments and agencies are also involved in the implementation. **Layer Cake Federalism,** on the other hand, describes clear and established differences between the powers of the federal and state or local governments. The name suggests that there are two separate layers of responsibilities that are distinct from each other. An example is the airport of the city of Venice, Florida, a small municipal facility. The city has control of the airport and its functions, but decisions regarding maintenance (and in the case of Venice, its very existence) are made solely by the Federal Aviation Administration (FAA). Thus, each level of government operates at a different, independent layer of responsibility.

When it comes to relations among the various states of our nation, the theory of **horizontal federalism** comes into play. We know we have 50 individual states, each distinct from one another. But we also know that as Americans, we can travel between them relatively unimpeded and accept that many of the laws of our home will be recognized and maintained in the other states as well. For example, driver's licenses and marriage licenses from one state are usually recognized as valid in the others. This falls under what is known as the category of **Full Faith and Credit** in which all civil laws are upheld and enforceable in all states. We further expect that our rights extend to all citizens and non-citizens alike. This falls under the category of **Interstate Privileges and Immunities,** which presumes that a state cannot impose stricter requirements on the citizen of another state.

Currently, there is one major exception to interstate privileges and immunities—same-sex marriage. Because the legal determination of what constitutes a marriage is currently considered a state matter, rather than a federal one, the issue of same-sex marriage is still undecided and remains a touchy area within horizontal federalism when it comes to enforcement throughout the nation. President Obama's declaration of support for same sex-marriage in May 2012 was couched in terms of being a civil rights matter, one deserving federal protection under the Fourteenth Amendment. The First Circuit Court of Appeals ruled in late May 2012 that the federal Defense of Marriage Act (DOMA) was unconstitutional as it denied those in same-sex unions the same rights and privileges granted to heterosexual couples, saying the law violated the privileges and immunities provided in the Fourteenth Amendment.[5] The issue was finally addressed by the Supreme Court in 2013 in its 5 to 4 decision invalidating DOMA.

There is a simple way to distinguish **Full Faith and Credit** from **Privileges and Immunities**. Full Faith and Credit applies whenever a law or state regulation is called into question, whereas Privileges and Immunities pertains whenever a constitutional right is involved. For example, it might seem logical that driver's licenses would fall under the banner of Privileges and Immunities—because driving is a privilege—but they actually come under the principle of Full Faith and Credit because the license itself is a product of a state law and/or regulation relating to driving.

When it comes to commerce and the Commerce Clause, it is important to understand the differences between **inter**state and **intra**state (see ***Gibbons v. Ogden***). *Inter*state refers to transactions *between* different states; *intra*state means *within* a single state. The issue becomes significant in determining the extent or limitation on the authority of the federal government regulating such matters. Segregation was the first major test of intrastate vs. interstate commerce. It happened during President Lyndon Johnson's Great Society legislation when the Commerce Clause expanded application of federal law against racial discrimination in lodging and eating establishments along federal highways (see ***Heart of Atlanta Hotel v. United States***).

The federal government can also impose taxes upon all citizens, regardless of their state residence. All taxes are considered **revenue** measures. Sales taxes, excise taxes, value added taxes, corporate and individual taxes, inheritance taxes…why do we have them? How do they work? Chief Justice John Marshall once said in a ruling, "the power to tax is the power to regulate." Keep in mind that all *available* federal tax revenues are redistributed to the states ("available" meaning those not committed to mandatory budget spending items, the military and the running of the federal government). Poorer states may receive more than they pay in, while wealthy states may receive less. This is **redistribution of wealth** as monies are made available on an "as needed basis."

An obvious example of redistribution of wealth occurs after natural disasters. In the early summer of 2011, massive level-5 tornadoes ripped through Tuscaloosa, Alabama and Joplin, Missouri. Entire cities were wiped out. Federal relief funds poured in to help and aid those in dire need, funds which the states affected did not have. During flooding and certain destructive winter storms, northern states receive federal aid, too. Many argue such a distribution is inherently unfair and financially irresponsible.

Former Virginia Representative Eric Cantor (R), when he was House majority leader, suggested this very idea during the tornado relief efforts in 2011, echoing the popular political mantra of requiring a balanced budget. He stated that any money paid to help the victims must be cut out of funds that had been budgeted for other projects. Most reasonable observers would argue that it is impossible to predict the needs of a nation as a whole, and that our federal government must have the ability to deal with unexpected events that affect its citizens. It is also important to remember that fairness is not equality. Fairness from a national point of view is that states get what they *need*.

## Grants and the Redistribution of Wealth

Whatever the impact on our national debt, shifting tax dollars back to states can come in the form of funded mandates, direct disaster relief or **grants-in-aid**. Such grants typically come with relatively few strings attached. **Federal grants-in-aid** come in a variety of forms. **Categorical grants** identify and target specific purposes and objectives with certain restrictions. These grants apply to particular categories, such as transportation, environmental programs, Medicare/Medicaid or education. There are two types of categorical grants. One is a **formula grant** where the cost of a project is shared by the federal and state government according to a predetermined formula (for example, 80% to 20%). The money will only be provided by the federal government if the state meets its share of the obligation, similar to a matching fund drive. Examples include constructing and/or maintaining airports, bridges and highways. The other is a **project grant**, where the entire cost is carried by the federal government, but implemented by the state or locality on its own. Typically, project grants are awarded to endeavors involving the construction of community colleges and universities, university research grants, or for health research.

Another type of grant, known as a **block grant,** is equivalent to a blank check. While the federal government identifies projects, it allocates money with little to no strings attached, leaving states to determine how and when the money will be used. This is perhaps the most popular of all federal grants. In general, conservatives widely favor the use of block grants, while liberals prefer project or formula grants wherein some powers are reserved to the federal government.

The federal government can use the dispensation of grants to place effective federal controls on the states. **Direct orders** require states to abide by federal laws, rules and regulations (and/or related agencies) or face a cut-off of funding. This threat can equate to millions of dollars that a state might lose, so it is quite a big stick for the federal government to wield. It is often utilized in the areas of regulating water and air pollution, and environmental cleanup. It has also been employed to ensure an end to racial, sexual and gender discrimination. Needless to say, its application is often controversial.

There are also **cross-cutting requirements** in certain instances. For example, the added requirement to hire minorities on a highway project according to federal standards would be considered cross-cutting because it is not part of the actual design and construction of the highway. Another example is a requirement that a workplace funded with federal dollars be drug-free. In other instances, **crossover requirements** are imposed when federal money given for one program comes with preconditions set in another. An example would be insisting that a particular state raise the legal drinking age to 21 or else lose highway funding on other pending projects. The requirement "crosses over" to the other project.

One area that especially raises the ire of politicians is the **total preemption requirement.** Under total preemption, states must comply with all federal standards and requirements imposed on all projects by the government and/or its related agencies. To clarify how federal preemption works, consider the relationship between a Varsity football team with its Junior Varsity squad. The federal Government is the "Head Coach" running the Varsity and the States are the Assistant Coaches running the JV. Only the Head Coach has the authority to determine if both teams will share the football field. If he chooses to take the entire field, the Assistants and the JV Squad must yield the Varsity exclusive use. The same goes for Federal Preemption. When the federal Government exclusively takes the field, the States have no right to be on it. Partial Preemption allows forms of cooperative or shared federalism, yet States are always under the sole authority of the federal Government. An example would be wastewater treatment plants, where states have no leeway in enforcing federal standards.

**Partial preemption** usually comes in the form of unfunded mandates which entail some federal requirements, but give the states some room to intercede, for example in the area of hospital and medical services to the poor, uninsured citizens and undocumented aliens. Partial preemption also applies to police enforcement of portions of the Patriot Act, which mandates initial investigation and enforcement by state and local law enforcement officials.

Perhaps there are reasons the framers of the Constitution never envisioned requiring the federal government to maintain a balanced budget. Unfortunately, political demagogues use the argument that redistribution of wealth is a "socialist" concept that should be proscribed in our society. Opponents of social relief programs prefer to have disaster victims look instead to the private sector to alleviate their suffering. But what are tax dollars for? What does it mean in the Constitution when it requires the government to see to the "welfare" of the American public? Many conservatives target redistributions when they involve aid to the poor or aged, but conveniently ignore tax subsidies to agribusiness, oil companies and petrochemical industries. Meanwhile, Democrats pander to the needy with promises of further entitlements in return for their electoral support. This is just another example of the clash between political ideologies and the demagoguery of our political system. It is another reason American citizens must learn how their government really is structured and how it is supposed to work.

Let's begin by looking at each branch of the federal government in more detail.

# 4

## ❈ CONGRESS ❈

### HOW DOES IT OPERATE AND FOR WHOM?

When people describe our system of government as a **democratic government**, they mean we all have a say as to who our representatives are. But the direct election of our members of Congress (including the Senate) does not mean that we have a **direct democracy** in which citizens have a say on every piece of legislation. Imagine what mayhem would arise if we all had the right to debate and vote on every bill and measure—what name to give to a stretch of highway, how much money to allocate to a study on the migration patterns of sandhill cranes, or whether to fund long-term NASA proposals for the exploration of deep space. Instead, we employ the classic **Representative Democracy Model** (Republican form of government), wherein we elect our representatives and expect (and hope) they act in our interests when dealing with legislative affairs. If we determine that we do not like their deeds or decisions, we simply can use the ballot box in the next election cycle to remove them from office.

Thus, under Article I of the Constitution, both Houses of Congress are primarily responsible for representing the public. Legislators' responsibilities include overseeing the **bureaucracy**—the non-elected members of agencies and bureaus that actually run the government—and building consensus for policy and lawmaking.

As mentioned earlier, the **House of Representatives** was designed to be the government institution closest to the people, with its constituency determined by population based congressional districts. Moreover, by limiting the terms of office to two years, the framers sought to curtail the powers of representatives. Voters would have the ability to remove and elect new representatives on a regular basis, if they wished to do so. The framers knew abuses of power would only be held in check by the implementation of regularly scheduled elections. They also recognized that restricting representatives' constituencies to districts based on population would encourage them to act on behalf of the interests of the voting public in order to stay in office. Although the number of representatives to the House changed over the years (as have the requisite population numbers), it currently (and perhaps from now on) will remain set at 435.

To keep that number constant, the House adjusts the number of members for each state from time to time. This process, known as **reapportionment,** divides the 435 seats among the 50 states based on the population figures collected during the **census**, which is conducted every 10 years. Based on the U.S. Census Bureau and the 2010 census, congressional seats for each state were reapportioned as follows:

Accordingly, reapportionment affecting representation in the House by changes in population were as follows: Massachusetts −1; New York −2; New Jersey −1; Pennsylvania −1, South Carolina +1; Georgia +1; Florida +2; Ohio −2; Michigan −1; Louisiana −1; Missouri −1; Illinois −1; Iowa −1; Texas +4; Arizona +1; Utah +1; Washington +1; Nevada +1.

The continuing trend of population shifts will result in demographic changes that not only affect the House of Representatives, but also the number of electors allotted in the Electoral College (see Chapter 11), as well as the affiliation to political parties by regions of the country.

Unlike the House, the **Senate** was not originally designed for its members to be elected by the public. Instead, the framers felt it necessary that the "elites" or "propertied" voters who held statewide office select their two members of the Senate. As a result, the influence of local party bosses and patronage issues clouded the selection of senators. These abuses led to the passage of the **Seventeenth Amendment** to the Constitution in 1913, which required senators to be *directly elected* by voters of each state, just like members of the House. Since 1959, when Hawaii became the 50th state in the Union, membership in the U.S. Senate has remained steady at 100.

Because there are only two senators per state, their constituency is considered to be "at-large," or across the state rather than within designated districts based upon population. The framers felt that this arrangement would make senators better able to deal with matters of national importance rather than local issues. In addition, since they are elected to **six-year** terms of office, they would be more capable of establishing the strong and lasting ties necessary to contend with concerns that affected the country as a whole. Thus, they were given the authority to review and ratify treaties.

Under Article I of the Constitution, the **Senate** has exclusive power to confirm presidential nominations by a **simple 51% majority**. Nominations by the president include appointments to the Supreme Court, the Cabinet, federal district judges, ambassadors, U.S. marshals, and most federal department chairs.

In the case of federal judges, the Senate has a custom known as **senatorial courtesy**, which allows it to give the president input on naming potential nominees to the U.S. district bench. The president may consult with those members of the Senate whose states are affected by an opening in a federal district. George Washington himself proclaimed that senatorial courtesy was simply a courtesy and not required of the president when choosing appointees. But by allowing the Senate to have input into the nomination process, the president will also then expect support from those same Senators when the actual nominee faces confirmation. In the case of nominees to the Supreme Court of the United States, although the Senate must confirm them, no senatorial courtesy is involved in their selection.

The president may also bring **treaties** to the Senate for exclusive **ratification,** requiring **a two-thirds vote** majority. This falls under the constitutional principle of "Advise and Consent."

The House of Representatives also has exclusive responsibilities under Article I, notably "the power of the purse," which includes all measures relating to the federal budget, including the collection of **revenue** (taxes) and **appropriations** (spending). All financial bills must be initiated in the House, although the Senate has to approve them, too, before they can go to the president to be signed into law. In order to accomplish this requirement, the House maintains a **standing committee** (one that always exists) known as the **Ways and Means Committee**. Because this committee deals with income for the federal government, it is obviously one of the most important and powerful committees in all of Congress. The House also has the equally important standing committee known as the **Appropriations Committee**, which decides the nation's budget expenditures.

When it comes to **impeachment**—a formal process to deal with unlawful activity by the president and federal officials—the two chambers of Congress share responsibility. The House brings charges of "Treason, Bribery or High Crimes and Misdemeanors"—or Articles of Impeachment—by a simple majority vote. The Senate hosts the impeachment trials with the Chief Justice of the Supreme Court presiding when the accused is the president. Conviction requires a two-thirds vote. In our history, only two presidents have been impeached, and both were ultimately acquitted in the Senate.

Impeachment proceedings against presidents are typically politically based. Andrew Johnson was impeached by the Radical Republicans in Congress following the Civil War and was acquitted by a single vote. President Clinton was impeached for lying about an affair with Monica Lewinsky, a White House intern, by a Republican-controlled House in an effort to delegitimize his presidency, and was acquitted by a substantial margin in a Democrat-controlled Senate. Richard Nixon did not wait for the House to impeach him in matters related to the Watergate Affair and, in all likelihood, for the Senate to convict him, becoming the first U.S. president to ever resign in office.

It is perhaps easiest to compare the differences in the nature of the offices between the House of Representatives and the Senate by listing them alongside each other and then breaking them down accordingly.

| HOUSE | SENATE |
|---|---|
| Two-year term | Six-year term |
| 435 members | 100 members |
| Congr. district based upon equal population | State-wide, not based upon equal population |
| Smaller constituency | Larger constituency |
| Rules Committee | No Rules Committee |
| Strict rules | Flexible and few rules |

| HOUSE | SENATE |
|---|---|
| Debate determined by Rules Committee | Unlimited debate |
| Policy staff specialists | Policy staff generalists |
| Powerful committee chairs | Fewer powerful committee chairs |
| Less prestige | Greater prestige |
| Riders to bills not allowed | Riders allowed |
| Less media coverage | Greater media coverage |
| Closed rules w/no amendments to bills | Amendments allowed (see riders) |
| Closer to the people of district | Closer to national constituency |
| No power review and ratify treaties | Power to review and ratify treaties |
| All appropriation bills start here | Amendments only on budget bills |
| More committees | Fewer committees |

## CONGRESSIONAL BILLS

Congress operates using a traditional system of committees based upon rules established by its leadership. In general, bills originate within committees specifically designed to deal with their area of concern. In other words, appropriation bills originate in the Appropriations Committee; bills relating to the military originate in the Armed Services Committee, banking in the Banking Committee, environmental issues in the Environmental Committee, etc.

All non-revenue legislation begins in a House or Senate subcommittee that specifically deals with the areas of concern addressed in proposed bills. Each committee creates subcommittees more "specialized" in knowledge and expertise regarding the areas contemplated by a particular bill. Subcommittee meetings deal with all aspects of a bill, down to its most minute details, including how it would affect other legislation and how it would be implemented and enforced.

Perhaps the most powerful House committee is the **Rules Committee**. Composed of those members who have the most leadership seniority in their respective political party, it sets the timeframe for all debate and voting on proposed legislation and also determines whether any amendments to the proposed bill will be allowed for consideration by the entire House. The makeup of the Rules Committee always overwhelmingly favors the current majority party.

In the event the Rules Committee decides to advance a bill for consideration, it does so under the **open rule** or the **closed rule.** All open rule bills may be amended; closed rule bills may not. Open or closed rules can also determine the amount of debate allowed on a bill, should it make it out of committee for a vote by the full House.

Since the Senate does not have a Rules Committee empowered to regulate the process of legislative creation, all its bills may have **riders** and/or amendments attached. Riders are additions to bills that are not germane to the original area of concern of the proposed bill. For example, a rider that proposed legislation requiring the building of the Keystone Pipeline from Canada to Texas was attached to a bill dealing with an extension of payroll tax cuts and Medicare rates during the 2012 session of Congress.[6]

Besides determining how debates on the floor of the House are conducted, the Rules Committee also controls the calendar of the House, and the scheduling of committee meetings, presentations or investigations. It may also require a **quorum** of representatives, meaning a simple majority, be physically present in House chambers before a formal vote may be taken on a proposed measure. Calls for a quorum happen rarely, however, as House leadership usually makes sure it has the required number of members present before scheduling a vote.

When a bill is in committee, it is either prepared to be pushed forward into the legislative process by its sponsors and the congressional leadership, or it remains there to suffer a slow death. To **pigeonhole** a bill means forcing it to die in subcommittee or committee without further consideration, affording it no chance of ever making it to the floor for a vote. Most bills are pigeonholed and are never seriously considered to be passed into law. One way to ensure a bill does get out of committee and to the floor for a full vote is to utilize what is known as a **discharge petition**. If supported and approved by a simple majority of the committee, such a petition will force the bill out of committee to the floor for full voting consideration over the objection of those opposed to it. More recently, conservatives criticized Hurricane Sandy aid in late 2012 and the proposed immigration reform bills of 2013 as laden with unnecessary pork barrel spending.

**Christmas tree bills** are those loaded down with many amendments and/or riders in the form of **earmarks**, also known as **pork barrel projects**, which represent additional spending on plans designed to benefit the home state of a particular legislator. Although the Troubled Asset Relief Program (TARP) passed into law in 2008 under President Bush is now criticized as "sinful and wasteful spending" by members of Congress, at the time representatives of both political parties were happy to load up the legislation with pork barrel projects galore.

Trading of interests in the form of pork barrel projects or earmarks is known as **logrolling.** The name refers to two men on a spinning log in a stream who must work together or they will both fall off and into the water. In Congress, logrolling happens when legislators gather votes for their pet projects by promising others to support their projects. It is a classic example of "I scratch your back, you scratch mine." Political favors and debts are how the system really works.

After a bill has been debated on the floor of the Senate or the House, it only requires a simple majority to pass. The process can be quite lengthy, though, especially if the bill is controversial or legislators tack on a number of amendments and riders. As a result, there are ways to limit or cut off debate in both chambers of Congress.

In the House, the Rules Committee has the authority to limit debate. In the Senate there is no such mechanism because of the **filibuster** (from the word "filibustro" or "buccaneer'). Created by Senate rules, a filibuster is a parliamentary procedure that permits unlimited debate and allows a minority to hold up legislation or a presidential nomination indefinitely. The only way to stop it from taking effect is to invoke **cloture.** This currently requires **60 votes** or a **supermajority** in most instances. In the event the cloture vote is successful, the Senate will have no more than 30 hours to debate the bill before a full vote must be taken. As a result, just having a majority of votes is not enough to carry the day, and accommodations must be made to ensure a floor vote on a particular bill or a nomination.

A filibuster is one of the most effective ways to force a bill, nomination or treaty off the floor to face a slow death back in committee by causing all Senate business to come to a screeching halt, making it a potentially dangerous mechanism available to the minority party. The use of the filibuster to block the confirmation of a presidential nominee is also known as the **nuclear option.**

In the summer of 2011, Senate Minority Leader Mitch McConnell, a Republican from Kentucky, boldly stated his Republican conference would not vote to confirm *any* nominee to the recently created Consumer Financial Protection Bureau (CFPB) because the Democrats passed the laws that created the agency over strong GOP opposition. McConnell and his fellow Republicans opposed the bureau because it was to be headed by one individual, while they preferred a controlling board led by several members. That way they could choose a board which would ensure regulations in line with those desired by Congress and not simply authorized by the act that created the bureau. McConnell made good on this pledge on December 7, 2011 when the Senate Republicans exercised the nuclear option and refused to allow a vote on the nomination of Richard Cordray as the new bureau chief.[7]

When opponents of President Obama point out that nothing was accomplished during his first six years in office, although his party had control of both chambers, and therefore his presidency must be labeled a "failure," they conveniently ignore certain realities at the time. Although the Democrats had a majority in both chambers, they often could not muster enough votes in the Senate for a supermajority—60 votes—to overcome the Republicans' threats of filibuster. Nowadays, minority parties all too often use the filibuster to "lock down" the Senate and block the president and his party from realizing policies in the form of legislation or appointments, all the while taking advantage of the public's ignorance of the fact that only cloture and a supermajority confer actual control of the Senate.

Thus, all presidential appointments to the federal judiciary—during both the George W. Bush and Barack Obama administrations—were subject to obstruction by the minority. Finally, in November 2013, Senate Majority Leader Harry Reid obtained a vote to alter the supermajority cloture requirement, lowering the number to confirm presidential judiciary appointments to a simple majority of 51 votes. It is important to note that this Senate cloture rule change affects only presidential confirmations for the federal judiciary, U.S. attorneys, federal marshals and Executive Branch appointments. It does not apply to appointments to the United States Supreme Court or any legislative bills proposed in the Senate.

## HOUSE AND SENATE CHECKS AND BALANCES

Despite the recent gridlock in Congress and politicians taking advantage of procedural means to prevent anything getting done, there can be no denying that the framers provided a remarkably effective blueprint for creating legislation. It ensures that any measure discussed, debated and eventually voted into law is subject to a system of **checks and balances** between the House and the Senate. Any non-revenue legislation proposed, regardless of which chamber of Congress initiates it, must be approved in exactly the same language by both. To accomplish that, a **Conference Committee** comprised of members of originating committees from the House and Senate is convened to hammer out any differences between the proposed bills in an effort to create a final version for full consideration and passage by both legislative bodies.

This process of joint negotiation, compromise and drafting language accordingly is called the **mark-up** stage. Once a bill is **marked up**, it cannot be amended in any way. It is now in its final form and ready for submission for approval by both chambers. Once it passes both the House and Senate, it goes to the White House for the president's signature to become law. Further checks and balances mechanisms exist at that stage, as the president has the power to ignore the legislation and allow it to become law without his signature, or to reject it by using his **veto power** (for a more detailed discussion of this, see Chapter 6). A further check and balance exists in the form of judicial review, in which the final arbiter, the Supreme Court, rules whether or not a law is constitutional.

## CONGRESSIONAL COMMITTEES

Because the committee system is so important to getting things done in Congress, it has evolved into a complex network. In both the House and Senate, committees are defined as either **standing, exclusive, joint** or **select**. Each plays a significant role in the legislative process. **Standing** committees are **permanent** specialized committees that exist in every session of both chambers of Congress. Currently there are 18 such committees in the House and 20 committees in the Senate. Examples include the already mentioned House Ways and Means Committee and the House National Security Committee. The Senate's standing committees include the Judiciary Committee, Senate Armed Services Committee, Homeland Security and Governmental Affairs Committee, Senate Committee on Foreign Relations, and the Senate Finance Committee.

**Joint committees** are made up of members from both the House and the Senate. They don't have legislative powers and usually do not initiate bills. Their purpose is to conduct investigations or generate non-binding resolutions to make political statements for public relations purposes. Joint committees are usually formed in the areas of the economy and taxation. A current example would be the recent Simpson-Bowles committee, where former and current members of Congress attempted to work out a deficit reduction plan.

**Select committees** are created to address specific issues and are therefore considered **temporary** in nature. They are often called on to investigate specific political abuses. Past examples include the House Watergate Committee, the Senate Committee on Unfair Campaign Practices and the Iran-Contra Select Committee.

**Conference committees** have been mentioned already as a mechanism for both houses to meet and work out the differences in content and language between bills passed by both chambers.

The House divides its committees into three categories: **exclusive, major** and **non-major.** Only the Ways and Means Committee, the Appropriations Committee and the Rules Committee are considered exclusive because their members *cannot serve* on any other committee. This is one of the few rules that ensures ethical and fair play in Congress, as no one in the exclusive committees can potentially influence legislation in other committees by promising spending and/or taxation benefits to its members.

**Major committees** deal with important national issues, such as national security. **Non-major committees** are concerned with day-to-day issues. An example would be the Small Business Committee. Members of a major committee may only serve on two non-major committees. Members of non-major committees may serve on as many as three.

The House has more committees than the Senate because representatives have to deal with a myriad of issues that affect their local constituency. That includes assisting with problems their electorate brings to them, collectively known as a representative's **case-load**. As a result, committees and related subcommittees attract members that share common interests related to their communities. Representatives from farming states, for example, will gravitate toward an agriculturally related committee, while legislators from states with large urban areas and heavy commuter traffic are likely to favor committees that deal with transportation issues.

Senate committees, on the other hand, are far more generalized in their approach—making it possible for senators to serve on more committees than their House counterparts—and their staffs are not nearly as large as those of House committees.

Regardless of interest, however, the political party holding a majority and a controlling number of seats in the House or Senate will determine who chairs each committee. At the same time, party affiliation will *almost always* determine how members of committees vote on issues.

## CONGRESSIONAL OVERSIGHT

A significant power granted under Article I of the Constitution is **congressional oversight**. Committees review bureaucratic agencies and bureaus to ensure they are implementing laws according to the intent or policy of the legislature that created them. They will also meet to review the efficiency or shortcomings of legislation after it has been passed and handed off for implementation and enforcement by the governmental bureaucracy. Not every bill is perfect and may need to be "tweaked" in order to maximize its effect. As a result, additional bills may be enacted to rectify problems, clarify certain aspects of the original bill or make its administration more efficient.

Overall, congressional committees have broad powers. They may create rules as they relate to the administration of laws (a further check and balance on the executive branch); they have influence on budget issues related to their committee's focus; and they can initiate investigations in an effort to provide adequate oversight of all related bureaucratic agencies. Each committee has the ability to **subpoena** or compel witnesses to appear at its sessions, provided there is a legitimate legislative purpose. A *subpoena duces tecum* is an order to compel not only a witness to appear, but to also bring along documents the committee may wish to review. Failure to appear before a committee after being subpoenaed can lead to being cited with **contempt of Congress** and may result in a fine and jail time.

Congressional committees may compel witnesses to testify, however, only if they grant them **use** or **transactional** immunity. By doing so, they protect witnesses against prosecution for wrongdoings they disclose to the investigating committee. In the event there is any suspicion of criminal intent, witnesses may invoke their Fifth Amendment rights against self-incrimination in an effort to avoid post-hearing prosecution. One exception to compliance with congressional subpoenas is the invocation of executive privilege by members of the executive branch (see Chapter 6).

In recent years, GOP members of the House of Representatives have been using Congressional oversight committees to hold repeated and seemingly endless hearings into the IRS and Benghazi "scandals" (Congressional Intelligence Committee) without unearthing any significant wrongdoings on the part of the federal bureaucracy or the Executive branch. I leave it to you to decide whether these continual "investigations" are legitimate or, as some would claim, "politically motivated."

## CONGRESSIONAL LEADERSHIP

When it comes to **leadership** and **seniority**, politics rears its head, as the majority party holds most of the important positions of power.

In the House, the overall leader is known as the Speaker of the House. Traditionally, the Speaker is chosen from among the most senior members of the majority party. Naturally, some elderly representatives may not be suited to lead the House, so the slate of potential Speakers is usually narrowed down to a select few. Politics again comes into play as the party regulars must throw their support behind one of the representatives coveting the Speaker's office. Many of the candidates maneuver to obtain support by calling in favors and making promises of future promotions to other representatives (see logrolling). After an intra-party vote by the entire majority party caucus determines which representative will be Speaker, the entire House affirms the choice. Since the political party in control has already ratified the selection made, the final vote is simply an administrative "rubber stamp."

The office of the Speaker bestows considerable powers on its occupant. Speakers have ultimate authority during floor sessions of the House, directing all debate and designating who may speak on any pending matter. They also wield great influence over the Rules Committee, which routinely follows their agendas. Speakers further have the informal power to decide who serves on special or select committees (which offer opportunities to enhance the public image of their members), conference committees, and standing committees. As a result, representatives coveting a specific committee, besides seniority must demonstrate loyalty to the Speaker. Once a Speaker has made the committee selections, the entire House then votes along party lines to confer "formal" approval on the appointments.

Because Speakers (and hence the majority party) determine the assignment of bills to particular committees, they also exert considerable influence on the shaping of legislation. In many cases, they decide which bills are pigeonholed or set for a discharge petition. An important member of the Speaker's inner circle of power brokers in the House is the

**majority leader**. The position usually goes to one of the most senior members of the political party in power. As "lieutenant" to the Speaker, the majority leader assists in keeping all party members in line when it comes to the handling of proposed legislation and helps to shape the public policy and strategy employed by the Speaker. **Minority leaders** serve similar purposes for their party.

Two significant positions—the **House majority whip** and **minority whip**—are also considered members of their respective political party's inner-circle. Their names refer to their responsibility to "whip" all of the party "rank and file" into shape so they comply with the efforts initiated by leadership and present a unified legislative front regarding objectives and political agendas. Whips are essential for the legislative process, and they take their position very seriously. A strong majority leader and/or whip can use the office as a stepping stone to become Speaker at some point in the future. Similarly, the leaders of the minority party, or **ranking members**, in the House and Senate are the most likely to ascend to the highest leadership position in their respective chambers if their party attains the majority as a result of an election.

Representatives that oppose their party leadership—in the case of the majority party, the Speaker—run the risk of being labeled "renegades" and punished accordingly. Punishment may take the form of lost opportunities to serve as members or chairs of prized committees, or a withholding of financial and other important party support during reelection campaigns down the road.

**Senate leadership** operates in similar fashion to the House, except there is no Speaker. Although the vice president of the United States is considered the president of the Senate, the position is largely ceremonial, limited to casting deciding votes in the event of a tie in a Senate floor vote. In his "figurehead" role, the vice president also presides over the Electoral College and at joint sessions of Congress, for example, during the president's State of the Union Address. At such events, the vice president is always seated next to the Speaker of the House.

In the modern era, vice presidents rarely appear in the Senate and the job of officiating the daily sessions and debates is handled in their stead by the **president pro tempore** ("pro tempore" means "for a time"). Although it is the second-highest position in the Senate and third in line of succession to the presidency behind the vice president and Speaker, it has very little real authority and is most often held by one of the most senior members of the Senate. Often, the task of presiding over the day-to-day sessions is assigned to less senior members in order for them to learn to preside over Senate matters and procedures.

The most powerful position in the Senate is the **Senate majority leader**, who is selected to lead the political party in control. Similar to House Speakers, the majority leaders are chosen by intra-party vote with a formal affirmation by the full Senate. Initiating all policy matters in the Senate, majority leaders direct committee assignments and, like the Speaker, control what legislation comes to the full Senate floor for consideration and voting.

The ranking members of the minority parties in the House and Senate, or **minority leaders**, are also selected in an intra-party vote. In the event that control of the chamber switches from one political party to the other during an election cycle, they eventually may become Speakers or majority leaders. In recent years this occurred when Nancy Pelosi lost the Speakership after the GOP gained control of the House in the 2010 mid-term elections. Then House Minority Leader John Boehner took over as Speaker of the House and Pelosi occupied the minority leader position.

Republicans in both chambers of Congress identify themselves as members of the **Republican conference and/or caucus.** Democrats in both chambers of Congress, on the other hand, consider themselves members of the **Democratic caucus**. In recent years, some legislators have declared themselves to be independents, for example, Connecticut Senator Joseph Lieberman, who started out as a Democrat but caucuses as an independent with the Republican Conference, and Vermont Senator Jim Jeffords, who started out as a Republican, and caucused as an independent with the Democrats until his retirement in 2007.

In the House, the Democratic caucus and the Republican conference/caucus meet early on in each new session to determine permanent or standing committee assignments. The majority party, as mentioned before, will follow the direction of the Speaker; the minority party often follows the wishes of the minority leader, although there can be considerable jostling for plum assignments. The members of a committee have no ultimate say in who becomes chair. That prerogative belongs to the majority party (and hence the Speaker).

**Seniority** is perhaps the most important determining factor in who ends up chairing committees, but fund-raising capability and committee staffing and management figure as well. The longest serving senior member affiliated with the minority political party is known as the **ranking member** of that committee. It should be noted that seniority is measured not by the length of time a legislator has been in the House or Senate, but by the length of service and membership on a specific committee. If congressional tenure alone were the standard, then the longest serving member of the House and Senate would chair *all* committees. Instead, the tradition is that the chair goes to the longest serving member of that committee, so long as he or she is a member of the political party in power. Recently, however, fund-raising capability has become a new element in the selection of committee chairs by both Democratic and Republican parties. Having the largest fund-raising machinery (loosely tied to Super PACs, PACs, etc.)—is now considered an important credential for chairmanship.

The use of seniority and fund-raising to determine committee chairs is a reliable, routine system that encourages unity and efficiency. With little competition for the chairmanships, the committees can instead focus on providing continuity from one legislative session to the next.

The only troubling issue in this process is the alliance between committee chairs and their campaign financing benefactors, which creates potential conflicts of interest and a sense that many legislators are in the pockets of moneyed campaign contributors. It raises the question that although Congress is vested with the authority to represent the people, how does it really go about deciding what is in everyone's best interest? It is important to keep in mind at this point that everything Congress does when it comes to **policy issues** is driven primarily by **political agendas**, which then formulate **legislative agendas**, and that both are closely tied to the political ideologies held by the major political parties in control.

Public policy issues frequently include, but are not limited to, arguments relating to illegal immigration, abortion, education reform, Medicaid reform, health care, environmental protection, national defense, drug laws, etc. During the 2010 mid-term election campaign for Congress, Republican candidates told voters that if elected, their number-one priority would be unemployment and jobs. Voters in turn elected enough Republicans to allow them to take control of the House. But instead of following up on their campaign pledges, the representatives immediately moved on legislation to deal with cultural issues by attempting to further limit abortion rights, protesting against contraception and birth control, and cutting entitlement spending.

As of this writing, the parties are in an incessant struggle focused primarily on reducing the size of the federal government, cutting the deficit and limiting spending without regard to increasing sources of revenue. Although jobs, unemployment and the economy continue to be favorite topics of political rhetoric, little of substance is being done to solve the problems associated with them. Knowing these issues, it is not difficult to imagine how political ideology comes into play when determining the areas that will garner the most attention by the Congress. This is not unique to Republicans; the game of politics is played using tried and true strategies by both political parties, whose only goal is to attain power through elected office-holding.

Nor is this a new development. Historically, the framers' efforts to curtail emotion and politics in the creation of laws and overseeing our government have had limited success in the face of ideology, relentless self-interest and power mongering. We are currently in a particularly extreme period, in which party politics, ideology and money seem to trump any sense of what is truly important to our country. Congress is getting historically low marks of confidence by the public during polls. One can only hope that this situation does not go on too long.

# 5

# ❂ THE EXECUTIVE BRANCH ❂

## DOES THE PRESIDENT LEAD OR FOLLOW?

**Article II** of the Constitution lays out the framework for the **executive branch** and the powers granted to the **president**. Unlike leaders operating under other democratic forms of government, for example a prime minister in a parliamentary system, the U.S. president is not a member of the legislative branch. His election involves Congress only if he does not obtain the 270 electoral votes required by the Constitution (see more in Chapter 11). The president is not empowered to directly initiate legislation in pursuance of a policy agenda. His immediate advisors, also known as the "Inner Cabinet," include his chief of staff, communications director, and policy advisors along with the department heads that make up his regular **Cabinet.** None of these advisors may be members of the legislative branch. Because of this arrangement, there is no guarantee that any of the president's policy initiatives will be enacted by Congress.

Moreover, Congress does not work directly *with* the president to create public policy. He alone is responsible to shape a policy agenda within the executive branch and the agencies administered through the West Wing of the White House. Policy agendas are shaped by a variety of factors, including but not limited to public opinion, media and interest groups (which lobby directly with the executive branch).

The **modern presidency** wields considerable power over our government. It has not always been that way. We have a varied history of electing strong or weak presidents, and discussions about the issue of executive authority are often disingenuous. When pundits advocating a specific ideology object to the expansion of presidential power, they conveniently ignore the role of political parties, which originally were not intended to play the strong role they do today. There is no mention whatsoever of political parties or factions in the Constitution; they evolved on their own over time.

To counter some of the rhetoric, let's look at the original intent of the framers when they drafted Article II of the Constitution.

From the beginning of our democratic republic, the framers debated the role our president would play as leader of the executive branch. Having just fought a prolonged and lengthy revolutionary war against England, many delegates to the Constitutional Convention worried that a president would quickly become another king. They hoped that regulations favoring the dominance of Congress would suitably constrain the leader of the executive branch.

Thus, the presidency was created having limited authority, as the most explicit powers were granted in Article I to Congress. The president was meant to cooperate, accommodate and enforce laws enacted by Congress, to handle foreign affairs and to act as ceremonial head of state.

It was perhaps fortuitous that the first occupant of the presidential office was George Washington, who acted as a unifying figure after the Revolutionary War. Although sensitive to concerns regarding abuse of power, he soon learned that no president could accept the limited role prescribed by the Constitution and successfully lead the executive branch. Most historians believe Washington ranks near the top of all U.S. presidents, not because he was first to serve in that capacity, but because of how he interpreted his role and constitutional authority, and implemented actions that forever expanded the functions of the executive branch. He recognized that presidential powers were subject to "Custom and Usage" under Article II, and once obtained would likely never be returned to any other branch of the government. But he also understood the limits of his power. Although he could probably have been president for life, he established the tradition of leaving office after only two terms.

## POWERS OF THE PRESIDENCY

Since Washington, a number of presidential powers have emerged that manage to circumvent the checks and balances envisioned by the constitutional framers. One of them is the current practice of **executive agreement**, which evolved from the president's right to negotiate treaties and trade arrangements with foreign powers (under the Articles of Confederation, the lack of a central negotiating figure caused all kinds of difficulties). In principle, agreements rising to the level of treaties require ratification in the Senate by a two-thirds vote, but because the Constitution reserves the realm of foreign affairs to the executive branch, courts for some time have held that the president has the inherent power to enter trade agreements that virtually have the same effect as a treaty. By utilizing such executive agreements, the president skirts Senate ratification and evades its "check and balance" authority. Of course, executive agreements remain in effect only for the term of the sitting president and may be extended, revised or revoked by subsequent presidents.

Perhaps the most controversial power wielded by the president is the issuing of **Executive Orders**, which represent an informal power arising under "Custom and Usage." (We will discuss **signing statements** on pages 89-90.) Presidents going as far back as George Washington have used them to by-pass an oppositional Congress. The practice has come under fire with President Obama, who threatened and then utilized them to move national policy forward according to his wishes. His opponents have called him a "tyrant" and "dictator" for his "imperial use" of Executive Orders, despite the fact that they are subject to challenge before the Supreme Court. Such was the case when the Supreme Court held unconstitutional

President Truman's efforts to nationalize steel mills through an Executive Order. (See ***Youngstown Sheet and Tube v. Sawyer***, 343 U.S. 579, 1952). The system of "checks and balances" applies to Executive Orders, and the president will always face legal scrutiny for them.

A related power is presidential imposition of **executive privilege**. As discussed earlier, Congress, with a legitimate legislative purpose, may subpoena individuals to testify during an investigation. Throughout our history, Congress has attempted to extend its role of oversight to include inquiries into matters of the executive branch (usually in an effort to engage in power plays). In an effort to maintain the integrity of his office and the executive branch, the president can claim all communication as "privileged"—hence, executive privilege—and withhold it from Congress.

One can imagine weak presidents rolling over to congressional oversight requests, but not someone like Andrew Jackson, who would have told congressional leaders what they could do with their subpoenas in no uncertain terms. Still, no one challenged the legality of executive privilege until Richard Nixon imposed it and refused to comply with Senate Watergate Committee subpoenas demanding oval office tape recordings and related documents. The issue was ultimately decided in the matter of ***United States v. Nixon***, 418 U.S. 683 (1974), when presiding U.S. District Court Judge John Sirica ruled that executive privilege did *not* apply to criminal investigations of wrongdoing. He then ordered Nixon to provide the tapes and related materials. When it was discovered that portions of the subpoenaed tapes were missing, Congress intensified its efforts to impeach and try Nixon for "high crimes and misdemeanors in office." On August 10, 1974, Nixon avoided certain impeachment by becoming the first U.S. president to resign from office.

One would have thought that the use of executive privilege might have diminished in the wake of Watergate, but it has actually intensified. In the modern age of terrorism, George W. Bush and now Barack Obama have frequently imposed executive privilege to avoid disclosing matters relating to secret intelligence and military actions for reasons of **national security**. That has also been the case when Congress inquired into activities at the military prison at Guantanamo Bay and the practice of **rendition** in which intelligence agents capture suspected international terrorists and transport them to unknown locations without formal criminal charge for "enhanced interrogation."

The legality of detaining suspected terrorists for years without formal charges or a hearing has not been heard by the courts. It can only be surmised that they would uphold the ability of the president as commander in chief to do whatever is necessary to secure our nation from threats of terrorism.

Along the same lines, despite some political rumblings, there have been no real threats of legal action relating to the deployment of troops to Afghanistan, the use of Navy Seals in the capture and killing of Bin Laden in Pakistan, or the imposition of U.S. fighter bombers over the skies of Libya—all ordered without Congressional approval. The arguments for such independent actions are that modern warfare and terrorism require swift responses unencumbered by public debate. Courts are slow to react, perhaps because they, too, recognize that traditional practices do not apply in the modern world. Hence, there are still no effective legal challenges to the constitutionality of provisions in the Patriot Act—warrantless physical and electronic searches and seizures. With the expansion of the president's powers to assassinate suspected terrorists, including U.S. citizens, a new realm of constitutional shaky ground has emerged. Coincidentally, it is opponents of the president who typically raise concerns, despite the fact that they themselves opened the door with the passage of the original version of the Patriot Act.

The office of the presidency is often identified as "the administration," and for good reason. As the nation's chief executive, the president is vested with the power to administer the operations of the federal government. From the West Wing of the White House, the president and his "inner circle" of advisors, led by his chief of staff, run the day-to-day affairs of the federal bureaucracy. As a result, presidents are implicitly granted a wide array of additional powers.

The president acts as the nation's **commander in chief**. The framers determined that he and the secretary of war (now secretary of defense) shall serve as **civilians** to ensure that military influence and power do not usurp our republican democracy. Every member of our armed services swears an oath of service to obey the orders of their superiors, including the commander in chief. Although the Constitution invests Congress with the right to declare war, it has been generally accepted that the president may commit military troops as needed to protect national interests.

## OTHER PRESIDENTIAL POWERS

The president may utilize informal powers not specifically enumerated under Article II, such as executive orders, executive agreements and his authority as commander in chief. This practice falls under the **prerogative theory,** which argues that the vesting clause of Article II includes the inherent powers of the president to use his best judgment in the event of a crisis, so that he can make decisions in the nation's best interests without interference by congressional "checks and balances." Such actions are always subject to review later on, but in an emergency, the president is expected to proceed with a "let's do this first and ask for forgiveness later" approach.

The president also has the unique authority to call Congress into session on an emergency basis, regardless of whether senators and representatives agree. Such an act can be an effective way to ensure legislation is dealt with. In the current media-oriented age, however, it is often viewed more as a political or public relations maneuver to show "who is in charge."

Under Article II of the Constitution the president is required to report on the **State of the Union** to Congress each year. From James Madison to William Howard Taft, presidents simply sent a State of the Union message to Congress to be read before a joint session. President Woodrow Wilson was the first president since John Adams to address Congress in person.

The president also has broad powers to nominate and appoint all heads of government agencies and bureaus, including independent regulatory agencies. Major positions, including Cabinet secretaries, federal judges (including Supreme Court justices), federal marshals, U.S. attorneys, the solicitor general and ambassadors, all require confirmation by the Senate. This is again a function of the intended checks and balances (see **Senatorial Courtesy** and **Confirmation Politics**).

The president may commute sentences and pardon convicted criminals, but only for federal convictions. The most well known pardon was issued by President Gerald Ford to former President Richard Nixon, exempting him from criminal prosecution for any crimes committed by him in the Watergate scandal. Because the tide of public opinion against Nixon was high at the time, Ford's pardon became a powerful factor in his failure to get elected after he finished out Nixon's term in the White House. He eventually lost to former Georgia Governor Jimmy Carter in the 1976 presidential election.

## QUALIFICATIONS

When it comes to eligibility for the presidency, Article II of the Constitution establishes the following requirements: A candidate must be at least 35 years of age, have spent the most recent 14 years as a resident in the United States and be a "natural citizen."

The last of these requirements has caused much turmoil during the Obama Administration. Far right-wing activists have insisted since the 2008 election that President Obama is not eligible to be president based on their belief that he was born outside the United States. The so-called "birther" movement gained national prominence when many Republican conservative leaders refused or failed to dampen its rhetoric. It took a national campaign demand by Donald Trump in the spring of 2011 to force Obama to release his long-form "Certificate of Live Birth," authenticated by Hawaiian officials. The issue was raised again in May, 2012, by Arizona Secretary of State Ken Bennett (who also served as Mitt Romney's campaign co-chair in Arizona) who questioned whether Obama should be on the presidential ballot because of concerns relating to his place of birth. Only after the State of Hawaii insisted that Obama was in fact born there did Bennett agree to the president being placed on his state's 2012 presidential election ballot.[8] The definition of "natural born" under the presidency requirements is still open to wide interpretation. For over a century, "natural born" meant that one became an automatic U.S. citizen by virtue of having at least one parent who was a U.S. citizen, regardless of where he was born. Now some critics claim that the parents must be of majority age before they can confer automatic citizenship to their offspring.

Moving down the list of reasons to question his constitutional credentials to serve, "birthers" and other opponents of Barack Obama then claimed that he somehow was ineligible to serve because he is a follower of the Muslim faith. Setting aside the absurdity of that claim, it is more important to note that one's religious faith is **not** an eligibility requirement for the presidency. Religion as a litmus test for eligibility for high office is specifically prohibited in **Article VI, Paragraph 3** of the Constitution.

Despite evidence to the contrary, opponents of Obama continue to argue that he is not eligible to serve as president, and that all of his appointments, including the two justices to the Supreme Court, are void. Despite these allegations, the facts are that officials and justices confirmed by the Senate are "legitimate" and therefore, regardless of their nomination, empowered to serve, provided they themselves meet eligibility requirements.

## THE PRESIDENT'S ROLE

Most Americans do not understand what a president can and cannot do while in office. They routinely give him credit for positive developments and achievements when it is not deserved. On the other hand, they also blame him for many negative occurrences over which he has little or no control. Perhaps the most important misconception is that the president has the power to initiate taxes or spend money independent of congressional authorization. Nothing could be further from the truth.

Citizens generally expect the president to cooperate with Congress in an effort to achieve legislative and public policy success. At the same time, they want the chief executive to be "in charge," regardless of the influence of special interests and rival political parties in the legislative chambers. Among the more "delusional" views of the chief executive's power and influence is the notion that the president can control and grow the economy, solving all economic troubles—not to mention keep the peace domestically and internationally, be smart and tough in dealing with foreign affairs, provide strong military leadership, protect our global interests, and lead with initiative to maintain the public's trust. We do not ask for much of a president, do we?

As a result, presidents routinely suffer from a cycle of positive and negative **job approval ratings**. Of course, this cycle is perpetuated by the political opposition and their ideologically based media supporters. History has shown, nonetheless, that in the event of a real crisis, the president is the one leader who has the ability to bring the nation together. Franklin Roosevelt offered hope to Americans during depths of the Great Depression with his radio "Fireside Chats." John Kennedy rallied the nation after the Cuban Missile Crisis, and George W. Bush did the same when he spoke from Ground Zero after 9/11.

For some time after a new president is inaugurated, he usually enjoys an interlude of calm with the public and the Congress known as "the first 100 days" or the **honeymoon period**. Even Obama benefitted from this break in political wrangling, as his approval rating during that time was at a 61% high. Historically, after the honeymoon period, the president's approval ratings typically begin to fall and then fluctuate. Each of the modern-era presidents have experienced such swings as their term progressed. George W. Bush's approval ratings soared immediately after 9/11, but fell considerably after his claim of "Mission Accomplished" in Iraq and Afghanistan. His ratings jumped when Saddam Hussein was captured, but then fell to their lowest point, largely because of bad economic news near the end of his second term in office.

Barack Obama's approval ratings have also gone up and down, soaring when Osama Bin Laden was killed and the details of his **executive order** to initiate the mission were made public. Later on, Obama's ratings fell dramatically as the topic of the weak economy came back to the forefront. As of this writing, the economy is continuing to recover and **public opinion polls** indicated that the 2016 presidential election cycle will be dominated by foreign policy issues, Russia, Syria, Iraq, Iran and the Israel-Palestinian conflict, not to mention the growing disparity between the wealthy and the shrinking middle class.

So far, this discussion may suggest that the "most powerful man on Earth," is anything but, and merely buffeted by the way the historical and economic winds blow. But that is not the case.

The president has a host of **informal powers** not specifically designated in the Constitution. These powers and responsibilities have evolved over time from the administrations of George Washington through Barack Obama. They include, but are not limited to, the president serving as the country's chief legislative leader (initiator of public policy), coalition and morale builder, recruiter for bureaucratic leadership, crisis manager, budget setter, world leader and, perhaps most importantly, communicator to the American public. The last responsibility happens through speeches and messages crafted in the West Wing by the director of communications and put forth by the press secretary in daily briefings to the media.

Although being a morale builder can be a purely symbolic function, a president's ability to convey a sense of hope and well-being to an otherwise troubled nation is of paramount importance. Having the opportunity to do so does not always correlate with the actual ability to do so. Herbert Hoover was an intelligent man, a successful engineer and organizer of large-scale international projects, but his inability to communicate and uplift the people during the Great Depression marked his presidency as an abject failure. Barack Obama, although capable of delivering moving and inspirational speeches during his election campaign, has frequently come off as too "professorial" when attempting to speak to and unify the nation as president.

Although Franklin Roosevelt is traditionally considered the best at building morale from the White House, the standard for excellence in the modern era is Ronald Reagan. Tagged "The Great Communicator," the former Hollywood actor understood the importance of television and had the ability to communicate news to the American public in a positive light even when the general perception ran counter to his optimistic version. This was most evident when Reagan dealt with the Iran-Contra scandal. Even though memos reveal that Reagan understood his actions to be unconstitutional and impeachable, he convinced the American public that his statements denying involvement were "wrong," but came from his "heart and not his mind." The public was quickly appeased and lost interest in the scandal. To this day, Ronald Reagan sets the standard for on-camera excellence, and many Americans still believe his public addresses came from the heart insead of the minds of his speechwriters via teleprompters.

When it comes to conveying a sense of stability and assurance to the public, the president is expected to assess dangers the nation faces and act as a capable leader in determining how to deal with them. He is also expected to provide comfort to victims of natural disasters and to show command in recovery efforts. President George W. Bush suffered greatly in the polls when his director of the Federal Emergency Management Administration (FEMA), Michael Brown, failed miserably during the Hurricane Katrina disaster. Bush had appointed Brown as a reward for his fund-raising support during the election campaigns. Unfortunately, Brown's resume was built on promoting national equestrian shows. He had no experience administering a large federal agency, let alone dealing with the tremendous challenges presented in New Orleans in the aftermath of the devastating hurricane. Bush came off as inept himself when he eventually made it to Louisiana and declared to the cameras, "Brownie, you're doing a heck of a great job," while thousands were still suffering.[9]

When Barack Obama became president, he obviously learned from Bush's failures. From the 2011 shootings in Tucson, Arizona to Hurricane Sandy, the shooting tragedy in Newtown, Connecticut, the Boston Marathon bombing, the explosion of a Texas fertilizer plant, the devastating Oklahoma tornadoes and the deadly California wildfires, the president has been swift and supportive in his response and successfully filled the role as "Consoler in Chief."

The president's ability to recruit talented people to work in his administration becomes important to his success. The federal bureaucracy is filled with policy wonks and experts, yet it is sometimes difficult to convince high-profile leaders who have been successful in the private sector to leave their well paying positions and serve in the public sector. Only the influence of a president can persuade such leaders to accept lower paying jobs in the government.

Clearly, the experience garnered while serving the public along with heightened access to senior governmental officials can produce a financial windfall for those returning to private sector leadership positions. This is clearly evidenced in what is considered the **revolving door.** The term refers to officials who come aboard in an administration only to master the job and then return to the private sector for higher pay based on their newly acquired expertise and access to high-level career bureaucrats. Often, they return to public service work at some point to reinforce their ability to access the bureaucracy and collect an even bigger paycheck when going back to work in the private sector again, hence the term "revolving."

According to *www.OpenSecrets.org*, the website of the Center for Responsible Politics, there were 12,389 registered lobbyists in Washington in 2012, of whom 316 were former members of Congress, not to mention an even greater number of former Congressional staffers. All in all, they spent $3.3 billion seeking to influence the federal government.

Because the revolving door has become commonplace, bringing with it charges of rampant **influence peddling**, President Obama signed an executive order entitled the "Ethics in Government for the Executive Appointees." It requires that appointees cannot have served as lobbyists in the two years immediately preceding their public service, cannot accept gifts of any kind from lobbyists, and are barred from returning to the private sector as lobbyists for a period of two years. After leaving public service employment, they also are precluded from lobbying any official in the executive branch until after the term of the president has ended.

It sounded great on paper, but it was impossible to enforce. Since just about every appointee with public policy expertise would be unable to meet these requirements, waivers were put into place that rendered the effect of the executive order negligible.

**Presidential appointments** can accomplish many objectives besides getting the work of government done. Appointments routinely reward political supporters. They can represent an attempt to mend political divisions by crossing the political aisle. President Clinton shocked the Democratic Party faithful by nominating and appointing then Republican Senator William Cohen to serve as his secretary of defense. Similarly, President Obama retained William Gates in the same job after President Bush had appointed him during his second term. Upon Gates' resignation four years later, he nominated former Republican Nebraska Senator Chuck Hagel in 2013 to serve as his Secretary of Defense.

Sometimes appointments reflect the ideological and philosophical views of the president. That is frequently the case with appointees to head the Environmental Protection Agency and the Department of Justice. At other times, appointments seek to convince the private sector that the president takes a positive view of policies affecting their interests. President Obama's appointment of General Electric CEO Jeffery Immelt to lead his Council on Jobs and Competitiveness was an example of this. Likewise, Obama's appointment of William Daley to serve as his chief of staff was widely viewed as extending an olive branch to Wall Street, as Daley was widely approved of by those active in the financial markets. Along the same lines, appointments may also intend to solidify support for a concerned interest group. When the appointment of Elizabeth Warren to lead the Consumer Financial Protection Bureau was opposed by Republicans—she is considered by many to be a strong, highly qualified consumer advocate—she withdrew from consideration for the post. President Obama then hired her as counsel to establish the structure of the bureau and made Richard Cordray chair using the recess appointment procedure over the opposition of Republicans. Warren later ran for the Massachusetts U.S. Senate seat in the general election of 2012 and won against a conservative Republican incumbent.

There are two areas where presidential appointments have major impact on our government and American society. One is the Cabinet, which affects how the federal bureaucracy is administered on a day-to-day basis. The other is the U.S. Supreme Court, where the effects of appointments can last decades after the nominating president leaves office.

## THE CABINET

Surprisingly, the **Cabinet** is not mentioned in the Constitution at all. Its origins date back to George Washington, who determined early on in his presidency that in order to function well, a government needed a group of "managers" to run day-to-day operations. He asked Congress to authorize the formal creation of department heads that acted as his Cabinet. Since then, while president-elects have a full plate of responsibilities prior to taking office, perhaps their most important obligation is to appoint the Cabinet secretaries to head the various agencies of the executive branch. Although Cabinet members must be **confirmed** by the Senate, they serve at the exclusive pleasure of the president. No consent or approval is required for him to remove or dismiss a member of his Cabinet.

The number of Cabinet departments has varied throughout American history, from four following George Washington's inauguration to the current 15, which are:

Department of State
Department of Defense
The Justice Department (Attorney General)
Department of Interior
Department of Treasury
Department of Agriculture
Department of Labor
Department of Commerce
Department of Housing and Urban Development

Department of Transportation
Department of Energy
Department of Health and Human Services
Department of Veteran Affairs
Department of Education
Department of Homeland Security.

The president may add others to sit in on Cabinet meetings, although they do not have formal recognition as Cabinet positions. Under President Obama, they include the White House chief of staff, the heads of the Environmental Protection Agency and the Office of Management and Budget, the United States Trade Representative, the Council of Economic Advisors, and the Ambassador to the United Nations.

## THE PRESIDENT AND THE EXECUTIVE OFFICE

Although some 3,000 people work in the White House, only about 1,600 of them are considered West Wing employees. They include a number of key aides and assistants who advise the president on a wide array of policy matters and are part of his **inner circle**, but are *not* members of the Cabinet.

Chief among them, as indicated by his title, is the White House **chief of staff**, who acts as the nation's chief operating officer. He possesses top level security clearance while actually overseeing the administration of the entire federal government; he works in an office adjacent to the Oval Office. The chief of staff generally attends all meetings held by the president, including Cabinet sessions and gatherings in the **Situation Room** (where all top secret military and national security measures are undertaken).

All of the following aides to the president answer to the chief of staff. The **national security advisor** possesses top level security clearance and advises the president on long-range military and foreign affairs. He provides the president with a daily **national security briefing** and also attends meetings as needed in the Situation Room.

To create a coherent fiscal policy, the executive branch has the **Council of Economic Advisors**, a group that works within the West Wing as consultants to the president on the economy and all related financial matters. Its members are also responsible for reporting to Congress on an annual basis. The council includes a panel of three economists who are supported by a staff of 25.

The head of the **Council of Economic Advisors** deals with major issues affecting the financial well-being of the nation. For the first two years of the Obama administration, he gave a daily economic report each morning to the president.

The **domestic affairs director** also works in the West Wing and is available to brief the president on issues relating to health, education and social services. The director helps to shape public policy and the White House's message as it relates to these issues. He also works closely with domestic affairs advisors, the communications advisor and the press secretary.

The **director** of the **Office of Management and Budget (OMB)** presents briefings as needed to the president. The OMB works closely with the president, the chief of staff, policy advisors and Cabinet secretaries to determine the budget that the president submits annually to Congress. This budget is a little like a Christmas wish list. The president knows he will not get everything he asks for, but he tries for big items nonetheless. The OMB also acts as the president's "oversight" office for all federal departments and agencies to ensure that spending adheres to budget guidelines and to eliminate inefficiency and operational defects. This makes the OMB a very powerful organization within the executive branch, as all departments and agencies must answer initially to it and then ultimately to the chief of staff and the president.

Two other top advisors to the president are the **director of communications** and the **White House press secretary**. They craft the message the White House wishes to communicate to the press and the public, and serve as buffers between the administration and the media. Both occupy challenging positions requiring strong-willed, skilled and tough personalities, because they are subjected to daily exposure to the press corps and often take the brunt of criticism aimed at the president. While the press secretary conducts the press briefings, the director of communications molds and shapes the message under the direction of the White House chief of staff.

Yet another important group of advisors is the **National Security Council**. Its members are not considered part of the inner circle, but have access to the president on an "as needed basis." They are directly engaged in using diplomacy and the military in foreign policy planning. They also develop emergency plans—command and control issues that affect civilian and military leadership—in the event of a national security crisis.

Also occupying offices in the West Wing and the Old Executive Office Building, located directly across the street from the White House, are the president's **economic advisors**, who plan strategies to deal with issues relating to inflation, tax policy, economic growth and job creation. They also answer to the White House chief of staff or his deputy.

Various heads of Cabinet departments as well as military and intelligence agencies who meet with the chief of staff and the president on a regular basis are the secretary of treasury, the secretary of homeland security, the national security advisor, the chairman of the Joint Chiefs of Staff (liaison leaders of the Armed Forces), director of the Central Intelligence Agency (CIA), and secretary of state.

Because the **Federal Reserve (the Fed)** operates as an independent regulatory agency, the **chair** of the **Federal Reserve (Fed chair)** is considered an *ex officio* (Latin for "out of office") advisor to the president. The Fed chair reports to the chief of staff and the president on current economic conditions and the Fed's position as it relates to monetary and interest rate policy. Members of the Federal Reserve serve staggered terms of five years and cannot be fired by the president.

It may come as a surprise, but a number of presidential candidates have made it clear on the campaign trail that they don't understand the role and functioning of the Federal Reserve. In 2008, GOP presidential candidate John McCain committed a major gaffe when he stated in response to the emerging financial crisis in the nation's banks that he would "immediately fire" Fed Chief Ben Bernanke upon being elected president. In August 2011, Texas GOP Governor Rick Perry, in one of his campaign speeches, called Bernanke's actions with the Fed "almost treasonous," as if he as president could change the Fed's policies.

## The President as Persuader

Because of his prominent position as leader of the nation, the president has informal ways to influence and persuade members of Congress, regardless of their political party affiliation. Both senators and representatives covet invitations to the White House because they confer instant credibility to their significant position in government. Being shown entering or leaving the White House by the media is always considered a public relations coup. It means *that* member of Congress is *important!*

Another gesture the president can make to develop good will is to invite someone to travel with him on Air Force One. Perhaps the best recent example was President Obama offering a ride to newly elected Congressman Ben Quayle (R. AZ). Quayle, while running in his first congressional campaign, repeatedly attacked President Obama as the "worst president ever." Shortly after the 2011 Tucson shootings that left several people dead and critically wounded Congresswoman Gabby Giffords (D. AZ), President Obama prepared to fly to Arizona to address the nation and the people of Tucson. Out of courtesy to all representatives from Arizona, he invited Freshman Congressman Quayle to join him aboard Air Force One for the trip from Washington. Imagine how awkward it was for Quayle after having publicly vilified the president for months.

Other forms of presidential persuasion may include invitations to a weekend at the most secretive and exclusive retreat in the world—**Camp David**—or to political occasions which afford multiple photo opportunities. There might be a mention in a national policy speech, a request to attend an international conference with the president, or simply participation in an event in a member of Congress' district during which the president announces a new federal project or public policy initiative. Such "soft" modes of political persuasion have been used since George Washington's tenure as president, and they will continue because they work!

## THE PRESIDENT AND THE PRESS

The media and press are often considered to be a part of the **fourth estate**. The term was popularized by Thomas Carlyle, a 19th-century British historian, based on a remark by Edmund Burke, an earlier political theorist and philosopher. Burke had apparently noted that in addition to the "three estates" in Parliament—king, lords and commoners—there was a "fourth estate," the press, more powerful than the rest.

As a result, its members consider themselves the "watchdogs and protectors" of our liberties and freedoms. They are not elected and frequently choose to take adversarial roles in order to question motives and issues undertaken by our government leaders. But because they enjoy unique access to the corridors of power, they are also vulnerable to undue influence. There have been many occasions throughout history when White House administrations manipulated the media to their advantage. Andrew Jackson had his own ally in the *Washington Globe*. The newspaper's editor, Francis Blair, was a personal friend. Jackson would include Blair in his "Kitchen Cabinet" and "allow" him to write favorable editorials in the newspaper. Theodore Roosevelt was the first modern president to recognize the power of the media by using the White House as a **bully pulpit** (a term he coined) to persuade the public or strong-arm policymakers in his favor. Ronald Reagan understood the advantage of staging events in front of national symbols of pride, knowing that the imagery portrayed in the media would boost his popularity and message.

Sometimes, administrations will "float trial balloons" before the press through unnamed senior White House officials in an effort to gauge public or congressional opinion without having to formally announce a new policy initiative. This grants the administration "cover" and deniability while it assesses the benefits or fallout from the trial balloon.

Most often, the media and the press can only report news if they have access to it. Being friendly to an administration allows them easier access. Reporters who don't play ball can be shut out of planned events and left to watch as rivals get advance scoops on news stories. Journalistic ethics sometimes get trumped by the ability to report news first. It remains up to the public to discern "news" from "commentary" and "punditry." Unfortunately, a large percentage of the public is unable to do so.

## THE VICE PRESIDENT

Based on Article II of the Constitution, the role of the **vice president** is limited to presiding over the Senate, certifying Electoral College results and breaking tie votes in the Senate. Since the establishment of the West Wing as the administrative center of the White House, the vice president maintains an office there and has his own chosen group of advisors, from chief of staff down to press secretary.

The *actual* role the vice president takes in an administration depends solely upon the president and his chief of staff. Many vice presidents have been excluded from the daily decisions affecting domestic and foreign policy. George Washington frequently left John Adams out of his inner circle, preferring to rely instead on the advice of Secretary of Treasury Alexander Hamilton. Harry Truman, vice president under Franklin D. Roosevelt, was sidelined to such a degree that when he became president upon FDR's death, the advisors were reluctant to disclose the very existence of the Manhattan Project to develop the atomic bomb to him.

The modern trend of the vice president actively participating in the government began when President Ronald Reagan included his vice president, George H.W. Bush, in administrative affairs. Bush, a former director of the CIA, attended all of Reagan's daily intelligence briefings to help decipher critical matters affecting our military and intelligence services. The practice prepared Bush well to serve as president following Reagan's second term in office. The trend continued after the Reagan presidency as virtually every vice president since—Al Gore, Dick Cheney and Joe Biden—has enjoyed an active partnership in administrative affairs.

## PRESIDENTIAL SUCCESSION

Prior to the enactment of the **Twenty-Fifth Amendment**, there was no established formal mechanism to replace a deceased president. The original framers simply required that an "officer chosen by Congress" would serve in his stead. Upon the death of President William Henry Harrison, many felt that Vice President John Tyler would serve only as an interim president, holding office until the end of Harrison's term. Harrison had died three weeks into office, so there was a long period left to serve. Tyler, however, insisted that he would become president in his "own right" and took the oath of office accordingly. His opponents failed to garner any support to effectively challenge him and Tyler's action set the precedent that the sitting vice president would be next in line of succession.

Because of the controversy over Tyler's action, no one was appointed to serve as his vice president, and that set a precedent as well. In every case since then, when a vice president has had to step into the president's office—whether it was Andrew Johnson succeeding Abraham Lincoln, Chester A. Arthur succeeding James Garfield, or Lyndon B. Johnson succeeding John F. Kennedy—the position of vice president remained vacant.

In 1967, the Twenty-Fifth Amendment finally codified the constitutional guidelines for presidential and vice presidential succession. Under its terms, the vice president becomes president upon the "death or resignation" of the president. Then the new president appoints a new vice president "who shall take office upon confirmation by a majority vote of both houses of Congress."

The amendment further clarified how to deal with situations in which the president becomes incapacitated for a period of time. In 1919, President Woodrow Wilson suffered a stroke while campaigning for ratification of the Treaty of Versailles. His condition was so serious that he was unable to speak or feed himself. The media were kept in the dark, as were Vice President Thomas R. Marshall and Congress. Wilson's wife, Edith, assumed his daily duties, advising the staff that the president was resting while she would routinely sign his name to official documents from the White House residence. Wilson would eventually recover from the stroke to finish his second term of office.

To deal with such events in the future, the Twenty-Fifth Amendment requires the president or vice president, along with a majority of the Cabinet, to claim in writing to the Senate president pro tempore and the Speaker of the House that the president is incapacitated and unable to discharge his duties. The vice president then assumes the position of **acting president**. This provisionary arrangement would end when the president informs the president pro tempore and Speaker of the House that his disability has ended and that he is ready to reassume the presidency, at which point the vice president steps down and resumes his original office.

Since 1967, the amendment, which is also known as the **Presidential Disability Amendment** has been invoked twice, both involving Gerald Ford. In 1973, Vice President Spiro Agnew was charged by the U.S. attorney with extortion, tax fraud and bribery. In an arranged deal with federal prosecutors, Agnew agreed to a plea of ***nolo contendere*** (or "no contest") with the provision that he immediately resign the vice presidency in exchange for receiving no jail time. The vacancy in the office allowed for the nomination and confirmation of then Michigan Representative Gerald Ford as vice president. When President Nixon in turn resigned in 1974, the Twenty-Fifth Amendment came into play again, elevating Ford to the presidency. Following the amendment's provisions the new president in turn nominated Nelson Rockefeller to serve as his vice president.

The Twenty-Fifth Amendment should have come into play in 1981 when President Reagan was shot, but no one except his closest advisors and physicians knew that his condition was critical and his life in danger. Technically, throughout his surgery, he was incapacitated and unable to perform his presidential duties. Fortunately, he recovered. But what if he hadn't fully regained his mental or physical capacities?

Imagine the **constitutional crisis** that would erupt if a vice president and a majority of the Cabinet wrote to Congress pursuant to provisions of the Twenty-Fifth Amendment and claimed the president was "incapacitated" and "unable" to discharge his duties, while the president himself disputed such claims. What if an incapacitated president felt he was ready to resume his duties, but the vice president and a majority of the Cabinet disagreed? Is this not what government takeovers are made of? In such cases, the Twenty-Fifth Amendment allows for the entire Congress to meet and decide the issue based upon a two-thirds vote. Congress alone has the power to resolve such a dispute. We can only hope in this day and age of extremist political fervor and ideological wrangling that we never have to face such a constitutional crisis.

From George Washington to Barack Obama, presidential powers have evolved and will continue to do so. Political rhetoric notwithstanding, our nation's chief executive plays a vital role in shaping the direction America takes in the world. Perhaps now more than ever we need stronger presidential leaders that can transcend party politics and rhetoric. Throughout history, America has had its share of strong and weak occupants of the presidential office. We can only hope that Americans employ clear logic and judgment, free of corrupting influences, when electing our future presidents.

# 6

# ❀ CONGRESS AND THE PRESIDENT ❀

## JOCKEYING FOR POWER

Shortly after taking office, George Washington was faced with an armed rebellion. Farmers in Western Pennsylvania felt that a new tax on whiskey was an unfair imposition on working Americans, and with support from many prominent politicians, including some within the Pennsylvania militia, they challenged the authority of the federal government to make such a tax "stick" in the face of armed opposition. Without hesitation, Washington called in troops from surrounding states and put down that early challenge to presidential authority. By suppressing the insurgent Whiskey Rebellion, he set the precedent that the executive branch could use military troops to quell domestic disorder while enforcing an act of Congress.

The constitutional framers anticipated that the presidents would have to balance the interplay for power that exists between the legislative and executive branches. In the process, the American public often erroneously assigns success or failure to the president when it actually should credit Congress and vice versa.

According to the Constitution, both the legislative and executive branches of government have the task of creating a **policy agenda**. Congress has the authority to enact items from this agenda into laws and the president is vested with the power to execute them accordingly.

The conflict arises when the president interprets and enforces the new laws in a different manner than Congress intended.

## CONGRESSIONAL POWERS AND LIMITATIONS

As discussed in Chapter 4, Congress possesses powers specifically delegated under Article I, Section 8 of the Constitution. In addition, there are implied powers as set forth in what is known as the **Necessary and Proper Clause.** Under Article I, Section 8, Clause 3, the framers gave Congress the power:

> *To make all Laws which shall be necessary and proper for carrying into Execution the foregoing Powers and all other Powers vested by this Constitution in the Government of the United States, or in any Department or Officer thereof.*

The Necessary and Proper Clause enables Congress to use implied powers or those not specifically enumerated under the Constitution to create laws deemed necessary for the governance of the United States. In reality, it is merely a catch-all provision allowing Congress to expand its power and authority as needed. As a result, it has also frequently been called the **Elastic Clause.** As early as 1819, the Supreme Court ruled in the matter of ***McCulloch v. Maryland***, 17 U.S. 316 (1819) that the powers of Congress may not be limited, but instead may be extended by implied powers based upon the Necessary and Proper Clause.

On the other hand, the Constitution also enumerates a number of prohibitions Congress may not overcome with legislation. Most of them are rooted in our historical distaste for abuses perpetrated by the English crown and its delegated colonial governors. The first of these expressly prohibits Congress from suspending ***habeas corpus***—the right to be formally charged with a crime if imprisoned—unless there is a clear emergency. Even then, the Supreme Court is reluctant to sustain such a measure.

The issue of the suspension of *habeas corpus* initially arose during the Civil War. In the matter of ***Ex Parte Milligan***, 71 U.S. 2 (1866) the Supreme Court ruled that no "emergency" was so important that taking someone's right to a hearing prior to imprisonment can be justified. Even in wartime, there must be a heavy burden placed upon the government to sustain the suspension of *habeas corpus*. The current court however, has not yet heard a case challenging the government's suspension of *habeas corpus* with regard to suspected terrorists or "enemy combatants" imprisoned at Guantanamo, Cuba.

Congress may not pass any **bills of attainder**, laws passed specifically to single out an individual or group for punishment via fine or imprisonment without first granting them a trial. Bills of attainder were common tools used by the British parliament to repress those perceived to be opponents to the Crown.

Similarly, Congress may not enact ***ex post facto* laws**, which make actions previously considered legal, punishable and apply them *retroactively*. Although not rising to a constitutional level, an example of this has occurred in Major League Baseball regarding players' use of steroids and other pharmaceutical substances which are now illegal, but were not always so. Although athletes like Mark McGuire, Barry Bonds and Roger Clemens did not violate any league rules at the time they used them, public opinion has condemned them nonetheless. The Constitution prohibits such an action *in law*. If someone acted legally and then years later a new law is passed making that prior act illegal, they cannot be charged now under the new law.

Congress also may not confer titles of nobility on citizens, such as "Lord," "Lady," or "Sir." Interestingly, during the 2010 midterm election campaign, Christine O'Donnell, the Republican senatorial candidate from Delaware, claimed that President Obama was in violation of the Constitution prohibiting the granting of titles of nobility because he appointed "czars" to head department agencies.[10] Of course, there is nothing sinister, "communist" or "socialist" in the use of that term. It was first applied by President Franklin Roosevelt to those members of his administration who provided leading policy decisions, as well as to department heads responsible for dealing with the unstable economy during the Great Depression. President Richard Nixon appointed the first **drug czar** in the **War on Drugs**, and since that time, every president, Democratic *and* Republican, has appointed "czars" to leadership positions within their administration.

When it comes to taxes, Congress is prohibited from passing **export taxes**. This is a direct result of the English Crown's imposition of economically debilitating export taxes on the American colonies. Similarly, Congress may not enact discriminatory **import taxes**. This prohibition also has historical roots. The English Crown would routinely disrupt free trade into and out of the American colonies by imposing harsh import taxes on a variety of necessities (leading to the famous Boston Tea Party, in which radicals under the leadership of Samuel Adams dumped bales of tea into the harbor to protest "taxation without representation"). In reaction, the framers prohibited Congress from enacting such taxes if they discriminate and single out a particular country. All import taxes must be applied equally to all countries.

## PRESIDENTIAL POWERS AND LIMITATIONS

There are powers conferred upon the president which Congress must accept. Some of these powers are difficult to limit because Article II of the Constitution leaves the chief executive with broad discretion in their application.

Under the Articles of Confederation, each state was authorized to negotiate its own treaties with foreign powers. Recognizing the need for a uniform and central government, the framers opted to concentrate all powers regarding foreign affairs in the office of the president and specifically recognize the chief executive as the supreme authority when dealing with foreign matters. George Washington himself formally organized these duties under the Department of Foreign Affairs led by Secretary of

State Thomas Jefferson. The department eventually evolved into what became known as the **Department of State**.

The power granted to the president dealing with foreign affairs is not absolute. Because Congress determines the budget for the State Department and provides funds for foreign aid and the military, it can use the power of the purse and its oversight authority to institute some measure of checks and balances on the chief executive. In addition, the Senate can reject treaties entered into by the president by not giving its two-thirds vote necessary for ratification. The most notable case occurred after World War I when Henry Cabot Lodge (R. MA) led the Senate in defeating President Woodrow Wilson's Treaty of Versailles. The United States ended up signing a separate treaty with the defeated Germany.

After years of fighting an undeclared war in Korea and then Vietnam, Congress in 1973 attempted to limit the president's power as commander in chief by passing a joint resolution called the War Powers Act over the veto of then President Nixon. Under the Constitution, only Congress has the authority to declare war. The War Powers Act requires the president to notify Congress within 48 hours of sending American military troops into action. In the event the military action extends beyond 60 days, an additional notification is required and Congress may then force the president to halt all affected military efforts if there has been no congressional declaration of war. Sounds reasonable on the surface, but it can also be viewed as a politically motivated usurpation of the constitutional powers granted to the president.

The constitutionality of the War Powers Act has not been determined by the Supreme Court, perhaps because of its reluctance to allow arguments to be heard before it that specifically pit the legislative and executive branches of government against each other. In today's charged ideological climate, such a dispute would rise to the level of being a political rather than a constitutional conflict, and the Supreme Court generally avoids such disagreements. In practice, every president since Nixon has ignored the War Powers Act.

Starting in 1983, President Reagan committed military actions in Panama, Granada and Lebanon. President George H.W. Bush involved the military in missions to Haiti and the first Gulf War to liberate Kuwait. President Clinton sent troops to Somalia and Kosovo. President George W. Bush fought undeclared wars in Iraq and Afghanistan. President Obama continued the commitment of troops to Iraq and Afghanistan and approved American Air Force fly-over protection to citizens in Libya. Clearly, the War Powers Act has had no effect whatsoever on the use of our military by our commander in chief.

In June of 2011, Speaker of the House John Boehner, (R. OH) claimed that President Obama was in violation of the War Powers Act because he did not seek congressional authorization for committing the U.S. Air Force over the skies of Libya. Political opponents and opposition news media joined the chorus decrying yet another of Obama's "wrongdoing" as president. Boehner seemed to have forgotten that he himself voted to repeal the act in 1995 as stated in a press release four years earlier:

> *Invoking the constitutionally-suspect War Powers Act may halt our nation snowballing involvement in the Kosovo quagmire. But it's also likely to tie the hands of future presidents.... A strong presidency is a key pillar of the American system of government—the same system of government our military men and women are prepared to give their lives to defend. Just as good intentions alone are not enough to justify sending American troops into harm's way, good intentions alone are not enough to justify tampering with the underpinnings of American democracy.* [11]

Up to now, at no time in our history has Congress garnered enough votes to force the president to do its bidding when it comes to the imposition of the War Powers Resolution.

## VETO POWER

Under Article II of the Constitution, the president was formally granted power to veto any legislation coming out of Congress. As soon as a final bill has been approved in both the House and the Senate, it is delivered to the president for his signature. He can either accept the bill as written or reject it outright by vetoing it. If he does the latter, contemporary practice requires him to notify Congress and to attach a veto message indicating the reasons for rejection. The legislative branch can override the president's veto by a two-thirds vote in both chambers (veto override). If that is the case, the president must then execute the bill as Congress originally intended. In the event one or the other chamber cannot muster the two-thirds vote, the veto remains intact and the bill dies. If Congress wishes to initiate the same bill again, it must begin from scratch in committee and go through the same lengthy legislative process as before.

The framers also left the president political "wriggle room" when it comes to accepting bills he does not agree with politically. If he suspects Congress has enough votes to successfully override his veto, president can elect not to sign or veto the bill for a period of 10 days after it reaches his desk, and it will become law without his signature.

The 10-day delay led to an interesting quirk in the process. In earlier times, Congress routinely presented presidents will bills for signature at the end of sessions (just preceding elections for a new Congress). Andrew Jackson, however, well versed in presidential authority, understood that if he ignored any bill that came to him during the last 10 days of a Congressional session and he ignored it, it would die. Jackson routinely stuffed his pockets with such bills, giving rise to the term "pocket veto." With Congress out of session and unable to override a veto, it had to watch helplessly as these bills expired. As a result, Congress, wise to this presidential tactic for some time, now rarely risks presenting bills the president doesn't like for his signature within 10 days of the end of a session.

## RECESS APPOINTMENTS

Another power the president may wield that frequently raises the hackles of members of Congress is the use of **recess appointments**. Although department heads typically must be confirmed by a majority of the Senate, Article II provides for the president to appoint them without the usual confirmation process, if Congress is in formal recess. Such appointees may not hold their office beyond the end of the current session of Congress, however. Presidents have historically used recess appointments to circumvent the entire confirmation process, either to speed up matters or to defy a recalcitrant Senate that refuses to vote in a nominee.

In January 2012, President Obama used this authority by appointing Richard Cordray to head the new Consumer Protection Finance Bureau. Immediately upon announcing the recess appointment, Republicans voiced outrage, ranging from claims that the president's action violated the Constitution or at the very least, violated the spirit of the Constitution. They bolstered their claims by insisting Congress had not been in recess, as pro forma sessions had been held on a daily basis, thereby rendering the recess appointment invalid. It seems that Republicans had at least one representative and senator go into each congressional chamber each day and gavel the session open, only to end it a minute later, thereby specifically avoiding a formal recess and affording the president the opportunity to make constitutionally authorized appointments without senatorial confirmation.

It should be noted that the efforts of the Republicans to use pro forma actions *did not* originate with them. During the administration of George W. Bush, Democrats first tried this ruse. Bush ignored them and made his recess appointments anyway. Obama went a step further, claiming his presidential authority rests on legal opinions issued by the Bush legal team. Thus far, Obama has made a total of 29 recess appointments, all to the chagrin of the Republicans in Congress.

Such appointments are hardly new. Recent presidents have taken advantage of the mechanism far more often than Obama. George W. Bush made a total of 171 recess appointments; Bill Clinton, 139; George H.W. Bush, 77 and Ronald Reagan, 243. The undisputed king of recess appointments thus far was Theodore Roosevelt, who made over 300 appointments in his two terms as president.[12]

However, in 2014, the Supreme Court ruled 5-4 in the matter of **_NRLB v. Noel Canning_** (#12-1281, decided June 26, 2014) that only the Senate can reasonably determine whether it is in session and capable of conducting business, including confirming presidential appointees. The Court ruled pro forma sessions—even limited to opening and closing, and no business being conducted—were enough to bar presidential recess appointments, so long as they lasted only up to 10 days. In the event they exceeded that time limit, the Senate would no longer be capable of meeting its "confirmation" authority, and the president could, under Article II powers, move forward with such appointments. This case is significant because the framers did not determine any time limits for when a president may execute recess appointments. In its decision, the Court artificially imposed a "short term" period in which such appointments may not be made.

## BUDGET ISSUES

A medical doctor once quipped, "the largest nerve in the human body runs through the wallet." Perhaps that is why the budget is by far the largest bone of contention between the president and Congress. As mentioned in the previous chapter, the White House relies upon the Office of Management and Budget (OMB) to work out all the budgetary needs of all Cabinet departments and agencies. They expect each secretary, department chair and agency head to fight tooth and nail for every penny they can extract from the proposed federal budget. It is the OMB's job to distill these requests into a working budget that also complies with the policy initiatives created by the president and his advisors.

Once a budget proposal is completed with presidential approval, the OMB submits it to Congress. As mentioned before, oftentimes the OMB proposes a laundry list of "wants" in addition to needs, knowing that Congress alone has the authority to enact a budget for the nation's upcoming fiscal year (October through the end of September). It is then up to the House to package a budget initiative and forward it to the Senate, which will in turn come up with its own version (packed with amendments and pork-laden riders). Pundits, political activists and the media love to lambast the president when it comes to federal spending and the budget, but it is Congress that deserves the "heat." The president ultimately can only operate on budget-related funds that Congress decides to provide.

In the event the House, the Senate and the president cannot reach agreement on a budget, an impasse results and the federal government may be forced into a **shutdown**. During a shutdown, all non-essential federal personnel, departments and agencies are closed and put on unpaid furloughs.

One such shutdown occurred in November of 1995 and extended into January of the following year when then President Bill Clinton vetoed a budget bill initiated by then Speaker Newt Gingrich (R. GA) because it contained extensive budget cuts Clinton would not agree to. Speaker Gingrich then threatened to block any effort to raise the federal debt ceiling, endangering the creditworthiness of the United States. Gingrich had campaigned on a platform he called **Contract for America** which demanded that federal spending be severely cut back and the size of the federal government trimmed. In retrospect, it has become clear, however, that what he really wanted was to minimize the power of a sitting Democratic president and harm his credibility.

Gingrich imagined that the political fallout resulting from the shutdown would be a windfall for the GOP-led Congress. He calculated that Clinton would be blamed for his inability to lead the country's economy and to curb the excessive spending habits of the Democrats in office. Unfortunately for Gingrich, the Democrats used the shutdown as evidence of the Republicans' play for power and suggested that the Contract for America had become the Contract *on* America. After a tremendous drop in the 1998 polls, Gingrich resigned both his Speakership and his congressional seat. Bill Clinton ultimately was reelected president to serve a second term.

The only way to avoid a shutdown when Congress and the president cannot agree on a budget is for Congress to pass a **continuing resolution** allowing the government to operate on a temporary basis under either the terms of the prior budget or upon newly negotiated budget provisions. In late 2010, a budget battle resulted in a standoff between Republicans and Democrats, threatening such a shutdown of the government. Ultimately, President Obama negotiated new budget terms with spending cuts, along with a two-year extension of the Bush-era tax cuts, and a continuing resolution was passed by Congress to carry the budget through the end of September 2012.

During the subsequent negotiations, candidates for the 2012 Republican presidential nomination engaged in extreme rhetoric, demanding that no further extensions of the debt ceiling be tolerated, at the risk of a full-scale financial default by our government. Political wrangling delayed the vote to raise the debt ceiling until barely less than 24 hours before the nation would in fact default on its debt. The freshman Tea Party members in Congress made it perfectly clear that they would sacrifice the nation's creditworthiness to prove their point that the federal government was "too big." Political figures such as Sarah Palin, Michele Bachmann and Mitt Romney each voiced stern opposition to efforts to raise the debt ceiling, even though it was to pay for funds already spent.

As a result, Standard and Poors, the international credit rating agency, downgraded the United States from AAA to AA, contributing to instability in financial markets. Some Tea Party-motivated members of the Republican Party were banking on President Obama being hurt by this, claiming he was solely responsible for the debacle.

But the clamor against the president's alleged lack of leadership on the economy no longer seems to resonate with most Americans, who blame the Republicans for the Congressional gridlock. Following the "fiscal cliff" in December of 2012, when GOP House Speaker John Boehner was unable to corral his caucus and get a vote to support a proposed alternative to Obama's earlier "grand bargain," it triggered automatic, across-the-board government spending cuts, known as **sequestration,** to all federal agencies and programs. At the same time, it meant that all extensions of the Bush tax cuts expired, resulting in the raising of income taxes on all Americans. Ironically, though spending cuts were maintained in all areas except the military and Federal Aviation Administration, so that air travel could continue unimpeded, the increased tax rates resulted in revenues of $800 billion, cutting the 2013 fiscal deficit in half.

Yet another GOP-led charge led to the shutdown of the U.S. government in the fall of 2013 when the radical wing of the Republican Party refused to consider any continuing resolution to finance the government unless it included provisions to defund or repeal the Affordable Care Act. Once President Obama declared he would veto any such measures, the government closed down for more than two weeks, until the GOP negotiated a continuation for federal funding without their demands being met. To this day, Obamacare remains a talking point for the far right and a litmus test for conservative political candidates that seek to limit the federal government and to reject anything Obama proposes as President.

## A RETURN TO MONARCHY?

Another bone of contention between legislative and executive branches is the widespread use of powers by the president. The subject matter was labeled **The Imperial Presidency** by historian Arthur M. Schlesinger in 1973. This idea suggests that although the framers clearly established Congress as having the most power in our government, over time the presidency has in fact become "imperial" and now occupies the most commanding position in our system of government. Such a notion raises two significant questions about the presidency: Does the holder of the office of the president exert too much power, and does this development violate the powers as originally conceived by the Constitution?

In the modern era, imperial powers of the president have extended to the frequent use of **executive agreements** (circumventing control by Congress), **emergency powers** to declare federal disaster areas allocating federal emergency funds, support and loans to the victims of said disasters (without seeking prior congressional approval), and the relatively modern use of what are known as **signing statements**.

A number of presidents have asked Congress for a **line item veto** to allow them to strike out provisions of a bill they disagree with, but the Supreme Court has ruled such a veto unconstitutional (see ***Clinton v. City of New York***, 524 U.S. 417 (1998)), although some state governors have that power. To get around that decision, presidents have begun to attach signing statements to bills, outlining how they will interpret the bill's intent and how they plan to enforce it. The idea is that the president can choose to enforce provisions that meet his approval and ignore provisions he would cross out had he the power to do so. Critics of that practice believe signing statements are unconstitutional, violating the independence of Congress and unlawfully extending the powers of the executive branch by allowing them to substitute the president's interpretation of the bill for what was intended by Congress.[13] Much to his opponents' dismay, President Clinton routinely used signing statements to deflect bills presented by a GOP Congress. President George W. Bush in turn endorsed over 750 signing statements during his tenure in the White House.

An example of President Obama's use of a signing statement occurred during the trade of five Taliban prisoners from Guantanamo Bay for Army Sargent Bowe Bergdahl. According to a bill passed by Congress, the president is required to provide notification in advance of any prisoner enemy combatant exchanges. In signing that bill into law, President Obama executed a signing statement allowing him to be exempted from the prior notification requirement, in the event he thought "exigent circumstances" existed that would necessitate immediate emergency action. Upon learning of the prisoner exchange, the right-wing media went into hyperdrive, Outraged by the president violating a requirement he himself had signed into law. But President Obama cited "emergency action" in the prisoner swap, thereby invoking the authority he maintained in the signing statement, rendering what he did "legal."

Signing statements are great when they benefit one's ideology, but bad when they do not. The Supreme Court has never ruled on the constitutionality of signing statements and perhaps never will, as it is a political dispute, not a "justiciable" dispute (more on this under the Supreme Court section).

Another way presidents have expanded their power and influence is by refusing to spend money allocated by Congress. This practice is known as **impoundment.** What really gets Congress' goat is when a president elects to shift money he refuses to spend as allocated for use in another area. To counter this practice the legislature passed the Congressional Budget and Impoundment Act of 1973, which allows Congress to insist that impounded money be spent as intended, but only if it musters a two-thirds majority vote.

There are additional ways for the president to "dance" with Congress over the budget. After the OMB submits its proposed wish list in the form of a proposed budget, the House Ways and Means Committee, along with a variety of related congressional committees, hold hearings and investigate how much shall be spent. These committees routinely interrogate officials from the OMB to determine how they arrived at their wish list. This is also the time when lobbyists come out of the woodwork and push their pet projects. After considering the budget requests, the **Congressional Budget Office** (CBO) reviews the accounting involved.

Created by Congress to review and investigate federal spending, the CBO is perhaps the only legislative branch agency that is non-partisan. It is not influenced by political ideology or party politics. The job of its financial and accounting experts is to present the "bottom line" on the budget and the spending it authorizes. According to the CBO's website, its mission is to provide "objective, nonpartisan and timely analysis to aid in economic and budgetary decisions on a wide array of programs covered by the federal budget and to provide information and estimates required for the congressional budget process."[14]

By mandate, the CBO has to produce a tentative budget and a complete analysis for submission to Congress no later than May 15. A revised budget must then be voted on in both chambers by September 15. Following that, a conference committee reconciles the two bills, and that version will be "marked up" for final presentation to both chambers for a floor vote. Once the bill is marked up; it can no longer be amended or altered. In the event a budget is ultimately passed by Congress, it still must be approved and signed into law by the president. If the president vetoes the budget bill, the entire process must start anew and negotiations are back at square one.

Once a budget bill has been signed into law, the president as chief executive can move money as needed within the departments and agencies he controls. If there is not enough to meet certain departmental needs, the president can cut funding from other departments in order to cover the shortfall. This method is known as the president's **reconciliation power**.

Because the Constitution clearly gives Congress the power to create the budget, it is wiser for a president to use his **rescission power** to cut congressional budget spending if he wishes to do so. Rescission power simply allows him to rescind the "offending" portion of the budget. Within 45 days both houses of Congress must approve or disapprove of the president's action. If Congress rejects the rescission, the president must then comply with the spending as originally authorized.

Another way for the president to respond to the budget is known as the **deferral power**, which refers to his ability to delay mandated spending for a period of up to one year without congressional approval. In the event the president elects to defer the spending for a second year, he must notify Congress, which may enact legislation prohibiting the further deferral.

The areas of the budget where the president has the opportunity to manipulate how monies are paid out are considered **discretionary spending**. This includes funding for the military (troops) and defense (missile systems, fighters and aircraft carriers, etc.). Discretionary spending also covers financial support for roads, education, all federal departments and agencies, and bureaucratic salaries.

There are also areas of the budget in which the president has no wiggle room, known as **mandatory spending**. It applies to such programs as Medicare, interest on the national debt (currently pushing $16 trillion), Social Security, welfare, Medicaid, veterans programs and to a large extent, federally guaranteed student loans. These are commonly known as **entitlements.** Required by law, mandatory spending cannot be reconciled, rescinded or deferred.

The president will keep some expenditures secret from Congress, claiming the monies are spent on items relating to matters of national security. Because there is no "check and balance" oversight, such spending runs the risk of being used for illegal purposes. Domestic wiretaps and secret investigations, including electronic surveillance, are areas of concerns.

However, Congress currently pays little attention to such matters once the president invokes the Patriot Act as justification for the expenditures.

Another way the chief executive has expanded his powers beyond what the original framers anticipated is the use of **presidential findings**. These are unilateral determinations by the president under emergency circumstances allowing him to approve actions that may be unlawful under non-emergency conditions. Examples are the presidential findings authorizing the payment of a bounty for the capture or killing of Osama Bin Laden and other al-Qaeda leaders. Findings also permit the authorization of agreements with foreign nations that would otherwise violate U.S. law (trading arms for hostages with Iran under Reagan, for example).

Congress has not sat by idly either. For years, it has attempted to expand various forms of control over administrative agencies. On more than one occasion, it has enacted general and vague laws for which the president then can determine guidelines, rules and regulations relating to their implementation. Congress then, pursuant to the original legislation, would have the ability to alter the president's efforts by amending his proposed guidelines, rules and regulations or by vetoing them all together. This effort was ultimately considered an attempt by Congress to create a **legislative veto** over the president.

The legislative veto issue was resolved in the Supreme Court when it ruled that Congress could not delegate regulatory control to the executive branch and then at some point attempt to re-take control via the legislative veto process. The Supreme Court agreed and ruled legislative vetoes unconstitutional (see ***INS v. Chadra***, 462 U.S. 1919 (1983)).

Congress continues to use other methods previously considered forms of legislative vetoes. By enacting **joint resolutions,** statements approved and voted upon in both chambers, it attempts to put political pressure on a president or to rally public support against the president and his policies. In the Joint Resolution on Libya in 2011, for example,

Congress demanded that President Obama comply with the provisions of the War Powers Act. Another way to do this is to issue a **concurrent resolution** wherein one chamber passes a statement or opinion and the other chamber agrees separately in its own resolution. Regardless of their public relations value, such resolutions have no effect in law and are not binding on the president.

While it may seem that the powers of the presidency have expanded to a much greater degree than those of the legislature, it must be remembered that the ultimate "check and balance" trump card resides in the hands of Congress—namely, the "Power of the Purse." Because Congress determines the federal budget, the president can only spend money it provides.

## Linkage to the Public

The struggle for power between governmental branches is also reflected in the way they connect to the public. Their linkage can often be measured by the impact and control our political parties have over the chambers of Congress. When the president's political party controls both the House and Senate, we wind up having what is known as a **unified government.** Although it may be easier to pass the chief executive's legislative agenda when both the chambers are aligned to his agenda (and enforced by the Speaker and majority leader), in response the opposition political party will usually dig in its heels and attempt to characterize the majority party as overreaching. In this scenario, the minority party will become the "Party of No," unwilling to accommodate or compromise with the majority, lest they lose any political edge for the next election cycle. Unified government can backfire and cause a slowdown in legislative affairs and lead to contentiousness and fighting between those found on the extreme left and right wings of their respective political parties.

Prior to the midterm elections of 2010, the Democrats controlled the House, the Senate and the White House. In classic response to this unified government, the GOP became the "Party of No." With its willing supporters in the media, it quickly pursued a political agenda to attack the ruling majority, no matter what legislation was under consideration. The GOP successfully took control of the House as a result, but still did not gain control of the Senate.

And so the jostling between government branches continues. The president enforces the laws created by Congress as he interprets them, while the Congress finds ways to override the power vested in the executive branch. This battling was anticipated and encouraged by the framers as a way to invigorate political discourse and compromise. True leaders in both branches were to work towards finding common ground in the best interests of all Americans. It is doubtful that the framers would condone the frequent head-butting and gridlock we see today between our president and Congress. No doubt, the system would work if we had the right leaders in place. The system is not broken, the people we elect to serve as our leaders are.

Since 2010, we had a form of a **divided government**, where the branches are not all of the same political party. Although compromise should be easier, it is still hard to come by. The ideologically driven media at both ends of the political spectrum prefer to create a tension of public distrust for government in an effort to gain control, power and increased viewership doesn't help. The primary objective of political parties is to get people elected to office to gain power, often at the cost of what's best for the American people. The sooner the public realizes this, the sooner we will demand that our elected representatives serve *our* interests and not the interests of the extreme wings of their respective parties and their corporate sponsors.

# 7

# ✦ THE JUDICIAL BRANCH ✦

## Rubber Stamp or Supreme Arbiter?

Although the framers granted Congress exclusive authority to establish the jurisdiction of the federal judiciary, they clearly intended the legal system to function independently and to provide checks and balances to the Legislative and Executive branches.

**Article III, Section 1** states:

> *The Judicial Power of the United States, shall be vested in one supreme court, and in such inferior courts as the Congress may from time to time ordain and establish.*

Recently, some members of the Republican Party, backed by members of the right-wing media, have determined that the judicial branch of the U.S. government should no longer be independent of congressional oversight. During the 2012 presidential primaries, candidate Newt Gingrich openly called for all judicial decisions of the federal courts be subject to congressional review with federal judges being subject to impeachment if their decisions ran contrary to the mood of the congressional majority. He and his supporters also claimed that Congress should have the authority to outright eliminate any federal court that defies its views on legal matters.[15]

What makes these assertions so amazing is the fact that the framers set forth the role and powers vested in the judicial branch in **Article III** with succinct clarity. Considering that conservatives usually argue for a literal interpretation of the Constitution, they are nothing short of astonishing, as they argue for deconstructing the very institutions the framers created with great deliberation.

Under the Articles of Confederation the nation did not have a central judiciary. Each state was free to establish its own judicial system and vest it with limited authority to resolve various legal matters, but there was no mechanism to settle disputes and controversies between states.

When the framers sought to address this problem, they realized that the fledgling nation had no tradition of established common law. They understood that they had a unique opportunity to create a new and reliable judicial system consistent with the principles of liberty and freedom fought for during the Revolutionary War. They further appreciated the need to develop an independent judiciary that would establish a new system of American common law. Common law or "case made law" is the accumulation of decisions made by judges that set precedents for future cases. The establishment of a judiciary based on the use of precedent, or **stare decisis**, is fundamental to American law.

## JUDICIAL REVIEW

The framers understood that constructing such a system would require a sustained and steady influx of case decisions that would take years to develop. In an effort to convince states-rights advocates to go along with their vision, they resolved to leave the task of creating all judicial rulemaking and jurisdiction to Congress.

The original intent behind the federal judiciary can be found in Alexander Hamilton's commentary in **Federalist No. 78**, in which he pointedly argued that although Congress was to be the "House of the People," it could not be entrusted with the responsibility to judge its own acts. Hamilton recognized that the legislature could far too easily enact new laws if it disagreed with a court's ruling, thereby controlling the creation of legal precedent or rule of law. Therefore, he demanded a strong judicial system empowered to provide the bedrock of support for the objectives of the infant democratic republic:

> *A Constitution is, in fact, and must be, regarded by the judges as fundamental Law. It must therefore belong to them to ascertain its meaning, as well as the meaning of any particular act proceeding from the legislative body…no other way than through the medium of the courts of justice, whose duty it must be to declare all acts contrary to the manifest tenor of the constitution void.*

In one simple paragraph, Hamilton laid out the argument that the judiciary and Supreme Court, independent of political influence, must have the exclusive authority to safeguard the Constitution from legislation that runs counter to its stated purposes, protections of liberty, and system of government.

He also advocated a cogent argument that jurists needed lifetime tenure by warning:

> *…courts of Justice can certainly not be expected from judges who hold their offices by a temporary commission. Periodical appointments, however regulated, or by whomsoever made, would in some way or other, be fatal to their (the Justices) necessary independence.*

Hamilton also applied the principal of *stare decisis* to the Supreme Court, insisting that:

> *…it will readily be conceived, from the variety of controversies which grow out of the folly and wickedness of mankind, that the records of those precedents must unavoidably swell to a very considerable bulk, and must demand long and laborious study to acquire a competent knowledge of them.*

As early as 1803, 15 years after the ratification of the Constitution, then Chief Justice John Marshall derived one of the cornerstones of the

Supreme Court's power from its own interpretation of **Article III**. In the seminal case of ***Marbury v. Madison***, 5 U.S. 137 (1803), he established that through the process of **judicial review** or *stare decisis*, the Supreme Court alone possessed the exclusive authority to determine if actions undertaken by the legislative or executive branch are "constitutional" and therefore legally valid. This decision cemented the intent of the framers that the court would be the third pillar of the checks and balances system of government.

Further expansion of judicial powers followed via a series of equally important rulings. In ***Fletcher v. Peck***, 10 U.S. 87 (1810), the young Supreme Court, still under Chief Justice Marshall, held that it had the authority to declare a state law unconstitutional. In ***Dartmouth College v. Woodward***, 17 U.S. 518 (1819), it ruled that it had the supreme authority to protect contract rights, even if the contracts had been entered into prior to the establishment of the United States and regardless of the intentions of a state to rule the contract null *ab initio* (from its creation). Once again, the Court in ***McCulloch v. Maryland***, 17 U.S. 316 (1819), held that although the Constitution does not explicitly empower the federal government to charter a national bank, it *implied* it as a part of the **Necessary and Proper Clause** when applied to the explicit powers enumerated in the **Commerce Clause.** From then on, any act undertaken by the federal government reasonably deemed "necessary and proper" would be validated as constitutional by the Supreme Court, regardless of its impact on any or all of the states. These cases validated federalism and confirmed the authority of the federal government, as established in both the Constitution and case law rulings by the Supreme Court, as the supreme authority of the Union.

Further applying the principle in *McCulloch*, the court in ***Gibbons v. Ogden***, 22 U.S. 1 (1824), established that the federal government's authority to control waterways was inherently a part of "interstate commerce," which could therefore be regulated by Congress.

It is now considered standard legal theory that once a law is determined "unconstitutional" by the Supreme Court, it is forever void. If Congress disagrees with the decision, it can either create a new law in accordance with the principles outlined by the court in established opinions or initiate a constitutional amendment. In order to pursue the latter course, Congress must first obtain a two-thirds majority of both houses of Congress. Then three-fourths of the state legislatures have to approve and ratify the proposed amendment before it becomes part of the Constitution.

Congress, with the approval of two-thirds of its members, can also call for the assembly of a **constitutional convention,** whose purpose it would be to draft specific amendment language. This amendment would also require ratification of three-fourths of the state legislatures before becoming supreme law. Since the ratification of the Constitution in 1788, there has not been a single constitutional convention.

Beginning with the Twenty-Third Amendment, Congress began considering a seven-year limit for proposed amendments to be ratified. Regardless, there is no set timeframe for the states to ratify or reject a proposed amendment set forth in the Constitution. The Twenty-Seventh Amendment regarding congressional pay raises was initially proposed for ratification in 1789, but it was not formally ratified until 1992! Some amendments also take a long time to fail. The Equal Rights Amendment, designed to guarantee women's rights, failed after a seven-year ratification process. It is important to note that once a state ratifies an amendment to the Constitution, it cannot rescind that decision.

## JUDICIAL JURISDICTION

In accordance with **Article I, Section 8, Clause 1** of the Constitution, Congress shall have the power to *"constitute the Tribunals inferior to the supreme court,"* subsequently known as Article III courts or legislative courts. As a result, the United States has separate legal divisions within the judicial system. At the most basic level is the **trial division**. At this level, courts render decisions after fairly hearing all disputes ("bench" or judge rulings and/or jury rulings).

Under the American system of law, the judge hearing the case on the merits of a claim and related evidence does not prosecute the case. The complaining party or **plaintiff** brings claims and evidence at trial against an offending party. That party is known as the **defendant**. Plaintiffs and defendants are collectively referred to as **litigants.** Trial judges are required to remain neutral in judicial proceedings, ensuring that all procedures are properly and fairly applied to the litigants. Trials may be decided either by a trial judge alone or by a jury impaneled to render a verdict with the trial judge merely acting as an impartial monitor of the proceedings.

A trial by jury is *not* automatic. Without a formal request, the federal clerk of the court will assign the matter to be treated as a bench trial—heard only by a judge. Either party in a lawsuit may ask for a jury trial, however. If that happens, the jury will decide the outcome of the case provided its decision is unanimous. Federal jury trials require a unanimous verdict of all 12 jurors. In the event the jury cannot reach a unanimous verdict, the judge will declare a **hung jury**, and the court will render a decision that the pending matter is to be considered a **mistrial**. In that event, a new trial may or may not be called. The decision rests with the parties involved. In a criminal case, it is up to the government prosecutor to decide if it wishes to go through the entire process again in an attempt to obtain a criminal conviction.

If the jury's verdict is so far perverted from the manifest evidence presented, the losing party may request the judge step in and override the verdict by filing a motion ***non obstante veridicto*** (**NOV**). Although this is a rare event, it can occur.

No case may be brought before an American judge unless there is an actual legal controversy or damage affecting a particular person or group. Such exposure to damages or injury gives the parties **standing**. Cases cannot be heard by a court in an effort to simply seek an advisory opinion. Courts must only hear **justiciable** disputes.

Although litigants must have standing to initiate a lawsuit and to be heard in court, others that would benefit from a favorable decision in a pending case may submit memoranda and briefs of law as **friends of the court.** These submissions are known as *amicus curiae* briefs and represent legal arguments supporting a plaintiff or defendant in an attempt to sway a judge's decision. Frequently, interest groups have their lawyers file an amicus brief in an effort to get a ruling favorable to their particular concerns. Examples would be women's groups filing such briefs in abortion litigation, favoring the right to choose; or the Sierra Club submitting an amicus brief in support of an environmental protection lawsuit.

The next level of the legal system is the **appellate division**. There, all rulings from the trial division may be appealed based on claims of improper application of law or technical violations of procedure (improperly admitting evidence, for example). Cases are typically presented before a panel of appellate judges, and juries are not allowed. Improper application of law may include claims that the law itself violates the Constitution. The highest appellate court in America is the **Supreme Court**, although it also may hear cases that originate before it. In the event a federal law is disputed, it can be heard only in federal court. The ability to hear cases is the application of jurisdiction. Congress has acted on only one occasion to limit the juristiction of the Supreme Court—**_Ex Parte McCardle_**, 74 U.S. (7 Wall.) 506 (1868)—and to do so today would certainly lead to a Constitutional crisis.

Courts at the **state level** are established by their respective state legislatures. Because there are 50 states, there are also just as many separate systems of courts, each with their own sets of laws, regulations and enforcing agencies. Each also has its own framework for appellate courts, including a state supreme court.

What if a dispute involves both a federal and state question of law? What if two or more states are directly involved in a dispute with each other? To deal with such cases, Congress divided our system of federal courts into 12 districts. The **federal district courts** have **original jurisdiction** to decide the facts of all cases involving federal law whether it is **civil** or **criminal** in nature. They are also empowered to resolve any conflict arising between two or more states, or where the federal government itself is actually a party to the dispute.

In situations involving states, the U.S. Supreme Court also has original jurisdiction and may hear "a case of first impression." Other instances of the Supreme Court exercising original jurisdiction include cases involving ambassadors from foreign countries whose diplomatic immunity precludes them from standing trial in any other American court, cases involving the federal government as a party, or cases questioning the constitutionality of a law. Original cases heard before the Supreme Court are quite rare. It is estimated the Supreme Court receives annually over 7,000 cases for review, but consents to hear no more than about 150 in any given term (October through end of June or early July), and only a small percentage of those are cases of first impression.

Except for the original jurisdiction granted to the Supreme Court under the Constitution, Congress has the power to define the jurisdiction of all other federal courts. In addition, it has expressly created courts authorized to enforce its **statutes** (codified laws) enacted into law. These **Article III/legislative courts** include the **U.S. Court of Claims**, which examines all property and contract claims against the United States, and the **U.S. Bankruptcy Court**, which hears petitions for individuals and businesses filing under available chapters of the U.S. Bankruptcy Code. The latter has received considerable criticism during the recent economic troubles because it allows large corporations to restructure and benefit from debt forgiveness under Chapter 11, but does not extend the same relief to individuals financially burdened with student loans under Chapters 13 or 7.

Congress also created **courts of military justice**, which enforce military codes that do not apply to civilians. There is also a **Court of Appeals for the Armed Forces.** Except in movies and television, the American people have traditionally ignored the use of military tribunals to deal with infractions of the Code of Military Justice by members of the armed forces. This recently changed as **enemy combatants** (a term coined by the Bush Administration) have been held without formal charges (*habeas corpus*). Although the United States is not formally at war (as declared by Congress), most terrorism experts believe enemy combatants should be tried before military courts and not in civilian federal courts. The constitutionality of these matters has not yet been determined by the Supreme Court.

All decisions rendered in federal district courts may be appealed to the **federal circuit court of appeals**. In criminal matters, however, only convicted parties may appeal decisions of the lower courts. If a defendant was acquitted by a unanimous jury vote, the prosecuting government has no recourse. To allow the U.S. attorney to appeal an acquittal would violate a defendant's Fifth Amendment right against **double jeopardy—** being tried twice for the same alleged crime despite a not guilty verdict in the first trial. The Circuit Court of Appeals is headquartered in Washington, D.C. and is staffed by 12 justices who are assigned "circuits" or districts to hear appeals from lower federal courts.

Federal circuit courts of appeal hear only appellate cases. They hear no facts of the case and limit arguments to allegations of misapplications of law or procedure only. There are no juries at the appellate level of law. Depending upon the nature of the matter, a single judge or a panel of judges may hear and decide the case. All decisions of the circuit court of appeals then may be appealed directly to the U. S. Supreme Court.

## APPELLATE PROCEDURE

The Appellate Courts act like the referees in a professional football game, making calls as they see them. The Supreme Court, on appellate authority, acts like the booth referees, reviewing the decisions and then rendering a final judgment, either upholding or reversing the lower court's decision.

Appealing a lower court's ruling requires filing a petition with the appropriate appellate court. Petitions, also known as **writs**, must specifically state the basis for the appeal and the remedy being sought. While all writs are reviewed by the circuit courts of appeal, not all of them are granted a hearing.

In order to appeal the decision of a federal circuit court of appeal to the Supreme Court, an **appellant** (the one seeking the appeal) must file what is known as a **writ of *certiorari*** (commonly called a **writ of cert.**). All such writs are assigned to the Supreme Court justices for review. Upon completion of this review the entire court, led by the chief justice, meets and determines which of the writs will be granted or rejected. Acceptance and agreement by the Supreme Court to hear a case requires the approval of at least four of the nine justices. This is commonly known as the **Rule of Four.** An appeal may allow for oral argument before the entire court or may proceed by written argument only. Obviously, the nature of the case will determine which form of argument is assigned. In the event the United States itself is a party to a matter before the Supreme Court, it is represented by the **solicitor general**. Approximately two-thirds of all Supreme Court matters involve the solicitor general.[16]

In all cases before the Supreme Court, written communications establishing the basis for arguments are submitted by the parties to establish and justify their legal positions. These are known as **briefs** and include legal arguments based upon relevant case law that established proper (or improper) precedent. In oral arguments, the attorneys for the parties involved stand before all of the justices—up to 30 minutes—and are subjected to interrogation by the entire court. The justices pose questions to force the attorneys to clarify their written arguments and to persuade the court to accept their interpretation of the law and the established precedent in question.

Following oral arguments, the justices each independently determine how they plan to rule in the matter and then meet to collectively hash out the court's decision. This is known as **the conference**. At that time, the justices vote on the merits of the case and reach a decision. Based upon their vote, they collectively determine which justices will write the **opinion of the court**. In the event the chief justice joins the majority, he can choose to write the **majority opinion**. He may also opt to assign it to a fellow justice who agrees with the majority. In the event the chief justice's opinion is in the minority, he can elect to write the **minority** or **dissenting opinion** or select the most senior of the dissenting justices to do so. In addition, any justice may write a separate opinion if he or she feels there is an argument to be addressed which has been ignored by either the majority or minority opinion writers.

The majority opinion represents the winning side of the argument and rises to the level of law. The minority opinion is the losing side of the argument. The dissenting opinion agrees with the minority but may have other arguments not addressed in the minority opinion. The concurring decision agrees with the majority, but reaches the agreement using other arguments of law. A *per curiam* decision is a unanimous decision that remains unsigned by the justices and provides little to no explanation for the ruling.

When all justices agree, the decision is called an **unanimous opinion**. Cases in which their verdicts are divided five to four are called **split decisions**. A split decision representing the slimmest margin of victory always has the potential to be overturned in subsequent court sessions.

Opinions of the Supreme Court become the **rule of law** and are relied upon as legal precedent (*stare decisis*) for future cases. There have been times in our judicial history when a dissenting opinion has eventually become the majority opinion as a rule of law. One of the most celebrated instances occurred in 1954 when ***Brown v. Board of Education***, 347 U.S. 483 (1954) overruled ***Plessy v. Ferguson***, 163 U.S. 537 (1896) ending the legal practice of racial segregation in public places and accommodations.

## JUDICIAL PHILOSOPHY AND APPOINTMENTS

One of the "unwritten" rules of the Supreme Court has been to only hear **justiciable** matters, cases with actual conflicts involving actual complainants. That way it can remain above partisan politics and keep the realm of the law. Obviously the Supreme Court does not operate in a vacuum, but until recently, it has done a good job of avoiding non-justiciable matters, using the "justiciability" argument as an excuse to steer clear of testy political cases. That changed, however, with the 2000 presidential election. It has started to ignore the rule and involve itself in some political disputes as well (see the matter of ***Bush v. Gore***, 531 U.S. 98 (2000)).

As previously discussed, the framers argued that an independent judiciary is necessary to create solid checks and balances against actions undertaken by the legislative and/or executive branches of government. To achieve this end, they decided that judicial appointees should also be free of any political pressure that could be brought to bear by Congress or the president. Thus, justices sitting on the United States Supreme Court have lifetime tenure (subject to impeachment) to ensure a stable high court of the land. One of the consequences—perhaps unintended—is a legacy of rulings that can have a profound and lasting impact on American law and society. As a result, presidents must give serious consideration to the individuals they nominate to sit on the high court bench.

Former president Gerald Ford wrote in 2005 how important his lone nomination to the Supreme Court was for his presidential legacy:

> *Normally, little or no consideration is given to the long-term effects of a president's Supreme Court nominees. Let that not be the case with my presidency. For I am prepared to allow history's judgment of my term in office to rest (if necessary, exclusively) on my nomination 30 years ago of Justice John Paul Stevens to the U.S. Supreme Court.*[17]

Modern politics however has changed the way justices are chosen in a way the framers did not anticipate. According to the Constitution, the president has the exclusive authority to nominate and appoint federal judges, and all appointments must be confirmed by a majority vote in the Senate. But because all appointees to the federal bench must be **confirmed** by a majority vote of the entire Senate, political ideology has become a litmus test for acceptability of nominees. The Senate judiciary committee initially interviews the candidates and hears witnesses speak for and against them before voting whether to recommend or reject the confirmation. A vote of the full Senate usually follows a positive recommendation of the committee. Membership on the judiciary committee confers elevated status to senators, and the effect of party wrangling has politicized the process to a high degree. Strong candidates with extensive lists of prior decisions and writings are now frequently disqualified from the high court because their views and judicial temperament may appear "too extreme" to the opposing political party (which are the very reasons they are being considered a "fit" for the court by the president in the first place). As a result, we may no longer be getting the very best jurists to sit on the Supreme Court and have to settle for relative "lightweights" who are so "plain" they can't offend anyone and be assured of confirmation.

In recent history, confirmation hearings often have been quite contentious, as ideology has ruled the day. The early beginnings of this political rancor can be traced back to the nomination and confirmation proceedings of Robert Bork in 1987.

Robert Bork was nominated to serve as an associate justice on the U. S. Supreme Court by then President Ronald Reagan. Bork, a former solicitor general and acting attorney general under Republican President Nixon, maintained a very conservative ideology in relation to minority and women's rights. During the confirmation process, Senator Edward Kennedy (D. MA) repeatedly traded jabs with Bork in an effort to paint him as a "radical" and unacceptable "extremist" whose views did not belong on the Supreme Court. It was an ideologically charged debate couched in vicious political rhetoric that resulted in Bork's confirmation being denied by the Senate. Needless to say, Republicans were outraged by the way the Senate judiciary committee under Kennedy's leadership treated "their" appointee. The entire fiasco surrounding his nomination led to the coining of a new word regarding American confirmation politics: To be **"borked"** means coming under personal attacks in order to have one's nomination derailed.

Four years later, President George H.W. Bush nominated Clarence Thomas, an arch-conservative judge, to replace Justice Thurgood Marshall, the first black American appointed to the Supreme Court. Although Thomas was also African-American, this created what is commonly referred to as a **wedge nominee**, someone who could split the interests of a single group of voters—in this case, black voters. President Bush, recalling the fiasco of the Bork nomination, figured that by nominating one black justice to replace another, even if he was a conservative candidate, the chance of having him confirmed improved. Although the hearings turned ugly when Anita Hill, a law professor, accused Thomas of sexual misconduct during the time she had been an intern with him—the allegations were never confirmed—the Senate barely confirmed Thomas to the court by a 52 to 48 vote. He remains one of the most conservative justices on the court.

As a result of the highly charged political atmosphere surrounding nomination hearings, judicial confirmations since that time have been mini-ideological wars, in which appointees wisely answer questions in only the broadest and vaguest of terms. Hearings have become primarily political exercises, grandstanding sessions on the part of committee members, and confirmation votes tend to follow political lines. Appointees now either have what it takes to survive the confirmation process or they do not.

Harriet Miers was nominated by President George W. Bush to the Supreme Court to replace centrist Justice Sandra Day O'Conner, the first woman on the court. When it became apparent she was unlikely to be confirmed, Miers simply withdrew her own nomination. Bush then nominated conservative John Roberts, a justice on the D.C. circuit court, to replace O'Conner. Following the death of Supreme Court Chief Justice William Rehnquist, Bush nominated conservative Samuel Alito, also a district judge, to serve in the seat vacated by O'Conner and Roberts to replace Rehnquist. Both avoided politically charged issues in the answers to questions about their judicial views and record, and both were confirmed (Alito by a vote of 58 to 42 and Roberts by a vote of 95 to 3).

Regardless of the framer's efforts, it is now just as difficult to shield the rest of the judiciary from the influences of politics. In the event the president is called upon to appoint a judge to fill a vacancy on one of the 94 **federal district courts,** he will first submit a list of potential candidates to senators residing within the affected district. Senators are then encouraged to submit a list of their own candidates for the federal bench. This system of **senatorial courtesy** has gone a long way to ensure the selection of a candidate for appointment that is acceptable to all Senators of the affected district, regardless of political party affiliation. In the past, it paved the way for a smooth confirmation process in the Senate.

Unfortunately, politics has continued to interfere with this process. President George W. Bush had 23 judicial nominees for the 94 different federal district courts blocked by his Democratic opponents. Many candidates never even received a confirmation hearing as Democratic senators put their nominations on hold or employed filibusters to prevent judiciary committee hearings from being convened. Under President Obama, up to 70 federal court positions were unfilled by his fourth year in office and only 14 nominations were pending. Cloture Rule changes since 2013 have allowed presidential appointments to the judicary to be "streamlined," but appointments to the Supreme Court still require a supermajority to overcome an oppostional filibuster.

## ACTIVIST VS. JUDICIAL RESTRAINT

Because the confirmation process is now contentious at best and rife with political maneuvering, justices with a track record of creating new law without regard to *precedent* run the risk of being labeled **activists** (hence the term **judicial activism**). According to Conservapedia.com:

> *Judicial Activism is when courts do not confine themselves to reasonable interpretations of laws, but instead create laws. It is when judges substitute their own political opinions for the applicable law, or when judges act like a legislature (legislating from the bench) rather than like a traditional court.*

In light of the accepted history of the Supreme Court, is there considerable bias in this interpretation? After all, if justices like John Marshall had not been "activist" in developing our system of judicial review and *stare decisis*, where would we be? The court had to start somewhere.

Justices that adhere to a strict interpretation of the Constitution, regardless of precedent, may be labeled as **originalists** or **strict constructionists**, practicing what is commonly called **judicial restraint.** They insist that their role is to refrain from overturning legislative acts and only interpret the Constitution in strict accordance with its literal terms. This leads to some interesting questions. Does this mean, for example, that the Second Amendment should be interpreted to allow Americans to only own muskets?

**Activists**, on the other hand, believe the Constitution was designed to be a "living document," capable of engendering decisions that reflect a changing society with a host of new needs and issues affecting our rights and liberties.

The question of whether the Constitution should be viewed as a "living document" or be interpreted in accordance with its literal meaning is often a topic of heated debate, but it is something of a red herring. In reality, whenever an opinion of the Supreme Court rubs someone the wrong way, it comes in for criticism and the justices are accused of practicing judicial activism, but when they rule in a fashion acceptable to critics, regardless of how activist the decision, the derogatory label is conveniently forgotten. Common sense would suggest that the framers left some of the rules of interpreting the meaning of the Constitution purposely vague. They grasped the concept that through time, what is considered a construct of the law may in fact change. Perhaps that is why they created the mechanisms to *amend* the document?

The trouble with a literal interpretation and strict constructionism is where to start. Taking the original Constitution at face value would mean accepting that African-American men count as only three-fifths of white American men. When arguing for judicial restraint, should we have accepted a decision like ***Dred Scott v. Sandford***, 60 U.S. 393 (1858), and continued to operate under a law which held that African

Americans who came here as slaves and their descendents born here were not U.S. citizens or protected by the Constitution? Or should we not have overturned ***Plessy v. Ferguson***? It was later reversed by an "activist" court in ***Brown v. Board of Education***.

It can be argued persuasively that the framers anticipated Supreme Court rulings would have to reflect contemporary societal mores and expectations to some degree. They understood that judges must play an active role in shaping the law to meet current norms and values. They recognized a **dissenting opinion** may one day become a **majority opinion**.

# 8

# ❀ THE BUREAUCRACY ❀

## PUBLIC SERVANTS OR A WASTE OF MONEY?

From the beginning of our nation, a small cadre of loyal public servants worked within our federal offices to run the day-to-day affairs of our government. As head of the nascent Treasury Department under George Washington, Alexander Hamilton oversaw a staff of 14 workers. Today, a huge federal workforce, numbering in the millions, is responsible to fulfill the requirements of government established by Congress and the president.

In modern times, the vast number of government employees has become a controversial issue among contentious politicians. Rhetoric abounds about the "bloated size" or "wasteful spending" of the federal bureaucracy. But rhetoric is just that, inflated oratory designed to incite the listener, often without any basis in truth or reality. Does our government really waste money paying all of those employees? Has the federal government continued to grow and balloon well beyond the size it needs? Can its size be reduced without diminishing the quality of life of our nation?

It may come as a surprise to the vociferous critics that the per capita size of the federal government has actually shrunk since the 1960s. According to the U.S. Department of Labor's Bureau of Labor Statistics (another bureaucratic agency), excluding the U.S. Postal Service, the federal government employs about two million civilians, of whom 85% work in the Washington, D.C. area. There are an additional 181,000 civilians working for independent agencies such as the Social Security Administration, NASA, EPA, and the Smithsonian. Another 33,000 work specifically in the judiciary and 30,000 in the legislative branch. The pay for an entry-level federal worker (GS 1) is capped at $21,944 per year. The maximum pay for a GS 15 employee is pegged at $127,000. In 2009, the average federal worker earned $74,403 per year.[18]

The federal government also employs 1,447,000 active members in the military, another 1,458,000 as reserves, and a sizeable number of civilians. The average starting pay is $30,810. The most experienced members of the armed services (depending on rank and combat experience) can receive wages on average as high as $93,800.[19]

Civilians working within the federal government are known as **bureaucrats.** They may obtain their position by appointment or by simply applying when a job becomes available. Bureaucrats do the day-to-day work in all of the departments and agencies that operate under the control of the executive branch.

The members of the **Senior Executive Service (SES)** of the federal government serve as managers of the civilian bureaucracy. Of the approximately 7,000 SES members, about 6,400 are **non-partisan**, which means that they work within the government regardless of their political party affiliation and regardless of the political party of the president. They are vested with the authority to manage departments and agencies of the executive branch without fear of political retribution based upon their personal political ideologies. Many are career governmental employees who are hired through the **merit system** based on their skills and ability to score well on the **federal civil service examination**. Pursuant to the **Civil Service Reform Act of 1978**, all available federal jobs must be published in list form and posted in available outlets, including government installations and websites.

Included in the 7,000 senior executive services of public servants are about 600 **partisan** political executives within the bureaucracy. These public servants are appointed by the president with or without Senate confirmation and serve solely at the president's pleasure. As beneficiaries of patronage, they receive their jobs in return for support and loyalty to the president, regardless of their qualifications. Take the earlier example of President George W. Bush's choice of Michael Brown as the head of FEMA. Because of their often limited prior experience, it behooves political bureaucrats to always work closely with career executives to implement the administration's policies.

The federal bureaucracy is organized in a hierarchical format, typically structured in a non-partisan fashion, from the low-end public worker all the way up to the Cabinet secretary. Bureaucrats conduct business using workplace rules and regulations that are uniform throughout the government.

Currently, there are 15 official departments under the executive branch. Each is headed by a **Cabinet secretary** (Justice is run by the attorney general) with assistance from a non-partisan senior career executive. Although leading a department is a high-profile job, most of the appointees pursue or accept it because of their loyalty to the president, not because of the financial benefits. In comparison, salaries in the private sector for jobs with similar responsibilities are many times what a Cabinet secretary earns. The post can be a huge career boost, however, with concurrent financial rewards when a secretary leaves office and reenters the private sector, where "access" translates into money.

Cabinet departments are broken down into bureaus that are categorized according to a couple of criteria. One is who the bureau is supposed to actually work for, or who is most affected by its policies. An example is the Bureau of Indian Affairs, which deals with all issues affecting Native Americans. Another criterion is subject matter, for example the obvious role of the Bureau of Land Management in overseeing national forests and other government-owned terrain.

Despite the political rhetoric we often hear regarding governmental intrusion, Congress will typically enact broad laws whose intention is often vague. As a result, many governmental departments and agencies are tasked with the responsibility of establishing their own policy-related directives in order to meet the objectives of congressional legislation. By establishing this process, Congress reserves the right to politicize bureaucratic policies and regulations for their political gain.

Sometimes the policy-related objectives of a department or bureau can run entirely counter to those initiated by Congress. That is when congressional committees and subcommittees provide **oversight** to help keep the agencies on their toes and implement policy. It is not unusual, though, for the president and his Cabinet secretaries to steer them back to the course they originally pursued. Virtually all disputes between government agencies and Congress are politically based. Although such conflicts may lead to a contentious relationship between the administration and Congress, the legislative branch has only a few options available to get its way. Congress may attempt to enact new laws which restrict the "offending" agency's ability to implement policies, or it may reduce funding in the next budget. The president, of course, has the option to veto such legislation and can manipulate the budget to get around congressional pressures.

## THE CABINET AND THE BUREAUCRACY

Cabinet secretaries are appointed by the president and confirmed by a majority vote of the Senate. Despite public perception, Cabinet meetings with the president occur infrequently. Instead, most communications routinely go through the chief of staff's office. Cabinet secretaries may meet one-on-one with the president and the chief of staff in the Oval Office on an "as needed" basis.

Although Cabinet secretaries are directly responsible to run all departments and bureaus, few have more than a "generalist's" background in administration and management, and more often than not, no direct prior expertise in the area in which their department operates. That is because their experience as former governors, former members of Congress, business executives, or perhaps deputy directors or undersecretaries of departments is limited to a particular constituency, rather than national concerns. In addition, most, but not all, are political appointments that share the political ideologies of the president. As a result, all Cabinet secretaries, regardless of their expertise, rely heavily on career executives within their respective departments, agencies or bureaus.

It is not unusual for the president to cast blame on a Cabinet secretary for a failed policy. In the event of public fallout over an unsuccessful or disastrous initiative, it is not unusual for a secretary to resign rather than expose the administration's culpability. Being asked to "fall on one's sword" as a loyal soldier seems to be part of the job description.

## Iron Triangles and Lobbyists

A tripartite alliance exists between members of Congress and their staffs, departmental and agency staffers and outside interest groups. This is known as the **Iron Triangle.** Interest groups representing their own constituencies lobby and use their influence to push for policy initiatives with congressional and bureaucratic staff who in turn lobby staff within the White House. Iron Triangles are considered a part of what are known as **Issue Networks.**

The way it works is that after listening to lobbyists make their case, a congressional staff member briefs his particular boss on the proposed policy, including the political and/or financial support he will gain. The members of Congress then directly lobby White House staff to consider formal support for the suggested policy initiative. The president, on recommendation of his chief of staff, will in turn call for a congressional bill with language favorable to the interest group. A sponsored bill will then be introduced into the House or Senate with the blessings of the interest group and the White House. Iron Triangles are the most familiar mechanism used for the creation and implementation of policy initiatives.

One concept governing the workings of iron triangles, in order to assure the best possible outcome in a democracy, is pluralism. The idea is to have many competing interest groups weigh in on a particular issue, with the government as mediator and ultimate decision maker taking into account all points of view and then creating laws based on what is most beneficial for the majority of the American people. Pluralism is considered a pragmatic approach in which the best legislation results from a struggle among conflicting, even opposing interests. It supposes that if each interest group has an equal opportunity to argue its case and influence the government, good policies will result. In practice, however, many groups simply don't have the resources to lobby members of Congress and their staff effectively, while others are able to spend millions of dollars to gain access and make their arguments heard (see also Chapter 12 regarding Interest Groups and money.)

## INDEPENDENT REGULATORY AGENCIES

Established by Congress to remain above the political influences of either Congress or the executive branch, **independent regulatory agencies** are typically led by multiple **commissioners** or **boards**. Examples of such agencies include, but are not limited to, the Food and Drug Administration (FDA), the Consumer Products Safety Commission (CPSC), the Environmental Protection Agency (EPA), the Federal Trade Commission

(FTC), the Federal Aviation Administration (FAA), the Federal Communications Commission (FCC), the Securities and Exchange Commission (SEC), the Federal Reserve System (the Fed) and the Corporation for Public Broadcasting (PBS).

Congress also authorized the establishment of government corporations, which operate independently from executive branch oversight. They all have their separate boards and chairs, although Congress is nominally responsible for regulating them. They include, but are not limited to, the United States Postal Service (USPS), the Corporation for Public Broadcasting (PBS), the Federal Deposit Insurance Corporation (FDIC), the Corporation for National and Community Service (CNCS), the Export-Import Bank, the National Railroad Passenger Corporation (AMTRAK), the Overseas Private Investment Corporation (OPIC) and the Pension Benefit Guaranty Corporation (PBGC).[20]

## OVERSIGHT OF THE EXECUTIVE BRANCH

Although the legislative branch has oversight powers to make sure the federal government operates effectively, the review hearings have become so fraught with partisanship that no department, agency or bureau voluntarily cooperates with congressional committee or subcommittee investigations. As a result, more often than not Congress will use its power to subpoena and order bureaucrats to appear and testify. The effectiveness of this process remains open to debate.

The one oversight office every department, agency and bureau is responsible to without a subpoena is the **OMB**, which works directly with the White House chief of staff and is vested with the authority to conduct internal audits for monetary *and* public policy compliance in order to ensure that funds derived from the budget are used efficiently. No bureaucrat can escape the scrutiny of the OMB. Everything in our government comes down to money.

## THE BUREAUCRACY AND ELECTION POLITICS

Although non-partisan government workers are supposed to be above politics, partisanship often permeates the West Wing; and presidential election campaigns throughout American history have been routinely co-ordinated from the White House. Following political upheaval during the 1930s, Congress enacted the **Hatch Act** to regulate on-the-job political campaigning and endorsements by all federal, state and local officials. Prior to its passage, government employees were pressured to use their positions to actively campaign in elections, frequently blurring the line between non-partisan employment and political patronage. While the **Hatch Act** curtailed many of the unsavory political practices surrounding campaigns within the bureaucracy, by the 1980s employees began to challenge it because its restrictions were so broad that some agency heads precluded election campaigning even away from the office. Congress addressed the criticism that the Hatch Act infringed on the right to political free speech and amended it in 1990 to allow government employees to work on partisan elections outside of their workplace. Then President George H.W. Bush, fearing a backlash against the new provisions, vetoed the legislation, and Congress was unable to override his veto.

By 1993 however, President Clinton signaled his approval of the measure and Congress, thus encouraged, passed the Hatch Act amendment again. Since it was signed into law, workers are now allowed to conduct political activity while on duty and within the scope of their employment, provided they do not use their position and office to coerce anyone to conduct political behavior against their will. There can be no retribution if an employee declines to participate in the political activity. The amended act does not preclude the president, though, from ordering his political appointees (Cabinet secretaries, department, agency and bureau chiefs) to refrain from participation in partisan political activities.

Federal employees are also allowed to join political parties and run for non-partisan office; they can also make voluntary campaign contributions and participate in voter registration campaigns.

The Hatch Act still prohibits federal employees from using their jobs to affect the outcome of an election or solicit campaign funds from people that work for them. They also cannot solicit money from outside businesses that work with them. The goal is to avoid any undue influence-peddling arrangement (although it routinely occurs in day-to-day lobbying). Unfortunately, despite laws prohibiting such activities, the use of government money to assist political campaigns is commonplace on all levels, including the White House. The Office of the Special Counsel charged with enforcing the Hatch Act as amended issued a report in January 2011 revealing that beginning in 2006, President Bush routinely violated the act by establishing a political campaign office in the White House, coordinating GOP campaigns throughout the nation. Known as the Office of Political Affairs and supervised by presidential advisor Karl Rove, White House staffers actively conducted unlawful campaign coordination and briefed candidates and Cabinet officials on how to assist in GOP congressional campaigns. In direct response to this finding, President Obama established his reelection committee headquarters in Chicago, but he also decided not to authorize a prosecution of his predecessor for the offenses charged.[21]

While there are examples of governmental corruption ineptitude—notably the bungling response to Hurricane Katrina—employees in the bureaucracy take their jobs very seriously. Without their dedicated work, the United States would quickly grind to a halt. The FDIC keeps a tight rein on banks with troubled financial circumstances, the SEC efficiently regulates the licensing of securities brokers and dealers, the U.S. Geological Survey does an excellent job of monitoring earthquakes and natural disasters, the National Weather Service tracks hurricanes and tornadoes while providing advance warnings, and the National Park Service acts as a steward for our natural resources. The number of federal agencies that perform their duties at a very high level is considerable, yet many citizens far too often take them for granted.

At the same time, conservatives "outside" of the administration rail against a bureaucracy as "broken" in an effort to rouse the public to the notion first presented by President Ronald Reagan in his 1981 inaugural speech that "big government is the problem." Contrary to this popular rally cry, perpetuated with the aid of sympathetic media outlets thriving on conflict, the actual size of the current federal bureaucracy as an actual percentage of our population has been declining over the past 20 years! The number of political consultants working within the Washington "beltway," though, has increased considerably. We do not hear similarly pointed rhetoric from pandering politicians about the "bloated" numbers of consultants and lobbyists because so many politicians rely upon them for contributions to their campaign war chests.[22]

# 9

## ❖ PUBLIC AND ECONOMIC POLICIES ❖

### For Public Consumption?

The revolutionary war against England, a massive and complex undertaking, had one overriding purpose—to achieve independence for the 13 original colonies. So long as the conflict remained unresolved, the founders pursued a single-minded goal that put all other concerns on the back burner. But once victory had been achieved, two critical issues confronted the fledgling nation. One was how to deal with large-scale matters affecting the citizens, the other came down to money—how to pay for the war and our new national government.

These two concerns never disappear—they are the lifeblood of a well-functioning nation—but can take different forms at different times, and they often result in contentious debates, struggles and evolving understanding at best.

## Public Policy

Put simply, public policy is the government's plan of action regarding matters that affect all of us—"the public"—on a daily basis. Throughout our rich history, we have dealt with a number of big policy issues that involved both our nation as a whole and each individual member of society. They have ranged from slavery to women's right to vote to civil rights of

African Americans and other minorities. Today public policies relate to the environment, abortion rights, gay marriage, the military, our national defense, education, expanded health care for the poor, Social Security, gun control and the right to use medicinal marijuana. All of these and many more can be considered a collective part of public policy. The questions to ask are: Do these policies benefit all Americans or only some of us? Do they favor special interest groups and the corporations that support them financially or the electorate that pays for them with its taxes? And how influential are those who shape public policy after all?

We can all agree that we want our government to create and enforce rules and regulations ensuring public safety. No doubt we see eye to eye on the need for the establishing of laws prohibiting murder, robbery, rape, battery, arson, theft, and so on. We probably even share the opinion that having policies that protect our food supply, preserve our environment, and provide opportunities for higher education is a good thing. The problem and disagreements come when we talk about the methods, approaches and actions to achieve these policies.

It is at that point that ideology rears its head on the political dividing line between members of the public and their elected officials. Democrats prefer our government to take an assertive, controlling role and use regulation and oversight in order to guarantee that policy initiatives succeed. Republicans believe that less regulation and a free market with private sector oversight is the best way to influence and guarantee a policy initiative.

In practice, a combination of some regulation and some free market mechanisms is a far better approach than the "all or nothing" approach our political parties advocate. It makes more sense for our government to work efficiently under a banner of cooperation and accommodation. The preface already quoted some of the cautionary words of one of our framers, James Madison, on the subject of applying ideology to government. Here is a more extended version of the argument he made in Federalist No. 51:

> *If men were angels, no government would be necessary. If angels were to govern men, neither external nor internal controls on government would be necessary. In framing a government which is to be administered by men over men, the great difficulty lies in this: you must first enable the government to control the governed; and in the next place oblige it to control itself. A dependence on the people is, no doubt, the primary control on the government; but experience has taught mankind the necessity of auxiliary precautions.*

Madison argued that people need government involved in their lives. In turn, we the people are the check on government. Do Madison's words sound too radical, too "activist?" He wrote them in 1788, long before the current debate on the proper size and power of the federal government.

It is obvious in current times that our government consists of political leaders with polarized views, which inevitably leads to potential conflicts between our citizenry. Differences of opinion are healthy in a democracy. Differences created to divide us all, though, can be dangerous to our democracy. There is but a fine line separating the two.

Currently, there is a strong political debate underway regarding the government's role in providing safety nets for the elderly and the nation's working poor. Opponents voicing outrage at money being provided to the less fortunate, especially in difficult economic times, like to apply the labels "redistributing the wealth" and "socialism." Their ideology basically boils down to: Less of *my* money should be taken in taxes, and only the money I pay in taxes should be spent on programs *I* benefit from. It sounds great as rhetoric to complain about taxes as it resonates with the political base, but imagine if everyone felt that way? Our government would grind to a halt and everyone but a very few would suffer.

Still it is important to ask questions like, "Who are we as a society? What collective obligations do we owe to our country? What is the role of government in terms of public policy that affects everyone? Again, these questions deserve a chance to be asked and answered.

Making public policy and creating the ways and means to implement it is a fragmented process. **Fragmentation** is a result of having so many levels of government and bureaucracy involved in policymaking. Each fragment has its own goals and objectives and stakes out its own "turf" demanding attention and money.

The carrying out of public policy is also impacted by **Issue Networks**, coalitions of interest groups and institutions that also wish to pursue particular policy objectives. The combination of fragmentation and issue networks results in slowing the process down to the point that our modern political machinery can rarely initiate a wide-sweeping policy that radically changes the government's approach to a problem. Elected officials who campaign for such changes—be they in health care, environmental regulations or any other large social program—are readily accused of "overreach" by their opponents, both in the political and private sector. In the realm of political rhetoric, such an allegation is tantamount to the kiss of death, and candidates and officeholders want to avoid that…like the plague. As a result, most of our policies change on an incremental basis only.

Incrementalism is seen as the only politically safe way to make any needed change, however urgent and critical it may be. It is acceptable to politicians because it virtually assures the status quo and doesn't "upset the apple cart." Those promoting such a method hope to attract a coalition of support and perhaps political momentum for broader policy change in the future. But while it is acceptable to most as a conservative approach to policy change, it usually does not do well in time of crisis. Current examples of incrementalism include the spreading out of spending cuts and deficit reduction over a period of 10 years, and not requiring 54.5 miles per gallon for automobiles until 2025.[23]

A rare example of actual crisis policy change occurred when President Bush initiated TARP (Troubled Asset Recovery Program) to bail out failing financial institutions in 2008. Seen as a necessary effort to prevent a global collapse of the financial markets, Bush garnered bi-partisan support for the plan. Once it went into effect, the opposition began to crank up the rhetoric to gain a political edge against those who signed off on the legislation, including, predictably, claims of "overreach." Tea Party advocates successfully ran opposition campaigns against incumbents claiming taxpayer money was "wasted" by TARP. We will never know what would have happened to the financial sector and our economy if President Bush and Congress had refused to bail out the failing banks and insurance companies.

President Obama is still being attacked by his opponents for authorizing stimulus spending to rescue General Motors and Chrysler. Once again, "overreach" is one of the accusations being leveled against him. Yet, the very same opponents claim Obama is a poor leader because he hasn't done enough for the economy.

According to the U.S. government, between Presidents Bush and Obama, over $1 trillion was invested in bailing out American banks, mortgage lenders Freddie Mac and Fannie Mae, and the auto industry, using TARP funds. As of July 22, 2014, not only was all of the money repaid, but the government realized a profit of $41 billion![24] Although TARP has been vigorously attacked by the Tea Party wing of the GOP, under ordinary circumstances most Republicans would agree that turning a business venture into a profit is a central part of their ideology and a good thing. They just don't like it when the public sector accomplishes something the private sector could not.

The Democrats do not come off smelling like roses either. When TARP was being debated, they wasted no time adding pork barrel pet projects to the bill, adding millions to the cost. Without the political will to whip its caucus to do more to stimulate the economy when they still controlled the White House and both chambers of Congress, the Democrats have contributed to our current economic anemia.

Traditionally, a government in which the White House and Congress have been controlled by different parties has been a time of compromise, requiring both sides to work together to implement policies beneficial to our nation. But this has not been the case in the current gridlock atmosphere in Washington, where extremist rhetoric and ideological purity has trumped all attempts by more moderate forces on both sides of the aisle to reach any kind of agreement. The heated political debates about the role of government in our society continue to sidetrack any serious efforts to deal with the significant problems we are facing today—from the deficit to health care, Social Security and tax reform.

With unemployment high, health care and education costs continuing to soar, and rising pressure on entitlement programs like Social Security and Medicare, we face a crisis severe enough to require bold moves. But we are currently mired in a political climate that is filled with wild political rhetoric and loud promises, but accomplishes very little. The reality is that incrementalism has solved none of the problems facing our nation, and that is not likely to change so long as most of our current political leaders prefer inaction and instead focus only on getting reelected.

## GAUGING PUBLIC OPINION

With public opinion being an important aspect of our political system, few politicians these days are willing to commit to any policy without first determining how it will fly with the voting electorate.

In one of the most prominent recent examples, using a combination of the media and public opinion polling, the Obama Administration took a calculated gamble when Vice President Biden disclosed on NBC's Sunday morning show, "Meet The Press," in May 2012 that the president was in favor of same-sex marriage. Immediately the media pounced on Biden's "revelation" as a gaffe or shocking surprise catching the administration off guard. Lost in the feeding frenzy for some time was the fact that Biden's appearance was taped on the Friday before the national broadcast, making it highly unlikely that his comments "caught the administration off guard."

It cannot be underestimated how many political strategists use polling to determine policy agendas and how they impact campaigns. In this case, with public opinion polls indicating a very close race between Obama and Romney, the Obama Administration's worst fear was that its liberal base of the Democratic Party had become disillusioned. A surefire way to "reactivate" that segment of voters would be to reach out to the, for the most part, liberal gay community. No better way to do this than to establish a firm position on same-sex marriage, especially since it had become even more of a wedge issue, potentially dividing the campaigns, because North Carolina was considering an amendment (which it ultimately passed) to its constitution defining marriage as a union between a man and a woman.

Knowing this, and the fact that over 52% of Americans favor same-sex marriage, the Obama Administration decided to use the wedge issue to its advantage. The following Wednesday, the president appeared on the popular television show "Good Morning America" to formally announce his support for same-sex marriage in terms of protecting civil liberties and civil rights under the Constitution. Predictably, his opponent, Mitt Romney, came out strongly against the issue. But within 90 minutes of Obama's announcement, as ideological battle lines were being drawn in the media, the president's campaign found itself on the receiving end of over $1 million in donations!

We can be reasonably certain that without polls favoring gay marriage, the Obama Administration would have soft-pedaled that issue for most, if not all, of the election cycle.

Subsequently, the Supreme Court in ***United States v. Windsor***, 133 S.Ct. 2675 (2013)struck down Defense of Marriage Act (DOMA), holding that states cannot limit the definition of marriage to opposite sex couples based on the constitutional principles of due process and equal protection under the law.

The following terms and characteristics are important to gain an understanding and appreciation of the impact of public opinion on policymaking.

**Intensity** is the strength of reaction of the public to an idea being floated. How strong will the electorate react to budget cuts to vital social programs? Think about the fierce reactions when politicians attempt to cut Social Security or Medicare. Nothing will get Grandma and Grandpa out on the street or writing e-mails of protest to their representatives more than those two issues.

**Latency** refers to potentially vacillating reactions. A policy idea being floated may not currently affect important sectors of the public, but may in the future. An example is the attempt to raise the retirement age to qualify for Social Security, or plans to alter Medicare for Americans under the grandfathered cut-off age of 55. It may not affect these Americans now, but it will in the future, eliciting strong reactions as well.

**Salience** describes the level of prominence or significance of an issue for a particular group of voters. If the issue personally affects them, they're more likely to have a strong reaction. If it does not affect them directly, they may not care one way or another.

**Consensus** happens when most people agree on an issue. Obviously, a politician floating a policy which has a consensus is not taking a very big risk in proposing the idea. Although many citizens may credit their elected officials for doing something bold, in reality their courage is the result of carefully pre-calculating the results and counting on collective consensual approval.

**Polarization** results from initiating a policy that divides public opinion. It may come about inadvertently or based on calculation. Some areas that stand out in this area are medicinal marijuana, same-sex marriage and abortion. Politicians may cynically seek to put any of these issues on a state ballot in order to rally a particular voting bloc for Election Day.

**Stability** is a concept involving matters that the public always responds to in the same predictable way, regardless of how they are presented. A good example is support for our military. Regardless of where one might stand on national defense spending and involvement in our military operations, supporting the troops is a sacred cow.

**Fluidity** is the ability to gauge how public opinion may be subject to change over time. Frequent updates via polling help to keep a handle on issues over which a fickle public may change its mind. When it comes to national energy policy, for example, Americans seem to fluctuate with the price of gasoline at the pumps.

## POLLING

All public opinion is collected and filtered via the use of **polling**. There are a wide variety of polls available to politicians and the media. One of the best known are **exit polls**, which are taken immediately after people have left the voting booth. Based on the answers to carefully chosen questions, pollsters draw certain conclusions, from which candidate is likely to win to what issues most affected people's choice. Obviously, there are inherent risks to exit polls: People lie.

**Census tracks** are another polling technique in which existing groups of targeted voters are surveyed. Based on voter registration lists—both major parties have them—pollsters tailor questions that most affect the voters likely to support a particular candidate's cause. Census tracks are typically used to gauge support from the base prior to primary elections.

**Universal polls**, the opposite of census tracks, question all voters regardless of political affiliation or demographics. Universal polls are commonly utilized by interest groups to determine support for particular issues or by political parties seeking backing once candidates have been selected for the general election.

**Sampling** is an effective way of questioning a smaller group of people or "a sample," without incurring the expense of a universal poll. Sampling is designed to question a cross section of voters to get a handle on how an issue will fly with the public. Because it saves time and money, sampling is the most frequently used polling technique.

**Random samples** question a *cross section* of different *targeted* demographic groups—youth vote vs. elderly vote, gun owners vs. non-gun owners, etc. Typically, such polling must question at least 1,000 voters before there can be any claim to accuracy.

While polls have become the bread and butter of American politics, there are limits to their accuracy—people lie or misunderstand questions, or poll takers don't gauge answers accurately. That is why the results for any poll always include a plus/minus count, also known as the **margin of error**.

Polling is the "thermometer" used for taking America's political temperature. The results influence how politicians frame their rhetoric in an effort to obtain public support. In some ways elections are the ultimate polls that determine how and by whom we want our nation to be led. Few Americans understand how much power they actually wield in determining the outcome—despite all of the simple-minded rhetoric, pie-in-the-sky campaign promises and negative attack ads—and how important it is that they make wise decisions at the ballot box come election time.

## Economic Policy

A related issue to public policy is its sister issue—economics. Somehow, all that government does has to be paid for. During the Revolutionary War, the Founding Fathers understood that we needed cold hard cash in order to wage a war against what was then the largest and most professional army in the world—the British red coats. Soon after independence, the framers realized that the new nation was mired in debt with little ability to pay it back to the creditors—other nations—that took a risk to see if America could, in fact, defeat England. As the first secretary of the treasury under George Washington, Alexander Hamilton proposed an intricate economic policy that included the structure of our currency, lending and trade, as well as the founding of a national bank. Although then Secretary of State Thomas Jefferson, initially opposed it, he quickly learned the benefits of a sound economic policy when as president he was able to borrow about $12 million from London banks to make the Louisiana Purchase in 1803 (the transaction also included a down payment of $3 million in gold).

Since economic policy is how our government controls our system of money—from collecting taxes to regulating our currency—it has a direct effect on all of us. To appreciate this system of interdependence of government and citizenry on money matters, a short summary of our economy and economic policy is in order.

The United States operates as a **capitalist economy**, in which the production and distribution of goods and services are owned and operated by the private sector. In theory, prices are determined by a **free market**, and established by supply and demand—what the public wants and needs—not by the government. The more there is of a product, the more can be sold. The more sold, the greater the chance that demand could drop. With less demand, sales would fall, leading to a lowering in prices. When prices reach a certain level, demand would increase again, leading to greater production and a rise in profits; and so the economic carousel goes round and round.

But producers will use other means in an effort to create demand. Often the public is inundated with products marketed as "new and improved," or with a "new fresh look," anything within a company's marketing department's ability to create a new push for demand. Some companies artificially slow production in order to create a run on demand, which leads to higher sales and higher prices, hence profits. This routinely occurs in the oil business, where manipulating refinery output and raising gas prices equates to higher profits.

Profits are the lifeblood of all companies. Accumulated profits become what are known as **capital** (hence the name "capitalism"). This money may be spent to invest in new equipment, new products, new marketing campaigns, give dividends to shareholders (investors in the company) or provide bonuses to corporate executives. Under American capitalism, most companies do everything they possibly can to maximize profits.

Another important economic term is **Gross National Product (GNP)**, which represents the total value of all the goods and services *actually* being produced in our economy. **Aggregate demand** is the amount of income individuals and businesses have to spend on goods and services. **Productive capacity** refers to the total of goods and services that may *potentially* be produced—meaning, an economy can afford to sustain the production at a constant and predictable level. It is not an absolute. By mid-2012, corporations were sitting on over $2 trillion in profits, but they did not see fit to release any of those funds for investments in the form of new equipment, plant renovation and hiring of new employees.[25] *Potential* is the economic measure, even if it is not reached.

## FISCAL POLICY

**Fiscal policy** is how governments create plans to either raise or lower taxes and/or governmental spending. This has a direct effect on how much money consumers will have to spend, which in turn affects aggregate *demand*. As much as politicians publicly rail against governmental spending, they routinely embrace it in other less obvious ways, for example, creating "tax holidays" by suspending sales taxes for a period of time for a specific group of goods (school-related items before the start of the new school year, etc.). Lowering taxes may seem like an odd way of describing spending, but it is considered expending money on taxpayers, putting money in their pockets by giving them a tax break they did not have before.

To create a coherent fiscal policy**,** the executive branch has the **Council of Economic Advisors**, a group that works within the West Wing as consultants to the president on the economy. It is also responsible to report to Congress on an annual basis. The council includes a panel of three economists who are supported by a staff of 25. One of its responsibilities is to advise the White House

The British economist John Maynard Keynes promoted a macroeconomics theory that has been embraced by administrations since President Franklin Roosevelt. Under **Keynesian economics,** government should actively impose regulation in the form of fiscal and monetary policies in an effort to smooth out erratic business cycles and to directly control mechanisms to adjusting aggregate demand. It can create an increase to aggregate demand, for example, by spending more money, even more than it has. This is called **deficit spending**. The theory is that government will be able to repay the debt from the gains in the economy it receives as a result of deficit spending. In the meantime, it has to borrow money to finance its spending by issuing bonds, notes and treasury bills, each paying interest on the principal, which is guaranteed and backed by the U.S. government. This form of economic theory diametrically opposes *laissez-faire* (free market "hands off") capitalist economic theory. Needless to say, support for either theory tends to break down along political party lines.

Nowadays, **deficit spending** is a white-hot issue. We currently have a federal deficit approaching $17 trillion, an unimaginable sum. One trillion dollar bills laid side by side will get you to the moon and back 200 times. It almost gets you to the sun. $17 trillion in debt is actually "out of this world!" By 2011, the greatest fiscal crisis to face our nation was underway, yet political ideology and a thirst for power blinded our representatives into playing a dangerous game of "chicken." A large number of freshman Republican representatives to Congress were elected with support from the Tea Party movement to cut the federal deficit. To do so, they signed pledges to cut taxes and the deficit without allowing any increase in revenues (taxes). Not surprisingly, these very same folks believe there is no need for a federal government and therefore, the best way to shrink it is to *starve* it of finances.

Along comes the need to raise the debt ceiling, something that has routinely been accomplished without fanfare for decades. Raising the debt ceiling is not a "green light" authorizing the federal government to spend money like it has a blank check. The debt ceiling instead is the annual authorization to come up with the money necessary to pay our *existing* debts (which climb every day due to rising interest on existing debt and unforeseen expenditures for disaster relief, etc.). Unfortunately, many political leaders portray the debt ceiling debate as authorizing more spending rather than authorizing paying for debts our government has *already* spent and accumulated.

Can you imagine buying trillions of goods and services on credit and then down the road saying "sorry, we can't spend any more money, so we won't pay our current bills?" At the 2011 Ames Iowa GOP Straw Vote

Debate, Michele Bachmann (R. MN) came out and immediately stated she hoped the nation had gone into default in 2011.[26] And Bachmann won! Any economic default by the United States would crush pensions, Social Security and the nation's global economic standing. Do Americans really understand what politicians say? Do they grasp the influence of political rhetoric?

The consequences of having the United States default on existing debt are profound. It empowers our economic rivals, makes us a serious financial risk for borrowing further funds, and weakens the value of both our economy and our dollar. What do Americans need to convince them that their leaders are not talking straight? What happened to "American exceptionalism"? Do we really want to be considered a deadbeat nation instead?

## THE FEDERAL RESERVE

An independent yet major player in our economy is the **Federal Reserve System (the Fed)**. Established in 1913, the Fed was created to serve as an independent regulatory agency. Acting as a Central Bank for the nation, the Fed includes virtually all banks as members. The Fed is managed by a board of six governors led by a chair, who each have staggered terms so as to ensure continuity. Each "governor" serves a term of 14 years. The chair, however, serves a term of only four years. All members of the Fed board of governors and the chair are appointed by the president with senatorial consent and approval.

The difference between the Fed and other executive branch officials is that Fed appointees are independent of political ideologies, just like the Fed itself; and although the president may appoint them to office, he cannot terminate them. Hence the length of the term each governor maintains—they inherently serve longer than any sitting president. This ensures the political independence of the Fed. Note the chair's term coincides with the president's, so it may be viewed as a political position. However, history indicates that Fed chairs are frequently reappointed by subsequent presidents.

The Federal Reserve System was established with 12 regional banks, each in turn led by its own bank president. This ensures the monetary policy of each region conforms to the needs of the region, as opposed to a blanket national policy. When it comes to national issues, though, we have seen the principle of "one size fits all" simply does not work. Overall monetary policy is established by the Federal Open Market Committee—essentially all of the board of governors, large bank presidents and the chair working together to determine said policy.

**Monetary policy** is the power of the **Fed** to control changes in the amount of money in circulation (also known as the "money supply"). The Fed can control the interest rates charged for borrowing money. By raising rates, it lowers the money supply and in turns lowers aggregate demand. This creates a *deflationary* effect on our economy. By lowering interest rates with hopes to raise the money supply, the Fed is attempting to increase the aggregate demand. This creates an *inflationary* effect on the economy. Under a deflationary period, the value of the money in circulation rises. Under an inflationary period, the value of money in circulation drops.

The Fed creates and fosters economic policies so banks can in turn operate with predictability and stability. All interest rates relating to lending rates between banks and the Fed are established in an effort to control the economic impact of "inflation" or "deflation."

The Fed has many financial tools available to it in guiding the economy. By increasing or decreasing the interest rates of borrowed monies, the Fed can feed or starve the economic engine of the nation. The Fed may also purchase federal bonds by having more money printed. This tool is known as **quantitative easing**. Ironically, from 2009 through

2012, the Fed essentially lowered interest rates to zero in an effort to jumpstart a sluggish economy. All it has left is to buy more government bonds and flood the markets with cash (which in turn devalues the dollar). Devaluing the dollar has its own problems.

Unfortunately, banks have taken advantage of the lower interest rates to borrow large sums of monies to acquire other banking interests and to invest in buying back their own stock. They have not engaged in any large-scale lending to the public and as a result, providing low-cost Fed funds without restriction has resulted in large banks getting larger, and with little to no positive movement on the larger economic front. Other than quantitative easing, the Fed has no other real tools available to stimulate an already stagnant economy. Ultimately, economic woes must be addressed by an effective Congress and White House. The question remains: Will our political leaders return to some sense of responsibility in the foreseeable future?

# 10

# ✻ POLITICAL PARTIES ✻
## GETTING ELECTED AT ANY COST

When our framers sat down to write the Constitution, there were no **political parties**. Many realized, however, that regional alliances within the Continental Congress had the potential for coalitions that would give rise to powerful factions in the new government. This became evident when Southern members allied themselves to save the institution of slavery. Nonetheless, nowhere in the Constitution are political parties mentioned.

George Washington, as the "father of the country," was elected by general consensus for his two terms of office, but as early as John Adams' presidency, political parties with particularly stated political objectives emerged. The first was led by Alexander Hamilton and became known as the Federalist Party. Soon thereafter, other national parties evolved, including the Whig Party, the Democratic-Republican Party, and the two major parties we currently have, the Republican Party and the Democratic Party.

Political parties have one fundamental purpose: to get people of like ideologies elected to office. They also serve as **linkage institutions** connecting people and their interests directly to the government. Parties are comprised of party activists or **the base**, which can always be relied upon to support the party, its ideology, platforms and candidates. Parties also include political operatives who promote ideology in an effort to expand the base. Finally, they have a large number of members who do little more than provide support in the form of voting exclusively for party candidates.

In the course of American history, many parties have come and gone, some with colorful names like the Know-Nothing Party, the Mugwumps and the Bull Moose Party; others have more conventional titles, such as the Socialist Party, the Green Party, and most recently, the Tea Party (the latter is still an unofficial party, running its candidates under the banner of the GOP). In time, many disappear or evolve into a new party—the Federalists and Whigs have long disappeared from the American political scene—or remain as small splinter organizations.

For the past century and a half, there have been only two *major* political parties in the United States, the Republican Party (GOP) and the Democratic Party. It is interesting to note that Republicans hate identifying Democrats as members of the Democratic Party—they consider themselves "democratic" too—so they refer to them publicly as members of the "Democrat" Party. Both parties themselves have evolved over time. The GOP of Abraham Lincoln and Theodore Roosevelt is not the party we know today. The Democratic Party of Andrew Jackson in the Southern states has long disappeared, and if "Old Hickory" were alive today, he would not recognize its modern counterpart.

## Party Identification

For the most part, Americans either identify with one or the other of the two major parties and their ideologies, or consider themselves independents. How we see ourselves politically is based on our exposure to **political socialization,** which becomes the foundation for our **political culture.**

Perhaps the most influential factor in our socialization is **family,** and not just for political beliefs, but perhaps all belief systems, including morals, religion, social etiquette, the love of learning, and more. Politically, if your parents lean to the left, right or center, then you are likely to have similar inclinations. In some cases, children react strongly against their parents' social and political beliefs and end up on opposite sides of the ideological divide, but that represents powerful influence nonetheless.

**Religion,** through attendance at church, synagogue or mosque, and education in the form of Sunday school, Bible classes, Hebrew School, etc., all influence how we view society and the role of government. Protestants are equally divided between the GOP and the Democratic Party, but members of the "Religious Right," comprised of Evangelicals and Southern Baptists, overwhelmingly identify themselves as Republican and are by far the most conservative group. Catholics are evenly divided between the two parties and are equally conservative and liberal. They generally oppose abortion, but differ on the role of the church regarding political issues. Jews are predominantly Democrats and tend to be more liberal, accepting of others and concerned with social equality. The higher the attendance at religious services, the higher the affiliation with the Republican Party. Those with little to no religious affiliation are primarily Democrats.

Of course, **education** is a large contributor to shaping people's beliefs, but the influence of schools is as much due to the peers students associate with as to what they are taught in the classroom. It turns out that the less **education** people have, the more likely they are to be Republicans; the more education, the more Democratic. At the highest education levels—doctorates—party identification seems to be evenly divided. It should be noted, however, that although universities provide opportunities for the honing of critical thinking and exposure to a variety of divergent political views, even the most open-minded students usually hold on to their established beliefs and ideology despite the best efforts of educators.[27]

The type of **employment** or **job** we have seems to correlate strongly with party affiliation. While it may no longer be 100% true, most **blue**

**collar and lower middle class** workers continue to be for the most part Democrats. Medical doctors, bankers and business owners, representing **white collar** workers and members of the **upper middle** and **wealthy classes,** are predominantly Republicans. Here, the **level of education** also comes into play. Although higher educated citizens tend to be more liberal, they also become more conservative as their income levels rise. Accumulating wealth usually comes with paying higher taxes, hence the appeal of the Republican mantra for lower or no taxes.[28] An example of the impact of education can be readily seen in the presidential election of 2008 where the demographics illustrated this.[29]

But while higher income goes hand in hand with a more conservative political ideology, this is not true of the "uber-wealthy," who often become so rich that taxes no longer have a real effect on their views towards society. In many cases, they revert to "giving back to their fellow man" and become more liberal than they were while amassing their wealth. At the beginning of the 20th century, Andrew Carnegie, the Pittsburgh steel magnate, gave away all of his money to endow libraries, schools and foundations. In the summer of 2011, billionaire Warren Buffet went on public record insisting that all billionaires should contribute more to help our nation recover from its economic ills.[30]

**Age** is certainly an important factor as well. Younger voters have a different view of America and the world than the middle-aged or elderly, especially when it comes to issues like same-sex marriage, marijuana use and civil liberties. Prior to 2008, young voters considered themselves predominantly "independent" or "apolitical." The latter also meant they were "apathetic" and wouldn't bother to show up at the ballot box. That changed in the 2008 presidential election, as large numbers of young voters turned out and supported Barack Obama, a Democrat. The recent results of the 2012 presidential election established, at least in the short-run, that the youth vote remains an active element of our engaged political electorate.

**Gender** has some influence when it comes to issues like birth control, abortion vs. freedom to choose, and social welfare programs. Men for the most part are Republican (the more conservative also want to control the reproductive process). Women tend to be more liberal and are over-whelmingly Democrats; however, we are beginning to see an increasing crop of Republican women on the national scene.

**Race** and **ethnicity** continue to be important influences on politi-cal affiliation that can't be ignored. African Americans overwhelmingly support Democratic candidates, while Southern whites routinely sup-port white Republicans, as demonstrated in the last presidential election. President Obama won the Black and Hispanic vote by a vast margin, while Mitt Romney scored well among Southern and poor white males. The latter feel disenfranchised in today's society as Hispanics and Asian Americans continue to rise in our economic and political affairs.

Hispanics have traditionally related to the Democratic Party and continue to do so in large numbers. As long as the GOP uses the Dream Act and illegal immigration as a political football, that won't change. His-panics represent the largest minority in the United States and are poised to become the majority within the next two decades. So long as the GOP continues to paint illegal immigrants as a perilous menace to our society, it risks massive defeats at the ballot boxes of the future. Ironically, accord-ing to the Council on Foreign Relations, illegal immigration from Mexi-co has dropped sharply in recent years, even though the political rhetoric intensity level has steadily risen.[31] One thing is certain, as the numbers of minority voters expand, they will be more difficult to accurately classify when predicting their political beliefs.

Demographic indicators like **regionalism** were traditionally used as a barometer of party affiliation—Southern conservatives vs. Northern lib-erals; "rust belt" Democrats vs. Bible Belt Republicans—but the most recent census confirms that population shifts throughout the country have made the customary benchmarks less reliable. As population groups move from traditionally Democratic Northern strongholds to the South and Southwest, they will transform and dilute traditional Republican ties in those regions, turning "red" states "purple," as happened in Arizona and New Mexico during the 2012 national elections. This trend may not continue, however, if the migrating population also shifts its ideologies as it ages and becomes conservative, as seems to be the case among retirees in states like Florida and Arizona.

All of these factors in political beliefs and ideologies make for a complex matrix of party affiliations throughout the United States. Add to that a wide variety of issues, which each have their passionate adherents and detractors, and the ability to create a large "tent" that includes enough people to assure elections of party candidates is a daunting task.

Political party leaders understand and realize that the diversity of the electorate requires **coalitions**—collections of groups that have a single issue or cross-interest in common—to be forged and nurtured. Coalitions that traditionally identify with the Republican Party include veterans, the Religious Right, anti-abortion supporters, anti-homosexual and anti-gay rights activists, prayer-in-school advocates, hardliners on crime and punishment, pro-business advocates and supporters of anti-government regulation of business. Since the 1920s, the theme of the Republican Party has been "more business in government, less government in business." Coalitions that traditionally identify with the Democratic Party are labor unions, pro-choice adherents, environmentalists, homosexuals, women activists, the poor, artists and many members of the entertainment and movie industry.

One of the results of the identification with one of the major parties has come to be known as the **ideological divide.** Democrats believe in more government spending to advance social well-being and less on national defense (on obsolete systems). They are against school-mandated prayer and less likely to support school voucher programs for parochial and charter schools that diminish funding for public education. Democrats also are more inclined to pursue government regulation to end discrimination based on race, gender, religion and sexual orientation, whereas Republicans cling to the theory that government can only prohibit institutional discrimination, but has no authority to regulate personal behavior and beliefs. Democrats routinely defend government support for medical programs and health care, and seek tax relief for the lower and middle classes. Most Democrats describe themselves ideologically as **liberals**.

Republicans believe in spending less to advance social welfare, supporting increased national defense spending, offering school vouchers and cutting funding for public education. They oppose any sort of gun regulation, resist universal health care programs, and prefer a tax code offering percentage reductions for all Americans, for example a flat tax (which inherently favors the wealthy). Republicans identify themselves ideologically as **conservatives.**

## THIRD PARTIES

Although not a large factor in our political system, **third parties** occasionally have an impact on elections and, as a result, the platforms of the two major parties. They tend to be groups of voters and candidates disgruntled with the status quo and often pursue an ideologically centered campaign. Traditionally, third parties represent single-issue interests such as environmental protection (Green Party) or anti-government, pro-libertarian principles (Reform and Libertarian Parties).

Third party candidates often run to keep certain issues on the table, for example, Ron Paul continuing in the GOP primary long after it was clear that he had no chance of being elected. His loyal supporters, however, put pressure on the front-runner, who knows he needs their vote in the general election and will have to accommodate their beliefs and interests as reflected in the 2012 GOP platforms. Third party candidates also act as "spoilers," siphoning votes from one or the other major party candidates, leading to their defeat. Ross Perot played that role in the 1992 and 1996 elections, appealing to conservatives and helping Bill Clinton get elected and reelected, while Ralph Nader, carrying the banner of the Green Party, assured Al Gore's ultimate loss in Florida and with it, the presidency to George W. Bush.

**Bolter parties** come about when trends indicate members of an existing party feel disenfranchised or underappreciated and choose to literally *bolt* from the party to start a new one. The Tea Party, which started as an anti-tax, no-big-government movement, joined the Republican Party but could become a bolter party if its members feel that the larger GOP won't serve its interests.

In the wake of gridlock in Washington, many voters have declared themselves to be independents, and there are occasional calls for a third party to represent them. Whether or not the United States will give up its two-party system remains to be seen. Since the established parties control state legislatures that in turn determine election regulations, such a development is highly unlikely.

## POLITICAL ORGANIZATIONS

Each political party has its own form of organization at the local, state and national levels. Depending on the state, they vary, although each has its own national, state and local committees. These do not necessarily work together all the time, as they each have their own set of constituents. Elections are guided by the principles of the Constitution as it evolved under the **Equal Protection Clause** of the **Fourteenth Amendment**, but selecting candidates for office is controlled by regulations promulgated by each state—a "weeding-out" process from a slate provided by the party via the primary election process.

The two major parties on the national level each share similar hierarchical structures. Each assembles a national convention wherein a **platform**, designed to create and tailor an **issue agenda** (and accompanying policy), will be the foundation of the party's focus for the next four-year presidential election cycle.

National conventions are also the places where the party's leadership is chosen. Each party's nominee for president is vested with the authority to select the new chair of the party. Approval by the entire convention is routine.

The winning presidential candidate in the November elections alone dictates who will be the party chair and how the platform and policy agenda will be shaped during the next four years in office. The chair becomes the "administrator" for the party, handling the day-to-day operations, but still answering to the White House and its political advisors. In the event the party's presidential candidate loses in the fall presidential election, a new chair is then selected from an available pool of party officials, whose job it is to develop a slate of potential national candidates for offices ranging from congressional seats to the next presidential contender.

The party chair also nominates and seeks the appointment of members to the national committee for the party, typically comprised of elected officials or appointees from each state. Currently, there are approximately 400 members of the Republican National Committee (RNC) and 150 for the Democratic National Committee (DNC).

Despite the rhetoric of party activists, both major political parties recognize that the majority of Americans consider themselves to be **moderates** or ideologically **center-right** when it comes to overall public policies. They are seen as **swing voters** or **independents,** capable of swinging an election to one candidate or another, regardless of that candidate's political party affiliation. As a result, national elections require parties to change from polarizing ideological campaign rhetoric that have become the bread and butter of primary elections to a more middle-of-the-road approach. Ideology can carry a party and its candidates only so far, and everyone except the most extreme left- or right-wing party members understand that. Remember, the main goal of political parties is to get people elected. Pushing and pursuing an ideology comes only after, when they can influence policy through the people in office.

# 11

# ❈ ELECTIONS ❈

## "AND THE WINNER IS...?

Former Speaker of the House Tip O'Neill allegedly once quipped that "all elections are local." And they still are, as they were when the framers created our government. Much of what people complain about regarding the process of running for office has been with us since the beginning of the United States. Malicious, personal attacks both direct and from behind the scenes, for example, have been a staple of American electoral politics going all the way back to the presidential contest between John Adams and Thomas Jefferson. The medium may have changed, giving rise to attack television ads, but any student of history can tell you the level of viciousness, vindictiveness and personal vilification has been extreme all along. The moral high ground and gentlemanly approach have been the exceptions rather than the rule.

On the other hand, there have been a number of changes, notably in the degree to which moneyed interests have become a significant part of campaigns and in the way the media have turned many elections into personality contests largely devoid of substantive issues. For many in office seeking reelection, the campaign for the next race has become a protracted process. U.S. representatives, whose term is limited to two years, start running for reelection virtually the day after they take office.

Contenders opposing a sitting president now typically start their campaign strategy to defeat the incumbent the night of his inauguration.[32]

## MODERN CAMPAIGNS

Not too long ago, candidates for public office had to rely upon party bosses in order to even be considered for office. These power brokers controlled party purse strings for fund-raising and held great sway over votes of party loyalists and activists. In the modern era, candidates no longer have to kowtow to the traditional bastions of power and influence. Developments such as the Internet, expanded electronic and print media, and campaign election laws all make it easier to run for office without the party's control.

That doesn't mean that when it comes to elections on the national level, people can simply declare their candidacy and expect to make any impact. They still need a network of volunteers and financial supporters. They must have an advisory staff keeping them informed and in front of the media to maximize efficient and effective exposure to the electorate. In many ways our two major national parties are still the most effective means to provide all that.

It is commonplace today to have a horse race filled with a diverse slate of candidates, all seeking the nomination of the party well before the onset of the primary season. Having a wide array of choices may be healthy for the party, but it has the potential to become a divisive and negative process when heading into the crucial primaries. As a result, party bosses have been replaced by professional media and political experts. Modern national campaigns spend over half of the money they raise on consultants![33] Routinely, these media consultants are Washington "insiders"; after the election cycle is completed, they frequently return to new or existing roles as "talking head" pundits on cable television networks.

## THE ART OF THE SOUND BITE

Media consultants are experts at honing the political message of candidates. They know how to manipulate the various forms of media available to create effective positive and negative ads. They are also masters of the art of the **sound bite**, a short phrase that makes promises or touts an accomplishment and can be used repeatedly to resonate with the electorate. In 2012, Vice President Biden tossed out a sound bite of his own: "Bin Laden is dead and GM is alive." Although short and sweet, this quip may find repeated play in general election campaign ads. This is very different from traditional campaign slogans, for example, "I like Ike," which was coined for use in Dwight D. Eisenhower's 1952 election campaign and had nothing to do with the issues of the time.

A good example of an effective sound bite occurred during Rick Scott's recent run for governor of Florida. Even though Scott espoused no concrete plans for economic recovery, his campaign slogan was "Let's Get to Work," and was that sound bite ever effective! He was elected in a close race with citizens citing his campaign to create jobs as the major reason they voted for him, even though he had said nothing substantial about how he would deliver on his promise.

Not surprisingly, the electorate has not been pleased with the actual result, and within a year after he took office, polls indicated that if the election were held then, more than 40% would switch their vote to Scott's opponent, who lost to him by a slim majority. This phenomenon is not unique to Florida, as voters in Wisconsin and Ohio also have had "buyer's remorse" regarding their governors, whose campaign slogans are miles apart from their actual behavior since they took office.

Along these lines, the voters of Wisconsin actually decided to force Republican Governor Scott Walker to face a recall election (allowed under the Wisconsin constitution). Over one million petitions were signed and certified demanding his recall and a special election was held on

June 5, 2012 resulting in Walker being retained. It is interesting to note that he won the recall election after donors and super-PACs supporting him spent over $31 million in his behalf (70% of the money was raised within a month of the election from out of state donors) versus only $4 million raised by his Democratic opponent. Once again the message seems to be: the more money you have, the more chance you have to win elections.

Another example of the sound bite, supported by a dramatic visual image, was President George W. Bush's "Mission Accomplished" banner welcoming his staged television arrival aboard an aircraft carrier in 2003. Bush exultantly claimed that the aims of the Iraq and Afghani Wars were met. In his case it backfired and became the butt of jokes, because it took until after he left office before our troops started to withdraw from Iraq, and as of 2013, they were still entrenched in Afghanistan. The list of pithy promises unfulfilled could go on and on, but the fact is that sound bites work and will continue to be used by media consultants to promote their clients.

The use of media, especially television, is extremely expensive. As a result, modern campaigns must raise large amounts of money in order to wage a competitive campaign. In 2008, the two Republican and Democratic candidates for the presidency spent over $1 billion collectively. Four years later in the 2012 election, Barack Obama's and Mitt Romney's campaigns and supporting Super PACs spent in excess of $2 billion!

Because elections are now more personality-driven and less dependent or centered on party, the candidates themselves must lead fund-raising efforts. Every party has its base of supporters or activists, but they do not represent a large enough number to assure election to office. Candidates must reach out to **swing voters** or **independents** who are not affiliated with any particular party or political ideology. During the primary elections, candidates will jockey for **front-runner** position and will seek the support of the party faithful, also known as the **base**. It is only after the primary election that the nominee of each party will refocus his message to target the swing voters while uniting the party base temporarily divided during primary season.

## THE PRIMARY PROCESS

The purpose of primaries is to ultimately select the delegates that will choose the presidential nominee at the party's national convention. There are no national standards, however, dictating how primary elections are administered. Each state is free to establish and maintain its own form and rules. Most institute standards and regulations, but leave the political parties in control when it comes to ballot design and qualifications required to be placed on the party's ballot.

In general, candidates for public office gain access to the slate for the **primary ballot** by collecting signatures of registered voters or by paying a **nominating fee**. They may include party affiliation on a primary ballot, but some local races are considered non-partisan and therefore no party affiliation is required. When party affiliation is mandatory, winning the nomination by ballot may also necessitate acceptance by a party's central committee, not just a victory in the primary itself. Although states create regulations controlling how primary elections are conducted, they all allow the prominent political parties to decide how the slate of candidates are to be selected and the method of electing them to the general election ballot.

The following types of primary elections exist in our states. In an **open primary** any registered voter, regardless of stated party affiliation, may vote for any candidate on the ballot. This allows for **cross-ticket voting** and enfranchises the highest number of primary voters.

Many states hold a **closed primary** in which only voters registered to a particular party may vote: Republicans may only vote in the Republican primary, Democrats may only vote in the Democratic primary, and so on. Although this option maintains **party loyalty** and inhibits raids by rival parties from voting to put the worst candidates on the rival's general election ballot (a favorite Nixon campaign method in the early 1970s), it ultimately leads to suppressing voter turnout as registered **Independents** are not allowed to vote in a party-oriented primary. Most states and political parties prefer closed primaries, and only a handful of states maintain open primaries.

In some states, the actual delegates may be chosen instead by the party leadership and they alone will ultimately decide who will be the nominee in the general/fall election. In others, primary voters actually pick a slate of delegates, which is then committed to vote for a particular candidate at the national election. This is known as a **delegate selection** primary.

Some state primaries follow **proportionate representation**, assigning delegate votes to candidates based on the number of votes received. Proportionate representation primaries tend to be favored by the Democratic Party as they promote minority candidates for consideration and allow for a more inclusive group of delegates at the national election.

Then there are the **winner take all** primaries in which all delegates are awarded to the candidate who wins most votes, regardless of the margin of victory. These delegates are then bound to cast their vote for the winner at the national convention.

In the past, some states offered **blanket primaries** as a way to open up early voting to all registered voters. But with all candidates listed on one ballot, many voters were confused, and political parties didn't like the erosion of their control over primary ballots. *California Democratic Party v. Jones*, 530 U.S. 567 (2000), challenged the State of California's use of the blanket primary on the grounds that it violated party member's collective First Amendment rights to associate. The Supreme Court ruled in favor of the plaintiff. It also held blanket primaries unconstitutional in the case of

*__Washington State Grange v. Washington State Republican Party__*, 128 S.Ct. 1184 (2008). Blanket primaries are no longer utilized in any state.

## Caucuses

Perhaps the most unusual type of primary is the **caucus**. Only a handful of states use this method, in which participants don't cast their vote at a polling place, but attend private meetings held throughout the state run by the political parties. During these caucuses, supporters of candidates make final pitches to the party faithful and leadership in a last ditch effort to grab their attention and votes. If successful, delegates bound to that candidate will be chosen at each of the caucus sites. Caucuses started out with only party officials attending, limiting the decision-making of who would be on the fall ballot to the elites within the party, but today the meetings are generally open to all registered members of the party, who all have voting rights.

Some consider this process a mere **beauty contest** in which party regulars choose who they would "prefer" to be their candidate for the general/fall election, but no delegates for the national conventions are actually selected and required to vote for the winner. An example of a beauty contest is the **straw vote** selection undertaken in Iowa several months in advance of the actual caucuses in early spring. By tradition, Iowa is the first state to select delegates during primary season, and the straw vote beauty contest is utilized by the Republicans more than the Democrats as a way to declare their candidacy and to get an edge in campaign fundraising and media attention as an early front-runner.

Currently, some Republican candidates choose to focus on other primary states to throw their hats in the ring, depending on where they think the announcement will have the greatest impact. Thus, conservative Republican Texas Governor Rick Perry announced his run for president in South Carolina, while ignoring the GOP Iowa straw vote.

Still, both the Republican and Democratic parties place a great deal of emphasis on the Iowa caucus, as it is the earliest primary and bestows the mantle of early **front-runner** on the winner. One thing the Iowa caucus is not, however, is representative of all Americans. Iowans tend to be white, rural, Christian and very conservative. As a result, candidates from both parties will invest a lot of money and organization in Iowa well before election season actually begins because a candidate can gain considerable momentum, not because so many delegate votes are at stake, but because of the symbolism of being the front-runner. In a sense, all roads to the White House begin in Iowa and New Hampshire, the home of the second primary contest.

Besides the Iowa caucus and the New Hampshire primary, another important event in the season leading up to the national convention is what is known as **Super Tuesday**, on which 24 states hold their primaries simultaneously. Since 41% of Republican Party and 52% of the Democratic Party convention delegates are chosen that day, Super Tuesday has a major impact on our electoral process, sometimes clinching the nomination for a candidate. A **Junior Tuesday** follows Super Tuesday with four more states holding their primaries.

As a result, we have a very **front-loaded** nomination process. Early momentum is critical for eventual party nomination and a successful general campaign in the fall. Early wins clear the field, allowing the prime candidate to focus his attention on fund-raising and honing his message by studying and preparing against his rival. The idea is to develop effective campaign strategies, clarify the differences between the candidate and his opponent, and test attacks and campaign messages that will activate the party base and grab the attention of swing voters.

In recent years, some states have jockeyed for early position on the calendar in order to increase their influence on the primaries outcome, as no one wants to hold a primary after a candidate has sewn up the nomination. Neither of the major parties has appreciated these attempts, since it can throw a wrench into well-honed campaign strategies, and they both have penalized such efforts. In 2008, the GOP punished Florida for moving its primary up into the third spot, right after Iowa and New Hampshire, and refused to seat 49 of its delegates at the 2012 national convention. A similar move by the Democrats was averted in a compromise brokered by Barack Obama, who did not want to alienate the voters of the fourth-largest state before the November election.[34]

The loss of delegates was particularly embarrassing for Florida, as the 2012 Republican National Convention was held in Tampa. Since then the state's GOP has formally announced that it will be moving its 2016 presidential primary so that it will not be held before March of that year and the full delegate slate will be be recognized and seated at the next convention.

## NATIONAL CONVENTIONS

The final stage in the candidate selection process is the **national party convention,** an assembly in which designated electors or **delegates** selected by the primary voters and **super delegates** empowered by the party itself vote for a nominee to carry the party banner in the full election. Delegates also initiate and approve party **platforms** or policy agendas linking the party with the voters in the upcoming election cycle.

Although both parties require delegates to vote for their designated candidate on the first ballot only—allowing them to freely switch support to another candidate—gone are the days of **brokered conventions** when no single candidate could marshal a majority, leading to major floor fights, wheeling and dealing behind the scenes, and surprise **dark horse** nominees. (In 1859, Abraham Lincoln became the standard bearer of the Republican Party that way, one of the most unlikely candidates to ever run for presidential office.)

Instead, nothing very interesting or surprising happens at national conventions anymore. Arguments over party platforms have been worked out well ahead of time and selection of the vice presidential candidate to join the national ticket is now left up to the nominee and his staff. **National conventions** are all pageant and regalia now, carefully choreographed for media exposure to fire up the base and hopefully draw in undecided swing voters. As a result of this pageantry, each party can expect a bump or **bounce** in the polls signaling public awareness and approval. Sustaining the bump depends on which party holds its convention second and how much of a lasting image it can create for the public via the media.

Typically, conventions follow the same format each election cycle: Day one is dedicated to the keynote address, usually assigned to an up-and-coming star within the party. At the 1988 Democratic convention, Bill Clinton bombed, while Barack Obama "hit a home run" in 2004. Day two is for platform reports and presentation of by-laws for the next four years. For media purposes, especially television, videos glamorizing primary candidates and ultimately the nominee are shown that evening.

Day three is usually dedicated to the nomination of the vice presidential candidate. It is usually again a love fest with videos and speeches given to frame the new VP candidate as "right for America" and "a true patriot." Surprisingly, at the 2008 Democratic convention, Barack Obama actually took the stage to congratulate Joe Biden upon his vice presidential nomination. It was spectacular political theater.

With the nomination of the presidential candidate and his acceptance speech, Day four is the culmination—the grand finale—of the convention. It is carefully orchestrated to be a star-studded media event, replete with handholding between presidential and vice presidential nominees and their families, to create the requisite imagery and momentum leading into the general election. Since the 1992 convention, when Bill Clinton and Al Gore danced with their spouses and families on stage, the finale has taken on the quality of a love fest, a celebratory, made-for-television event.

## HOUSE AND SENATE CAMPAIGNS

There are differences between campaigns for the presidency and campaigns for the House and Senate. Usually, the political parties stay out of the primary process in an effort to avoid conflicts between party loyalists, supporters and activists that have their own favorite. Only party regulars vote in primaries and voter turnout is usually low. Typically, House elections are more contested than Senate elections, but that is not always the case. Because incumbents have a considerable edge when they run for reelection, the party strongly urges other contenders to "wait their turn" in order to push for a safe outcome in the fall election. Republicans use that approach more than Democrats in House or Senate nominations. When there is no incumbent running, it is considered to be an **open seat election.**

Why do incumbents win so often even if there is a primary fight? The main reason is **name recognition**. Incumbents use their office in order to keep their name before the voting public. Other factors include holding town hall meetings, publishing in local papers under their bylines, maintaining public profiles by promoting constituent services, taking advantage of committee memberships for greater media exposure, and the use of the **franking privilege,** which allows free use of governmental publishing and postal services to communicate with constituents (as long as it has a governmental purpose, which is loosely defined these days). Additional advantages for incumbents come from having access to their party's congressional campaign committee staffs and committees, which assist them at election time, and connections to powerful fund-raising groups.

Because Senate races are statewide campaigns that have national implications with widely diverse constituencies, they are very expensive.

The average Senate campaign costs are in excess of $6 million and spiraling. The races are usually highly contested between the parties and a lot is at stake: Think of the national implications of gaining one of only 100 seats. Seniority matters—committee memberships improve and increase profile and media opportunities—and senators' terms are six years, the longest term of office among elected offices, with a responsibility to more than just their state constituency. They must also be responsive to national constituency concerns.

House races on the other hand involve narrow constituencies within clearly defined districts, focused on local voter issues. There are more safe seats in the House and therefore, House races are far less expensive to run than Senate races. At the same time, since House members serve only two-year terms, they are in effect always running for reelection. Incumbency brings with it seniority and important committee memberships, and access and influence are vitally important to lobbyists. As a result, protecting the status quo will get most of the attention of national PACs and 527 groups.

## Debates

The nationally televised **debates** are not really "debates," but staged events designed to present an impression of the candidates and to check how well they have rehearsed their tried and true campaign talking points. Most front-runners or incumbents have little to gain from these occasions. Many presidents detest debates because they have to share a stage with an opponent lacking the standing of being in office. Opponents love debates because it gives them the chance to share the limelight and status with a sitting president. Viewers usually have lower expectations of opponents, and if they can answer any debate questions without tripping up, they are awarded some measure of status. This is critical in the **spin room** where media consultants or **spin doctors** work their magic to portray their candidate as a genius, "presidential" and deserving election. Debates rarely become "game changers" in the opinion of most voters. Although debates have led to gaffes, their impact is usually temporary. Big gaffes though, will be used in negative campaign ads and can lead to an eventual erosion of credibility. Thus, George H.W. Bush's campaign pledge, "Read my Lips, No New Taxes," uttered at the GOP national convention in 1988 came back to haunt him four years later because he raised taxes during his presidency.

For some presidents, honesty and integrity are more important than political leadership and policy skill. Since the Clinton era, the economy has become the overriding issue in the public's approval or disapproval of our presidents. As the details of the economic downturn of 2008 came to light during the presidential campaign, John McCain, the GOP Candidate, and Barack Obama were within one point of each other in public opinion polls. Then McCain committed a blunder by stating he did not have a great deal of expertise in economy matters. Compounding the problem, he confidently argued that the fundamentals of the economy were sound, only to witness details of the bank failures emerge and the economy head into a free fall (what talking heads now call the "Great Recession"). Voters reflexively moved into the camp of Barack Obama, helping him to be elected president.

An example of a catastrophic campaign blunder occurred during the 2012 presidential election when a video of Mitt Romney addressing a group of financial supporters in Florida was leaked to the media. His comment that 47% of the American electorate are the victims who believe that government has the responsibility to care for them and "his job is not to worry about those people" had a profound negative impact and played into the Obama camp's painting Romney as "out of touch" with ordinary Americans. Romney himself later admitted that his statement was probably the major reason for his monumental loss of the presidential race.

## THE FALL CAMPAIGN

Unlike the primaries, the general election in November produces greater voter participation, and Republicans routinely have a better turnout than Democrats. As a result, "get out the vote" efforts are always more of a concern to the latter than the former. When exit polling indicates a high voter turnout, it usually presages a Democratic victory. Factors that impact voter numbers range from the likeability of the candidate, the nature of the issues the campaigns focus on, the record of the incumbent, weather, traffic, the number of polling places and voting machines available—long lines vs. shorter lines at polling stations—and most importantly, how well the candidate appeals to independent or swing voters.

The majority of Americans who are independent and swing voters are moderates looking for a candidate that can lead from the middle and not from the extremes of any given political ideology. But while these voters are needed to win an election, they are considered unimportant in the long run and are often ignored once office is attained. Our electorate is notorious for its short memory and remarkable ability to vote against its self-interests. The best explanation for this phenomenon is ignorance or lack of interest in the political process as evidenced in voting patterns and manifested through voter apathy as reflected in very low turnout numbers (going back many decades).

Presidential, Congressional and state elections throughout the United States generally follow **plurality** or **winner takes all** rules, which means the candidate with the most votes wins, even if he or she gets less than 50% of the votes cast. Imagine having four candidates running for the same public office who get 42%, 33%, 20% and 8% of the votes, respectively. The one with a plurality of 42% wins. This is true in just about every part in the country. (There a few place where run-off elections are required when none of the candidates get more than 50% of the vote.)

Having a plurality is different from needing a majority of 50% or more of the votes to win. Since we have **single member voting districts**, as endorsed by the Supreme Court in case law, plurality means you can win by a single vote over your nearest opponent and end up representing the whole district.

## THE ELECTORAL COLLEGE

Every strategy for a presidential election must be created, maintained and implemented with the ultimate goal of achieving success in the **Electoral College**. According to the Constitution, there is no direct election of our president and vice president. Instead, citizens vote for a candidate, and **electors** in each state are then committed (on the first ballot only) to cast their vote for the winning candidate in the Electoral College. Each state is awarded a number of **electors** based on the total number of members in Congress.

There are a total of 538 delegates in the Electoral College—for 100 senators, 435 congressmen, and three representatives of the District of Columbia. Some states allow for a **plurality vote**, assigning electors based on the percentage of a candidate's vote total. However, most states employ the **winner take all** system, whereby a candidate who wins the state's popular vote, no matter how slim the margin, gets all of the electors. Altogether, it requires a majority of 270 electoral votes to win the presidency.

What is the impact of the Electoral College on campaign strategy? Essentially presidential campaigns must calculate the fastest and most efficient method to reach the magic number of 270 to win the presidency. This translates into expenditures in the forms of money and time spent by the campaign and candidate. As a result, modern campaigns establish fewer ground troops in states with lower electoral votes—also known as "fly-over" states—and focus more attention on states where they'll get a bigger "bang for their buck."

In the event no single candidate gets the requisite 270 votes in the Electoral College, the election of the president then goes to the House of Representatives, where each state receives **one** vote and a majority of **26 votes** wins the White House. The election of the vice president takes place in the Senate, where **51 votes** elects.

The Electoral College holds its formal vote on the first Monday after the second Wednesday in December following the November general election. Its votes are tallied and reported to a joint session of Congress in January where the president of the Senate (the sitting vice president) then certifies the Electoral College vote. Imagine how Al Gore must have felt in 2001 when he had to preside over a vote certifying his opponent, George W. Bush, as president.

It is important to understand that winning the popular vote does not correlate to winning the White House. There have been several occasions where candidates have won significantly more popular votes but still lost the election. This first happened when Andrew Jackson scored a popular vote victory over John Quincy Adams, but Adams won the presidency; and more recently in 2000, when Al Gore won the popular vote by over 500,000 over George W. Bush.

From time to time, there have been arguments against the modern use of the Electoral College, but reforming the process would be cumbersome. To do so would require a constitutional amendment. It would also alter tradition put in place by the original framers. Reform sounds great, especially when the outcome of the Electoral College is skewed from the popular vote totals; but it happens rarely, and more times than not, it is still an effective and efficient method to elect our presidents.

## ELECTION PATTERNS

Pundits opine that a single election demonstrates this or that development in the body politic, but no one really knows what election results mean until some time has passed. One impact of a single election cycle, however, can be determined—the **coattail effect** when a strong leader of a political ticket pulls along lesser known candidates (they "ride his coattails" to victory). This is usually caused by **straight ticket** voting, meaning voters mark all the candidates on a ballot along party lines. Often, uninformed voters will vote with a straight ticket because they like the personality of the main national candidate and don't know enough about the other candidates. Obviously, political parties encourage straight ticket voting.

There are a few other election categories that suggest patterns, usually identified after the fact. One is **maintaining elections,** which confirm previous election results and establish and maintain control of one political party over another. They are characterized by the reelection of incumbents, ensuring the status quo.

**Critical elections**, as defined by the pioneering political scientist V.O. Key, represent shifts of power to a party in a specific election year if that party had not been in power before the particular election cycle. In a critical election, a major shift occurs with lasting impact on the power held by one party over another. Elections also may be considered to be **deviating** when one party temporarily obtains power, but it does not last beyond the next election cycle.

**Realigning elections** reflect a shift in coalitions of voters from one political party to another and impact all levels of government (national, state and local). No election can be considered "critical" until the passage of time. Pundits will jump on each other to be the first to claim the significance of an election; however, no reputable political scientist will do so until well after the passage of time.

## COMMON VOTER MISCONCEPTIONS

The characteristics of those running for federal office are fairly established and known. Polls suggest members of Congress have a lower approval rating then used car salesmen, insurance agents and lawyers. Most Americans when polled will say Congress is ineffective and filled with lowlives. There is one glitch, however. Americans actually favor their own representative in Congress; the other guys' representatives are the ones who are no good. This fact is borne out in an August 2011 *New York Times*/CBS poll when the approval rating for Congress fell to an all-time low. Although 87% of the respondents believed Congress was doing a poor job and should be replaced come next election, 56% thought their representative deserved to be reelected.[35]

Despite the distrust the electorate has towards Congress, more than 84% of incumbents are reelected to office repeatedly.[36] This routine reelection of incumbents from the same districts comes about because they represent **safe districts** where reelection is easier and they enjoy a **safe seat.**

The most dangerous attack on a safe seat is the ability of state legislatures to **redistrict** or **gerrymander** districts. The Constitution states that all representatives to Congress be determined by population, and that number is in turn to be ascertained with a nationwide census every 10 years. Congress then takes those population numbers and **reapportions** the number of representatives in each state accordingly. Based on population shifts, some states lose, while others gain congressional seats. Once the new number of representatives is determined for each state, the state legislatures then have the power to **redistrict** the state and create new district boundaries. It should come as no surprise that the party in power during the **reapportionment** year will draw the boundaries in its own favor.

This process is called **gerrymandering**—the creative, partisan way state legislatures define districts to favor the majority party and guarantee it stays in control. In the past, gerrymandering included drawing district boundaries that were extremely convoluted, often producing a crazy looking quilt on the map, but effective in ensuring the continuity of a party's power base.

In the process, districts were often designed to minimize the political effect and impact of minorities, depriving them of the chance for fair representation. Although redistricting was an exclusive power held by the states, the Supreme Court determined that in order to be constitutional, all representative districts must be comparably equal in population and must be contiguous to one another. This ruling ensured that districts would not be designed to give a small population disproportionate powers and eliminated the tortuous district lines that looked like they had been drawn by a drunken sailor (see *Baker v. Carr*, 369 U.S. 186 (1962) and *Wesberry v. Sanders*, 376 U.S. 1 (1964)).

Subsequent Supreme Court rulings have refined the redistricting requirements to guarantee that only these two standards be upheld to meet constitutional validity: equal population and district contiguity. There is absolutely no requirement that a district favor a particular social, ethnic or racial group, or that there be equal representation of men, women, blacks, whites, Hispanics, Chinese, Muslim, etc. Population is the only standard and measure. See *Shaw v. Reno*, 509 U.S. 630 (1993) and *Miller v. Johnson*, 515 U.S. 900 (1995).

Rarely have efforts to derail a majority's complete control of the redistricting process been considered real threats to the time-worn process of gerrymandering, practiced by both political parties when they're in power of statehouses. But we may be seeing a sea change. In 2014, a Florida Circuit Court ruled in *Romo v. Detzner*, 2012-CA-490 (decided July 10, 2014) that the majority party in the Florida statehouse (GOP) violated the Florida Constitution which requires an unbiased approach for a "fair redistricting process." In the wake of this decision, we can expect a more aggressive campaign in a number of other states to provide fairly drawn districts. It also has added momentum to efforts to create independent commissions capable of redistricting without favoring whichever political party is in power at the time.

There is another fallacy in our political system. We routinely hear politicians seeking the limelight by proudly proclaiming a need for a constitutional amendment to establish term limits for members of Congress. But we already have term limits. They are called elections!

Unfortunately, elections have become affairs involving fewer and fewer Americans. In the 2004 presidential election 45% of registered voters stayed home. In the 2008 presidential election, when Obama galvanized a new generation of young voters, still as many as 42% opted to stay home. In 2012, it was 42.5%. What will it take to re-engage disaffected American voters? What will it take for Americans to embrace the right of suffrage that so many have fought and died for? Perhaps these statistics prove that no one has taken our government from us, but that we have begun to give it away instead.

# 12

# ❖ INTEREST GROUPS ❖

## Follow the Money

Money has become a big issue in elections over the past few decades. Running a campaign without money is like driving a car without fuel. You can have the best equipment in the form of a turbo-charged organization, but without an infusion of cold cash, it will never leave the station or garage. All too often, the lack of money has doomed political desire and ambitions. Because it all comes down to finances in the modern era of politics, the question is what the impact of large contributions is on a campaign or candidate. Although some donors may be giving money because they truly believe in the candidate and his or her cause, many expect some form of return for their "investment." As a result, there is a fine line between campaign financing and outright bribery—investing for influence, access or potential favors down the road after the candidate is elected. Once again, money fuels campaigns and elections. Candidates with greater financial support are more likely to win at election time. But one has to ask: Is democracy being served if money becomes the primary factor for electability?

## INTEREST GROUPS

Representing a wide array of concerns and issues, **interest groups** or **special interests** have been around for years and provide important services to its members in addition to lobbying for their interests in Washington. They include such organizations as the American Association of Retired Persons (AARP), the National Rifle Association (NRA), the American Medical Association (AMA), the American Bar Association (ABA), the National Association of Manufacturers (NAM), the American Automobile Association (AAA) and the National Education Association (NEA), to name a few.

Although many interest groups have straightforward names, which reflect the makeup of their constituencies, more recently a substantial number have taken on flowery titles designed to hide their true intentions, objectives and interests. Many of them are issue advocacy groups, commonly known as **Political Action Committees (PACs)** or **527 groups** (named after the number of the section of the U.S. Internal Revenue Code granting them non-profit tax status).

Examples of 2012 Republican "Leadership PACs" include *Freedom Works* (Dick Armey/Tea Party); *Freedom Project* (John Boehner, R. OH), *Bluegrass Committee* (Mitch McConnell, R. KY); *Tea Party Patriots* (Koch Brothers), *Think Progress* (Koch Brothers), *Prosperity PAC* (Paul Ryan, R. WI); *Defend America PAC* (Richard Shelby, R. AL); *Fund for America's Future* (Lindsey Graham, R. SC.) and *Storm Chasers* (Steve Buyer, R. IN).

Some of the "Leadership PACs" aligned with the Democratic Party are *Working Americans United to Give Help* (Rick Waugh, D. VA), *Renewing Opportunity, Trust and Hope* (Stephen Rothman, D. NJ) and *Vision for America* (Jackie Speier, D. CA).

There are also **Super PACs,** which can raise unlimited funds from an unlimited number of sources. The largest of the Super PACs are identified and listed on the Internet by *www.OpenSecrets.org* along with their ideology and total expenditures in 2012. They include *American Crossroads* (conservative) at $104,746,670 million; *Club for Growth Action* (conservative) at $17,960,737 million and the *NEA Advocacy Fund* (liberal) at $9,135,952 million.

According to *OpenSecrets.org,* as of May 23, 2013, a total of 1,310 groups organized as Super PACs have reported receipts of $828,224,595 and independent expenditures of $609,417,645 in the 2012 election cycle. Of this total, 66.6% was spent on Republicans' 31% on Democrats, and 2% on "other." It is important to note that with the current push by states to front-load primaries earlier and earlier in the calendar year, some Super PACs may not have to disclose the source of their political funding until after the elections are held. This further clouds the transparency we typically expect during elections.

The obvious concern regarding any interest group is its ability to actually influence public policy. Each department in the executive branch of our government sets policy priorities and seeks to translate them into programs to create and pursue. Examples of policy would include pro-choice/anti-abortion, drug-free schools, gun restrictions, pollution controls, etc. There is nothing wrong with groups trying to influence our government to their point of view, even if their notions are not always good for our nation as a whole. The question is: How much access and say do interest groups have in the actual legislative process?

## HISTORICAL CONTEXT

Our framers anticipated and debated the impact of financial contributions to candidates for public office at the creation of our political system. James Madison wrote in Federalist No.10 that politics and the influences of money will lead directly to the existence of **factions,** in which rival politicians will seek the power created by high public office. As a keen student of human nature, Madison believed that such factions were inevitable and argued that competition would benefit our political system, as only the best could rise to the top to make a case for their positions. Overall, he thought that adapting those positions would lead to positive results for the young nation. He did warn, however, that government should be weary of factions, keep a close eye on them, and regulate them to prevent them from getting too powerful.

George Washington was less sanguine. When he left office in 1796, he issued this prescient warning about factions in his farewell address:

> *They serve to organize faction, to give it an artificial and extraordinary force; to put, in the place of the delegated will of the nation the will of a party...to make the public administration the mirror of the ill-concerted and incongruous projects of faction, rather than the organ of consistent and wholesome plans digested by the common counsels and modified by mutual interests.*

Washington meant political parties, but he might as well have been talking about special interest groups.

## Campaign Finance Reform

Congress has wrestled for decades with Washington's warning and Madison's call for oversight, notably in regard to campaign financing. The most recent such reforms installed a limit of $2,500 on how much an individual may donate to any one political candidate from 2011 to 2012, and they require public disclosure of all individuals contributing to a candidate's election committee.

Over time, campaign finance regulations have been dissected by legal experts, leading to loophole exploitation and sometimes, outright fraud. This phenomenon is not new. There have been many occasions in American history when elections were "bought." During the Gilded Age (1850-1900), many corrupt politicians and judges in New York City were in the pockets of Boss Tweed and the moneyed interests he represented. Flagrant party machine politics was the norm at the beginning of the 20th century, resulting in calls for progressive election reforms during the

Roosevelt, Taft and Wilson presidencies. In addition to ballot and party reforms, the **Seventeenth Amendment** was ratified allowing for the direct election of Senators in 1913.

Perhaps the most egregious recent campaign finance scandal was the disclosure of widespread corruption of Richard Nixon's "Committee to Re-Elect the President," whose acronym, CREEP, should have been the tip-off that something wasn't quite right. CREEP solicited and received huge sums of illicit contributions which it laundered into cash to fund illegal campaign activities. Among others, CREEP paid for the bugging of Democratic candidates and the Democratic National Committee offices located in the Watergate Building in Washington, D.C. The scandal, which became widely known as **Watergate** (and started the tradition of adding "gate" to every political scandal in Washington since), brought down two U.S. attorneys general and several top White House advisers, and ultimately led to Richard Nixon resigning the presidency.

As a direct result of the Watergate scandal, Congress in 1974 amended the **Federal Election Campaign Reform Act of 1971**. The Act limited the amount of presidential campaign contributions allowed and placed considerable disclosure restrictions on them if, and only if—and that was the loophole—the candidates accepted federal presidential campaign matching funds. These funds became available as a result of taxpayers checking off a $1.00 donation on their federal tax forms. By 2012, the voluntary tax donation was raised to $2,500, but taxpayer participation has steadily declined over the years, and Congress is currently considering terminating the program. Back in the early 1970s, the theory was that average candidates for the presidency would not have access to large sums of money, so to level the playing field, federal matching funds would be made available to candidates who obtained at least 5% of voter support at the polls. Interestingly, Congress exempted itself from any similar provisions of the act.

Nowadays, raising enormous sums of money is a basic requirement to run for national office. Members of the House of Representatives must raise tens of thousands of dollars per week to get reelected. Based on their current salary of $174,000, plus a maximum of $27,000 in outside income, how could they possibly come up with this kind of money on their own? More importantly, what kind of allegiance do they owe to their wealthy donors? Although senators do not have to run for office as often as representatives, being elected for six-year terms, it is no different for them. Their constituency base and national influence are much larger, and their election campaigns are that much more costly. These figures alone should suggest for anyone interested in the future of our democracy that when it comes to campaign financing, all candidates for public office should have a level playing field.

In the 2008 presidential election, John McCain trailed Barack Obama in fund-raising by a considerable margin and therefore needed the federal matching funds to keep his campaign afloat. Obama, rejecting matching funds, was free to raise as much cash as he could. As a result, just before the election, the Obama team was able to purchase 30 minutes of prime time on the major television networks and aired a campaign "infomercial." Unable to compete, McCain could only sit back and watch as the spots helped to push even more undecided voters into the Obama camp.

Obama was not the first presidential candidate to reject public matching funds. George W. Bush did the same during the primaries of the 2000 presidential election in an effort to outspend and destroy his rivals for the GOP nomination—he had a number of wealthy donors on his side. It was only after he secured the nomination that he allowed his campaign to accept matching funds and the restrictions that came with them.

The 1971 Reform Act also created the **Federal Election Commission (FEC),** which consists of six members—three Republicans and three Democrats. Nominated by the president and confirmed by the Senate, each commissioner serves a term of five years. The FEC's task is to monitor elections and make sure campaigns play by the rules, regulating all campaign finance contributions, fund-raising and expenditures.

Through the years, interest groups and corporations have sought to pour campaign cash into the election process unfettered and to utilize **lobbying** as a mechanism to directly influence legislation. With the creation of the FEC, however, Congress has from time to time placed limits on how much money corporations may spend on individual candidates for public office.

Moneyed interests did not take these restrictions on their rights to influence elections lying down, however. In 1975, they initiated a lawsuit arguing that the limitations on campaign fund-raising by interest groups violated their First Amendment freedom of speech protections. A year later, ***Buckley v. Valeo***, 424 U.S. 1 (1976) reached the Supreme Court, which ruled in the plaintiffs' favor, but upheld the FEC's authority to restrict the amount of money that may be given to any one individual candidate. In the court's opinion, unlimited campaign fund-raising could be used for "issue advocacy," so long as money did not go directly to an individual candidate's campaign war chest. As a result, Congress was forced to pass a new law in order to restrain interest groups and related corporations from flooding elections with campaign dollars.

The **Bipartisan Election Reform Act** of 2002, otherwise known as **McCain-Feingold** (after its two sponsors in the Senate), was an attempt to regulate the amount of financial contributions that could be made directly to individual campaigns. McCain-Feingold banned **soft money—** funds provided for a candidate without actually being donated directly to that candidate. Soft money could be cash or in-kind contributions directly to a political party, but could not be given directly to a candidate's campaign treasury. McCain-Feingold also placed limits on total individual contributions during an election cycle to $30,000 and prohibited labor unions from spending dues and treasury funds for advertising in support of a candidate within 60 days of the November election. It further placed an iron-clad prohibition against donations to political campaigns from foreign nationals, and banned soliciting political contributions on federal property. It seems Congress was concerned that too much money in the political campaign process might pollute the process itself.

Ironically, McCain-Feingold led to the creation of what we now call **Political Action Committees (PACs)** and **527 groups**, issue advocacy groups registered as non-profit organizations under **Section 527** of the Internal Revenue Code, which opened the floodgates to big money entering national races. In 2010, PACs spent more than $177,845,988 for House Democrats and $112,387,700 for House Republicans.[37] These numbers are now dwarfed by spending related to the 2012 general election. In the first four months of 2012, there were 434 groups organized as Super PACs from both parties, which reported total receipts of $201,979,896 and total independent expenditures of $91,143,259. One of the obvious advantages of the non-profit advocacy Super PACs, is that the names of contributors need not be disclosed.

Once again, conservatives went to court to legitimize their campaign contribution methods and gained a big victory. In the matter of ***Colorado Republican Party v. FEC***, 518 US 604 (1996), the Supreme Court ruled that unlimited soft money may be spent for advertising, as long as it does not mention the name of any individual candidate and deals with an issue, not a person running for election. Using soft money to portray an issue, which by implication treats a candidate in a positive or negative light, is permissible. As a result, we have seen an explosion of issue advocacy and negative advertisement related to candidates.

In 2004, Bob J. Perry, a Houston builder and T. Boone Pickens, a wealthy Texas oilman, used issue advocacy soft money to promote the presidential reelection of George W. Bush by paying personal funds to support the writing and publication of a book. While much of it recounted innuendo and untruths, the book provided the foundation for negative attack ads against John Kerry, the Democratic presidential nominee, questioning his distinguished service record in Vietnam as a swift boat commander ("swift boats" were a class of naval vessels used during that war). The negative media campaign by "Swift Boat Veterans for Truth" effectively destroyed Kerry's credibility as an experienced military leader. It also spawned a new political buzz word, **swift boating**, to describe a vicious, unfair and or untrue political attack.

In a more recent judicial case, ***Citizens United v. FEC***, 558 U.S. 08-205 (2010), the Supreme Court determined by a narrow vote of 5-4 that corporate-funded advertising that positively or negatively impacts an individual's campaign is also free speech protected by the Constitution. Now corporations have the same free speech protections as individuals. While the court upheld the restrictions on labor union spending, it freed up corporate ability to spend soft money without any restrictions and disclosures. More money than ever may be given anonymously to everyone but the campaign itself, including foreign capital. The Chinese government may funnel money to its candidate of choice for president, and the American people will never know it. Other developments have followed in the wake of the *Citizens United* ruling. In 2012, Republican candidate for president Mitt Romney received political contributions in the amount of $1 million from W. Spann, LLC, a corporation created solely to raise and spend that money. As soon as it paid out the cash to the Romney campaign, W. Spann dissolved and ceased all corporate operations.[38]

The *Citizens United* ruling was initially assailed by Democrats and welcomed with open arms by Republicans. However, the bruising GOP

presidential primaries of 2012 caused a number of the earlier supporters to reconsider, and many Republicans are now calling for Congress
to enact legislation limiting the effect of the *Citizens United* decision. In
May 2012, as many as 22 states joined Montana's lawsuit against corporations spending Super PAC-related campaign funds, claiming it violated
existing state campaign finance restrictions on corporations in an effort
to have the Supreme Court reverse the *Citizens United* ruling.[39] In June
2012, the court struck down the Montana ban, however, ruling that the
*Citizens United* decision applies to state and local elections as well.

The Supreme Court in the matter of ***McCutcheon v. FEC***, #12-536,
(2014) ruled that corporations have First Amendment protected "campaign speech," and therefore, no limits may be applied to their political contributions. In doing so, the High Court extended Bill of Rights
protections to corporations. In the majority decision, Chief Justice John
Roberts ruled that there is no quid pro quo connection between political donations and political favoritism. Justice Clarence Thomas stated in
his concurring opinion that there should never be any limits to political
contributions, equating money with free speech in the realm of politics,
equates money with free speech. I'll leave you to decide the merits of
such an opinion. With no limits on corporate political donations, will
there also be no limits allowed on lobbying expenditures? The age of
the SuperPacs has dawned since the Supreme Court decision in *Citizens
United*, and there is currently no end in sight to the unfettered influence
of corporations on our political affairs.

## PACs in Action

PACs are not always interested in promoting the advancement of a
single candidate. More often than not, they hedge their bets by contributing to politicians on both sides of the spectrum in the same fashion
that lobbyists spread their cash around in order to purchase as much

influence as possible. In general, PACs want to ensure effectiveness of their contributions, so they concentrate them on **incumbents**, those politicians already holding office who seek reelection. That is why more objections to campaign fund-raising and contributions via PACs come from **challengers**, those seeking to be elected to political office against incumbents.

Usually individual supporters of PACs and 527s favor candidates or causes that mesh with their personal ideology, but it is not unusual for PACs to engage in seemingly bizarre actions. For example, some big donors spend lots of money to destroy the reputation of one candidate during the primaries only to turn around and embrace that candidate wholeheartedly in the general election. In the 2012 election cycle, Las Vegas casino billionaire Sheldon Adelson did just that. He single-handedly kept Newt Gingrich's primary campaign going because he detested Mitt Romney, only to give millions to Romney to use against Obama once he became the GOP candidate.

Each effective PAC has a defined leader supported by activists—the die-hard supporters and "believers"—and a group that can be generously referred to as **free-riders**. These "fellow travelers" pay absolutely nothing into the PAC, participate in no formal role for the PAC, but spout support (sometimes when convenient) during elections on blogs, in letters to the editors, at parties, etc. Members in name only, they are nonetheless an important part in the success needed for the PAC to accomplish its goals. If a free-rider puts a candidate's political sign in his yard during elections, he's done enough to enjoy the benefits of a successful campaign.

An example of a free-rider can be seen in virtually any community. Citizens may never contribute a penny to a political party or attend a political meeting, but they will advocate for a candidate by putting supporting bumper stickers on their motor vehicles and signs in their yards or on their social media outlets. They pay nothing to support a political party, but seek the advantages of membership by providing basic free support to its candidates.

Interest groups also contribute **soft money** to candidates. Soft money does not come in the form of cash, but in the form of services, such as providing telephone banks for canvassing and targeting voters in a demographic area in order to influence them via **robo-calls** or actual phone calls made by organized groups of volunteers. Soft money can also come in the form of telephone or Internet-based **polling** in which the electorate may be asked directed, or **"push"** questions, in order to produce a favorable image of a candidate. **Push polls** are efforts to steer an answer during a telephone poll. Often pollsters will ask carefully phrased questions that have only one possible answer, which invariably fits the objective of the poll to show a certain candidate in the best possible light. Another example of soft money is informal get-togethers in people's homes for "meet and greets" with candidates, which is also an effective fund-raising method for campaigns.

When interest groups gain access to candidates, they move on to **lobby** them and their staffs once they become elected officials, promoting public policy initiatives that meet their objectives. The most common lobbying influence comes in the rule-making aspect of legislation in efforts to sway how governmental bureaucracies enforce policy and regulations. That occurs most frequently in situations involving deregulation by big business concerns vs. enforcement of rigid regulations by environmentalists.

## ISSUE ADVERTISING ADVOCACY

Another form of financial contribution to politicians is **issue advertising advocacy**. Under McCain-Feingold and the non-profit tax section 527, issue advocacy groups may use unfettered, unrestricted, and unregulated funds from donations for political causes. Such donations and expenditures are considered "protected free speech" according to the ruling in the case of ***Buckley v. Valeo*** just like political advertising in ***Citizens United vs. FEC***.

According to the Center for Responsible Government, as posted on *www.OpenSecrets.org,* conservative groups spent $858.8 million; liberal groups, $406.9 million; and other groups, $25.4 million. The following groups led the way in donations received and funds spent in 527 issue advocacy media advertising during the 2012 election cycle:

- Crossroads GPS - $175,928,610
- Restore Our Future - $142,087,336
- Priorities USA - $65,166,859
- National Republican Congressional Committee - $64,653,078
- National Democratic Congressional Committee - $60,545,352

The top five organizations giving money in 2012 were:

- United States Chamber of Commerce - $35,657,029
- Service Employees International Union - $23,011,004
- National Rifle Association - $19,767,043
- AFL-CIO - $8,210,268
- National Association of Realtors - $8,210,268

## THE INTERNET

Another way to fast-track donations to political causes and campaigns is via the Internet. No one prior to the first presidential campaign of Barack Obama utilized the Internet as a widespread and tremendous source of political fund-raising. Obama raised enough money over the Internet that he was able to reject federal public campaign matching funds and the strings that came with them.

The Internet is also a huge source of information and demographic data. Using e-mails and messaging during political campaigning not only makes communications smooth, widespread and efficient, it also provides instant feedback on political solicitation. Although the Bipartisan Campaign Reform Act limits personal contributions to individual candidates to $2,400 per year, no such limits apply to PACs and issue advocacy groups (527s). Obama raised in excess of $264 million in the third quarter of his 2008 presidential election cycle. McCain raised $212 million during the same period. Looking at these numbers, the importance of campaign financing becomes glaringly obvious. As predicted, Obama and Romney each raised well over $1 billion for their 2012 campaigns![40]

If an argument can be made that money is a corrupting force, the only solution would be to eliminate all special interest PACs, 527s and lobbyists. To do so would require a massive expenditure of public funds to meet the needs of candidates seeking public office. Would Americans be willing to sacrifice federal tax dollars in order to ensure the integrity of our electoral process? Certainly those in power would object, and most of those seeking influence from outside donors now would prefer the current system.

The sooner Americans realize that interest groups have infiltrated and overrun our politics and our system of government, both on a national and state level, the more likely we can begin to eliminate their undue influence on our representatives. Americans have traditionally had little patience for meddlers in our freedoms. Unfortunately, interest groups themselves have hijacked our political process with their infusion of huge sums of money, making it that much more difficult to separate real American idealism from biased political rhetoric aimed at poisoning an honest political discourse. George Washington would be amazed with how ignorant Americans are when it comes to the roles our government plays and how it operates today.

## 13

### ❋ THE MEDIA ❋

#### Lapdogs or Watchdogs?

Even before the invention of television and computers, media in various forms have held tremendous sway in American politics. Before the Revolutionary War, printed handbills and posters slapped on town billboards announced meetings and detailed grievances against the colonial governors. One of the founders, Benjamin Franklin, had an influential printing business in Philadelphia. Pamphlets like Thomas Paine's "Common Sense" and "The American Crisis," which begins with the famous words, "These are the times that try men's souls," were widely disseminated (George Washington had the latter read out loud to his soldiers to inspire them during the darkest times of the revolutionary conflict with England).

The framers of the Constitution believed that an active, independent press was essential to preserve our liberty by airing political differences and safeguarding our rights to complain about our government. That is one of the main reasons they felt it necessary to include freedom of the press in the first of the Ten Amendments to the Constitution that make up our Bill of Rights.

For nearly 100 years after the founding of the United States, print media—newspapers, gazettes, handbills and pamphlets—were the only means of sharing information. But that changed. New technologies, including the telegraph, the telephone, radio, television, computers and the Internet, have brought us ever more close to one another. The latest "breaking" news appears simultaneously on 24-hour television news channels and Internet websites. Blogs, Facebook and Twitter instantly spread the word to millions across the globe via laptops, cell phones, Droids and iPhones.

Yet, while the founders might welcome the many opportunities these new technologies provide to empower individuals, they would surely be dismayed at the way the increasingly powerful media forces are undermining our democracy. The consolidation of television and media outlets into a few global networks has resulted in news reporting and political discourse that are carefully managed and manipulated for public consumption. Today, the Internet Age brings digital media to virtually every household, from Net-based newspapers and blogs to social media. On the other hand, now more than ever, the media hold a tight grip on the dissemination of "breaking news" and provide a relentless 24-7 flooding of the airwaves with a glut of often insipid and irrelevant information.

## NEWSPAPERS AND MAGAZINES

The mass media of today still rely on newspapers and magazines for "serious" reporting, but their readership has been on the decline since the 1960s due to television broadcasts, reality dramas and the emergence of Internet news. Only a few valued newspapers with substantial daily circulation remain. They include *The Wall Street Journal* (over 2.11 million), *USA Today* (over 1.83 million), and *The New York Times*, which is considered the elite of all newspapers (nearly 1.5 million). Among weekly news magazines such as *Time, Newsweek* and *U.S News & World Report,* by far the most widely read is the *National Enquirer* (at over 1.05 million readers).[41]

Newspaper and magazine articles encourage readers to consider and think about the information they present. No doubt the "screaming" banner headlines announcing the elections of various presidents, the sinking of the *Titanic* and the end of World War II appealed to reader's emotions, but they pale beside the impact that electronic media and sensationalized news entertainment make. Through the use of satellites, Twitter, and Skype-relayed news from smartphone cameras, television news can now put a personal face on news events as they unfold. Many can remember watching the tragedy of 9/11 on television or more recently, the devastation of the tsunami in Asia or the uprisings in Egypt, Libya and Yemen during the 2011 Arab Spring and subsequent developments in 2014. The instant images of the civil wars in Iraq and Syria are immediate, dramatic and indelible.

Historically, the media has performed several roles, acting as "watchdog" in the nation's political arena and becoming a beacon of light to illuminate the dark sides of our society. The Progressive Era from 1890 to 1920 had its "Muckrakers," reform-oriented journalists who wrote for popular magazines at the time, exposing political corruption and social ills.

As recently as the early 1970s, the work of two investigative reporters for *The Washington Post*, Bob Woodward and Carl Bernstein, who looked into a petty burglary at the Watergate Building, led to the resignation of a U.S. president. Although many people look down on journalists, we as a society generally expect them to keep a watch on how the legislative process works, and a number of journalists still consider revealing corruption in government an important aspect of their profession. Unfortunately, most news is now filtered through a few limited sources, such as The Associated Press. We receive "standardized" news because the days of news bureaus independently reporting to each major newspaper on the political affairs of our nation are gone.

At the time this edition is being prepared, the FCC is considering petitions by Comcast, AT&T and other media companies to permit them to consolidate ownership of content and distribution via satellite and cable outlets. This development should make all Americans wary because liberty requires a free and open media. The deliberate bundling of data usage, Internet access and viewership would allow content providers to "tailor" the broadcasting of information to consumers, seriously limiting and manipulating what Americans hear and see, and steering them toward a collective, yet woefully uninformed, political consensus.

## RADIO

Radio, a powerful medium of mass communication, brought news into the living rooms of America starting in the 1920s. President Franklin D. Roosevelt used it creatively for political purposes by giving hope to people during the Great Depression with his "fireside chats." With the arrival of television in the 1950s, however, radio had to take a backseat. In recent decades, its importance continued to diminish as listenership fell off sharply, although it recovered some of its swagger with the advent of satellite subscriptions. "Shock" radio now reaches millions of listeners with daily broadcasts by talk show celebrities like Howard Stern and Rush Limbaugh (although most of the rest of programming is simply the audio portion of the televised edition).

As the airwaves have become crowded by talk show hosts who are "entertainers" rather than journalists, radio has become a polarizing format. Glenn Beck made a fortune voicing provocative comments about any topic under the sun he considered worth talking about. When it was revealed that he was a commissioned salesman for a company selling gold while claiming in his "news" segments that the world economy was looking to gold as the only safe hedge against economic global collapse, his only retort to criticisms of conflict of interest was to say that he was only an entertainer and not a real journalist.[42] He later had a television show on the Fox network, successful for some time, notable for airing his extreme rants and tearful breakdowns as he bemoaned the current state of affairs.

Rush Limbaugh is another talk show mogul who professes to speak to the concerns of the average white, working-class male. Limbaugh has become the *de facto* leader of the right-wing conservative movement and rallies public opinion against anything he doesn't consider conservative enough for possible political consideration. Soon after Barack Obama was elected president, Limbaugh actually told his listening audience he hoped Obama would fail. At the same time, Limbaugh calls himself a patriot, as if rooting for a president not to succeed wouldn't affect the United States negatively. More recently, Limbaugh attacked Georgetown Law School student Sandra Fluke for the comments she made to a Democratic congressional panel on the need for insurance coverage for contraceptives, repeatedly labeling her a "slut" and one "addicted to sex." This time, he found himself on the wrong side of listeners and eventually apologized when some of his corporate sponsors, concerned about angry consumers, pulled advertising support from his radio program. Limbaugh continues un-chastened and maintains a powerful voice that has captured the hearts and minds of the right-wing electorate. As a result, he wields considerable political influence; so much so, that moderate Republicans are afraid to speak out and criticize his most outrageous comments.

It is likely that radio will continue to be a venue for extremist political speech on both sides of the political spectrum, operating with half-truths and innuendo to push a certain ideology instead of serving as an objective source of political news.

## TELEVISION

Television remains the main source of information in America. There used to be just four networks, the American Broadcasting Company

(ABC), Columbia Broadcasting System (CBS), the National Broadcasting Company (NBC) and the Public Broadcasting System (PBS), but with the expansion of cable, there are now a number of other channels exclusively dedicated to news. CNN, the first 24-hours-a-day news television station, had its first broadcast on June 1, 1980. Fox News followed in 1996.

Although television is still the top provider of the news to the American public—via digital antenna, cable, satellite dish or the Internet—network news has fallen on hard times due to the emergence of cable-oriented news programs that can be found on channels like CNN, Fox, MSNBC or CNBC.

The drawback of television as an objective source of news programming is related to its commercial nature. Viewership numbers drive advertising dollars—audience support leads to advertising support, which in turn leads to financing broadcasting operations. As a result, there is little support for serious news and sensational entertainers crowd out legitimate journalists. Why else do we have serious news programs on Sunday mornings or late at night, while "Entertainment Tonight" airs during prime time, along with a spate of sitcoms and "reality" shows?

Television may be a vital venue for the projection of images, but the high cost of television advertising often closes the door to genuine political messages in favor of 30-second "sound bites." As any marketer will tell you, as soon as an ad on TV starts to annoy you, it has actually begun to work! Serious debate on serious issues may never again be presented on television due to the astronomical cost of fee based coverage and advertising.

At the same time, television has fallen prey to the same ideological divisiveness as talk radio. Fox has its Charles Krauthammer and Sean Hannity, two of the most overt right-wing conservative talking heads, followed in short order by Bill O'Reilly and his "No Spin Zone" (except for his own spin on issues).

On the liberal side, there are political show hosts like Chris Matthews ("Hardball") and Lawrence O'Donnell ("Late Night with…"), whose shows runs five days a week on MSNBC. Another example is Rachel Maddow, who holds a PhD in political science and attempts to cover news in an objective manner, but usually ends up pushing ideas favorable to the left side of the spectrum.

For the most part, however, news broadcasts are superficial, filled with sound bites and hyped-up events. We are easily distracted by the latest headline of breaking news without retaining interest in ongoing public affairs. News providers have taken advantage of this by presenting news in choppy, attention-grabbing details, admittedly knowing their broadcasts lack depth.

At the same time, the line between genuine news and entertainment continues to blur. Many younger audiences turn to the Comedy Channel for ongoing news and watch Jon Stewart and Stephen Colbert without realizing that they, too, are entertainers and not real journalists. At least Stewart is not confused about what he does. When asked in a serious interview after whom he modeled his presentation style, he answered, "Jerry Seinfeld." Surprisingly, the questioner was actually puzzled.

Yet, the public seems to like it this way. Most Americans prefer to obtain their news from a sensationalized format with talking heads and opinion pushers rather than from real investigative journalists. What else can it mean when MSNBC's ratings for its reality show "Lock Up" score higher viewership than either Fox or CNN for the same time slot?[43]

## WHO OWNS THE MEDIA?

While cable television has "dumbed down" news and political discourse, the ownership of large numbers of media outlets has consolidated to the point that just a few corporate players control most of the airwaves.

News Corporation is a conglomerate owned and operated by Rupert Murdoch. It in turn owns or controls the following outlets for news information: Fox News; 20th Century Fox Film with 10 subsidiaries; Fox Broadcasting with five subsidiaries; 17 television channels on cable alone; satellite access with a network in both Italy and India; seven magazines worldwide; 30 newspapers and information services and Harper-Collins, a worldwide publishing house.

Another media empire is Time Warner. Originally founded by Ted Turner, but no longer owned by him, it has the following media outlets: CNN, Home Box Office (HBO), Turner Broadcasting (TBS, TNT and 31 networks worldwide) and Time, Inc., which owns 125 companies and brands worldwide, including *Time Magazine*. In addition, the company owns Warner Brothers Entertainment and all of its subsidiaries. Although CNN aspires toward presenting an unbiased perspective in its news reporting, many conservatives contend that it favors a liberal view of the world.

Joining these two mega players is Comcast Cable and General Electric Corporation (GE). Comcast and GE combine to own 18 separate entertainment networks along with 14 other television stations. On the radio side, Bain Capital (Mitt Romney's company) and fellow venture capital firms collectively own Clear Channel Communications, whose 2011 earnings were $6.2 billion while operating 866 radio stations offering conservative talk shows along with the Fox Network and its stable of entertainers. CBS owns and operates CBS Radio with over 130 stations. These are the largest owners of radio outlets in America.

While the federal government through the **Federal Communications Commission (FCC)** issues licenses for broadcasters to utilize the "public airwaves," private ownership of the media really runs the show. The argument for this arrangement is that private media providers ensure that they are not controlled by the government, thereby guaranteeing independence and freedom. In theory, that would be true; but in practice that's just not the case. Anyone who does not understand and appreciate this is blind to the reality of modern television media. Fox television can be considered virtually an "arm" of the GOP.

In the United States, we only have one television and radio outlet owned by the public, the Public Broadcasting Service (PBS). Republicans routinely criticize PBS for its left-wing bias, and want all public support for it to cease. Yet, anyone watching PBS for news can quickly determine that political rhetoric is absent from its news programs.

Since many privately owned media outlets pursue a deliberate right or left wing political ideology, few can honestly state that they report news without some kind of bias. At the same time, bias is nearly impossible to prove considering how news is developed, written and ultimately broadcast. Yet it does exist. News coverage is created in direct response to market research conducted by the various networks. It is this type of internal polling that results in the broadcasters obliging and showing whatever the public wants to see, as long as they can make a profit doing so through the sale of advertising. That is why there is a "fluff" piece segment in just about every news broadcast. That is why local news always sensationalizes the broadcast with scenes from robberies, murders and car accidents. Like rubbernecking, audiences cannot get enough of this type of broadcasting. It is also why we have so little coverage on foreign news in our news cycles. American audiences generally don't care about what happens elsewhere, unless it has a sensationalist angle, like a tsunami, assassination or airplane crash.

The obvious bias of the media can also be seen in the way it uses demographics to reach different audiences. MTV's "Jersey Shore," for example, seeks a viewership the Christian Broadcasting Network would not touch. Different regions of the country also influence the nature of programming. In the Southwestern United States, for example, television channels are likely to carry more shows designed to appeal to Hispanic audiences than in the Pacific Northwest, and their news reporting will be affected, too.

## REGULATION OF CONTENT

With the FCC overseeing the use of our airwaves, how the media affects politics, in particular national campaigns, is subject to some regulation.

In the past, television and other electronic media had to operate under the **Fairness Doctrine** which required that access had to be equal in the amount of time made available on broadcasting networks. That meant that the television stations had to give a certain amount of airtime to all candidates. When the Fairness Doctrine was repealed during the Reagan Administration, it was replaced by the **Reasonable Access Rule**, which requires that all electronic media be *reasonably* available to persons with conflicting points of view. "Reasonable access" does not require media to offer free time, however; it just refers to the right to purchase airtime. It has come down to "pay to play."

As a result, using media to communicate with the masses can be an expensive proposition, but that has not stopped politicians from becoming adept at using it to its maximum potential. The issue facing us in today's political climate is that the amount of money a candidate spends on media coverage may very well impact the way the media treat the candidate, positively or negatively. "Pay to play" is likely to continue to blur the lines between honest and corrupt politicking, between someone who cares for our nation and its people and someone who is merely pursuing a self-centered ideology aimed at power for himself and his friends. It will take a diligent and knowledgeable public to discern the difference.

## MEDIA COVERAGE OF POLITICS

Obviously, owning and controlling the airwaves is a powerful asset for any political movement, and large corporate ownership of media outlets becomes part of the equation of who wields the greatest influence in our political system and government. But do the media actually determine public policy? Although they can influence how the public perceives public policy initiatives, they rarely can manipulate the agenda completely. The media, more often than not, inform the public about news, but they do not influence how that news is interpreted.

In fact, there is considerable jockeying from the camp of elected officials on how to present political messages favorable to their causes and ideology. The use of media however, is a vital tool utilized by politicians and interest groups to communicate policy initiatives and implementation. Some of this occurs directly when an elected official uses the power of his office to disseminate information, ideas and political agendas. Since President Theodore Roosevelt used the White House as a "bully pulpit" to appeal directly to the public (over the heads of reluctant congressional leaders), presidents and politicians have utilized media to get their message out to the people. From Franklin Roosevelt's intimate radio "Fireside Chats" to Ronald Reagan's legacy as "The Great Communicator," presidents have used the power of the media to appeal to the American people. Reagan, as a former Hollywood actor, knew how to come across as folksy and vibrant in front of the camera. But he also had a staff that worked on presenting him in the best light—literally—as when his outside photo ops were deliberately scheduled at times when the angle of the sun most flattered his looks.

A different method utilized by the White House is **institutional coverage,** an important aspect of dealing with the news. Reporters attend briefings by the president's press secretary, who works directly out of the West Wing of the White House and is the "mouthpiece" of the administration. It is his or her job to lay out a carefully crafted message, hoping reporters will convey the information without questioning or extensive investigation. And often they oblige, being content to just "report the news."

Modern politicians have become experts at utilizing the media in a multitude of ways to influence voters' perceptions and "sell" a favorable image of themselves. In the first three months of 2011, Florida GOP Representative Vern Buchanan had his congressional office spend over $142,000 to "communicate" with his constituents. Members of Congress have the **franking privilege,** which allows them to send out brochures and letters to their electorate regarding matters that affect them, so long as they offer information and not political campaign messages. Needless to say, the line between the two is often blurred.[44]

It is not far-fetched to suggest that nowadays one of the most important skills politicians have to learn early on is how to manipulate the media. One way is to take advantage of the desire of rival news organizations to **scoop** the competition—being the first to report on a particular event or item. This leads to efforts by reporters to gain access to political figures and receive favored treatment by them. Scooping rivals can become a problem when nurturing such access starts to blur the line between favorable and unbiased reporting.

For the politicians, cultivating a close relationship with members of the media (especially those pundits and reporters favorable to their ideology), can help them manipulate the message they want disseminated to the public. A favorite way is to use **leaks** as "trial balloons" to float potential new ideas while providing a cover of deniability. Another tactic is to **spin** the talk about certain events to turn negative news into positive news.

A good example of the latter was the GOP's handling of Representative Paul Ryan's 2011 legislative proposals to overhaul Medicare by creating a narrative that suggested his ideas would be the best remedy for the program's shortcomings, even though they would result in ending Medicare as we know it. After considerable public fallout, Republican Speaker John Boehner simply stated it was just a proposal "to jump start the conversation" about spending cuts and added, "We are not wed to them."[45] Ironically, the Republican-controlled House voted to *enact* the very same Ryan Plan in both 2011 and 2012, thereby moving it from a theoretical conversation starter to proposed law. Had the Senate been in the hands of the Republicans, the Ryan Plan would have become law.[46] Talk about spin!

Another aspect that makes the media vulnerable to exploitation by savvy politicians is their insatiable need for the latest, up-to-the-minute development. Since news reporting has become a 24/7 endeavor, network anchors and talk show hosts are always on the lookout for fresh items or tidbits they can package as "new" or "breaking" news. In order to satisfy this need, politicians are happy to rollout press conferences which in reality are only opportunities to capture political headlines and bask in the limelight. Photo opportunities, appearances on Sunday news programs, radio interviews, etc. all play into the marketing strategies of the politicians, all in collusion with the coterie of allegedly impartial and serious news journalists. Listen to any news program on any given night and you will hear pundits or politicians squaring off against their opposition reciting a checklist of **talking points**, designed in sound bite format for future use and reuse by the media.

## MEDIA AND ELECTIONS

We have already discussed the media's role in national elections in an earlier chapter, particularly the money aspect regarding campaign ads. Here I want to focus on the way the media like to cover the election process. Journalists consider any political contest as a "horse race" between individuals and not a campaign fought between political parties. This is reflected in their use of terms like "starting gate," "back stretch" and "home stretch," as well as the common description of the leader as the "front-runner."

When it comes to elections, the media take it to the bank in the form of advertising revenue because the contests draw viewership. No matter how early or mundane an election cycle may begin, news outlets will pile on as if they are the most significant events taking place. Take for example the early primary debates that are promoted as momentous media events—and reported and analyzed by talking heads ad nauseam, even though very few Americans care about them when they're held 10 months before the actual state primary (as is the case with the New Hampshire primary debate). Even when debates later on in the process garner genuine public interest, the media continue the horse race approach, focusing on "winners" and "losers" and not paying attention to much else, least of all the issues.

## APPEARANCE AND REALITY

Perhaps the first instance of television influencing political races happened during the 1960 presidential television debates. Republican candidate Richard Nixon opted not to use cosmetics to lessen the appearance of sweat on his upper lip and a pronounced five o'clock shadow. Unaware of how hot the television lights would be during the debate, he believed makeup was unnecessary. John Kennedy, his Democratic opponent, was advised that television would emphasize imperfections in his face and opted to use makeup to enhance his appearance for the debate. People who listened to the debate on the radio believed that Nixon had dominated Kennedy and was well on his way to winning the presidency. But the millions of American who tuned in to watch their encounter on television found Nixon's appearance distracting—his face appeared sullen, sweaty, unkempt, ill-humored and in need of a shave. Kennedy appeared younger, friendlier, engaging and without any sign of sweat. Those who watched the debate on television overwhelmingly believed Kennedy had won.

Since then, both sides in the presidential debates—or all three on the rare occasion that there is a significant third-party candidate who shares the stage with the front-runners (Ross Perot in 1991)—make certain to hire image consultants. They ensure that the candidates look right, from the color of their suits and ties to the appearance of their hair and make-up. The same goes for non-presidential national contenders for office.

In the past, the media, especially the national television networks, have been blamed in the past for the way they handled reporting elections. In many cases, the blame has been justified. In the 2000 presidential election, all of the major news outlets declared Al Gore the winner of Florida well before the polls closed throughout the state. As a result, many people chose not to brave the traffic or take the time to vote when they easily could have influenced the election. That happened in prior elections, too. In 1992, for example, the declaration of the national winner before the polls closed in the Western United States impacted the presidential voting results as well.

Sometimes the media are only partly to blame. In 2000 and 2003, media outlets relied upon the Voters News Service (VNS), a joint venture owned by NBC, ABC, CBS, CNN, Fox News and the AP and its subscribers, to provide up-to-the-minute exit poll data. As a result, they all proclaimed erroneous election results and VNS was shut down. The same news outlets then established the National Election Pool, a service that collects data from exit polls, but allows each individual television network to interpret the data and declare results based upon its own independent analysis.

## THE PUBLIC RESPONSE

How has the public reacted to the pervasive cheapening, manipulating and sometimes mistaken impact of the mass media? One obvious way has been to ignore the media altogether. Many Americans are so disaffected by politics they simply fail to read or watch any news dealing with the political arena. They become bystanders who routinely fail to vote in elections. It is no accident that the United States has some of the lowest voter turnout for national elections, ranked 114th out of 140 surveyed countries.[47]

Another result of the ideological divide of the current media is what is known as **selective exposure**—the tendency of people to tune into only those news outlets that spout commentary and rhetoric they *want* to hear. Watching their favorite pundits simply reinforces ideological positions they already hold. This is typical of viewers of MSNBC and Fox News. Selective exposure also determines the readership of certain newspapers and online magazines. *The Wall Street Journal* and *Forbes* magazine represent a conservative, pro-business slant, and their readers rarely check out liberal, pro-government regulation publications like *The Nation* or *The Huffington Post*, and vice versa.

Another thing people do is to tune in only when issues directly affect them. This "filtering" of information is commonly a direct result of political socialization. We are conditioned to learn what issues we want to scrutinize and only pay attention to them, ignoring the rest of the news provided (more on political socialization in the next chapter).

Yet another result of the negative influence of the media is **selective perception**, the tendency of viewers or listeners to interpret the news through the blinders of their narrow ideology. An illustration of selective perception occurred when Sarah Palin said in New Hampshire in 2011 that Paul Revere was famous as a patriot because:

> *He who warned uh, the British that they weren't gonna be takin' away our arms, uh by ringing those bells, and um, makin' sure as he's riding his horse through town to send those warning shots and bells that we were going to be sure and we were going to be free, and we were going to be armed.*

Most people simply brushed off her statement as just another example of her ignorance of American history. Some ideologues, though, vociferously supported her comments, claiming that when Revere was captured, he warned the British that the colonists were going to fight to keep their arms. Some of her supporters even went onto Wikipedia to change the real history behind Paul Revere's ride so that it meshed better with Palin's fanciful version.[48] This is a perfect example of selective perception, not to mention politically-motivated revisionist history.

## Social Media and its Impact on Society

With the emergence of Internet broadcasting, the "mainstream" media as we know it has begun to decline in interest and influence. The latest shaping of public opinion, not surprisingly, comes from bloggers and social media websites. Internet news includes "iReporting," which encourages bystanders to use their cell phone cameras and take instant video or snapshots of unfolding events. A variety of applications for communicating them, found on virtually every smartphone, feeds the demand for instant news.

The impact of what is referred to as "social media" has become all pervasive. Yahoo, Google and MySpace kicked off the trend, but **Facebook**, **Instagram**, **Skype**, **Snapchat**, **Tumblr** and **Twitter** now command the social media arena. Members using these web-based media can post status updates and send out messages any time of day or night. Each can spread information immediately to masses of people and garner instant response.

For political purposes, they make it possible to effectively take the "instant temperature" of the electorate on a wide array of issues. Each of these websites can be used to fund-raise and to create a network of supporters and campaign volunteers. During the 2008 presidential election, Barack Obama not only raised significant campaign contributions via the

Internet, but galvanized a young electorate of 20-year-old-voters for the first time in generations.

As with all media, there is a potential downside in the form of significant invasions of privacy. Misused, they can become a dangerous liability to a politician. In 2011, Representative Chris Lee (R. NY) used Facebook to seek out prostitutes and to send Instant Messages (IMs) and Twitter messages including images of his naked body. When his behavior became public knowledge, Lee was forced to resign. In a special election to fill his congressional seat, a Democrat won in the traditionally Republican district (NY 26th district).

On the other side of the aisle, Congressman Andrew Weiner (D. NY) was exposed by a conservative blogger to have sent lewd photographs via his Twitter account to numerous females across the country. Despite his initial, adamant denials and placing of blame on "hackers and jokesters," Wiener reluctantly confessed 10 days after the initial report that he was, in fact, guilty as charged, and he eventually resigned his congressional seat as well. This time a traditionally Democratic district went Republican.

Social media may also be used to keep a watch on politicians. In 2011, Senator Jon Kyl (R. AZ) gave a speech from the Senate floor in which he proclaimed that 94% of the federal funding for Planned Parenthood went toward abortion procedures. Social media gave the public an opportunity to instantly comment on his statement. It turned out that none of the federal funds granted to Planned Parenthood were ever used for abortions—federal law prohibits it—and only 3% of the organization's entire budget was allocated to such procedures. Senator Kyl's office responded by issuing an astonishing press release, which stated "his comments were not intended to be factual."[49] Needless to say, shortly after this fiasco, Kyl announced he was not going to stand for reelection at the end of his current term in the Senate.

More recently, Louisiana Congressman Vance McAllister, a "Christian Family Values" Republican, saw his credibility destroyed when he was caught on a security camera kissing an aide. The video was leaked and went viral on the YouTube, exposing his full-fledged extra-marital affair. McAllister, initially contrite, withdrew his name from the ballot for re-election, but then asked that his name be reinstated while seeking forgiveness for his "indiscretions" from his constituents. As of this writing, his political future is still up in the air.

While lightning fast access to information over the Internet can be used to keep politicians on their toes, much of the discourse tends to be personality-driven. We haven't yet seen any serious ongoing impact of the issues affecting our society via Twitter or Facebook, and it remains to be seen if they become a genuine asset in healing our divisive political discourse.

## What Is to Be Done?

Ultimately, the best way to limit the impact of negative political marketing in media and the pontifications of narrow-minded advocates of political hearsay is to have an educated electorate. Shortly after the delegates to the Constitutional Convention concluded their business, Benjamin Franklin was asked by a woman if they had created "a monarchy or a republic." Franklin's response was simple: "A Republic, if you can keep it." More to the point, Thomas Jefferson commented, "Ignorance and self-government could not exist together: The one destroyed the other. A despotic government could restrain its citizens and deprive the people of their liberties only while they are ignorant."

With the emergence of predominately partisan media—what I call the ideoligically oriented, for-profit media—the public continues to become more and more divided when it comes to understanding how our government really works, and what solutions may be in our collective best interests. So long as ordinary citizens continue to believe they know everything they need to know because they watch television and get their ideas from talking heads and politicians reiterating their talking points, there is little hope that we will resolve the impasse and dysfunction of our government in Washington. So long as entertainment trumps serious political discourse and our information comes to us in meaningless sound bites, we will continue to muddle along. The electorate, unfortunately, gets what it bargains for.

# 14

## ❧ FREEDOM OF SPEECH ❧
### YOUR RIGHT TO SAY IT OR MINE?

The framers and the delegates to the Constitutional Convention who insisted on a Bill of Rights before they were ready to sign on to the final document considered **freedom of speech** a fundamental right. They felt so strongly about it that they enshrined it in the First Amendment, entitling it to the highest level of protection. The language is brief but profound in its implications:

> *Congress shall make no law respecting an establishment of religion, or prohibiting the free exercise thereof; or abridging the freedom of speech, or of the press; or the right of the people peaceably to assemble, and to petition the Government for a redress of grievances.*

Numerous court cases and many books and articles have been written about the First Amendment, and this book is not intended to provide an exhaustive review of all the issues surrounding freedom of speech. To do so, an entire library of materials would have to be assembled, including philosophical texts and case books on constitutional law. Instead, this chapter presents an overview and seeks to counter the most basic misunderstandings. Most people know they have rights, but they can't tell what they are or why they have them. We often take our rights for granted, and we should not.

The constitutional protection of our fundamental speech-related rights is the envy of the world. The ability to pursue and protect them, though, has not always been easy. Perhaps the most important thing to realize is that our understanding and application of the amendment has evolved over the last two centuries and continues to do so. Freedom of speech acknowledges not only the right to speak our mind, but also to hold and maintain certain beliefs—that is one of the reasons why the First Amendment discusses religious freedom and the right to voice grievances against the government.

Although there are some limits on free speech, in most instances, we have a right to say just about anything we wish, so long as we don't promote dangerous or hurtful actions. What that means in practice, however, is not always clear. Consider an individual's right not to speak at all, or the fact that speech is not always spoken, but may be expressed in written and symbolic forms. Applying the First Amendment to case law regarding specific situations has broadened our rights and our understanding of them considerably. In fact, our rights to free speech have evolved ever since the Supreme Court began hearing freedom of speech-related cases.

Not all speech is protected under the law. Defamation of others in the form of libel and slander is prohibited; if speech includes a lie, it is not protected. If printing an article about an individual is untrue, it, too, is not protected. Sedition is also a questionable area of speech. Speech criticizing the government may be an inherent and patriotic right, but advocating the violent overthrow of the United States is not. Words that can incite an immediate call for violence—for example, saying the word "bomb" on an airplane or telling a TSA agent kiddingly that you are a terrorist—are not considered free speech. What constitutes obscenity, which is considered illegal, has been defined and redefined through the years as well.

All of these examples fall under the **Doctrine of Speech**, which has a number of different applications. In the event that normally protected free speech creates a dangerous, potentially violent situation, it can be censored, as it falls under the **Dangerous Tendency Doctrine**. When otherwise free speech creates a potential danger to society, the government through its legal system may punish the speaker, but it must meet the requirements set forth under the **Clear and Present Danger Doctrine**. Under this doctrine, any effort for the government to regulate, control or censor speech must first meet an exceptionally high standard before it can be tolerated in law. In fact, any law or action affecting free speech is considered initially, at face value, to be unconstitutional. The **Preferred Position Doctrine** establishes that the First Amendment and freedom of speech supersede any other amendment or law, and will be upheld by the courts in most circumstances.

It is important to understand that free speech has not always been interpreted the way it is today. From the Alien and Sedition Acts of 1798 during President John Adams' administration to Woodrow Wilson's 1918 Sedition Act, any speech considered critical of the government during a time of war was considered unprotected and liable to get the speaker arrested and thrown in jail on charges of inciting rebellion. A shift in attitude occurred during the Vietnam War protests. Now any attempt by the government to limit speech in the political realm, even during wartime, must meet the compelling interest/strict scrutiny test as part of our protected procedural due process rights (see next chapter). No doubt, this issue will once again face further legal review if and when the Patriot Act is enforced against U. S. citizens.

This is perhaps the best argument against the hypocritical claim that the legal system and the Supreme Court are controlled by "activist" judges, who make law without having been elected to do so. The facts are that the Supreme Court has been making law since it convened in

1789. The freedom of speech we take for granted today is the result of repeated changes in the law as it relates to communication, mostly in our collective favor.

Several 20th-century cases reveal the evolution of free speech. Cases such as **_Schenk v. U.S._**, 249 U.S. 47 (1919), **_Abrams v. United States_**, 250 U.S. 616 (1919), **_Gitlow v. New York_**, 268 U.S. 652 (1925), and **_Whitney v. California_**, 274 U.S. 357 (1927) all dealt with the imprisonment of speakers under the Sedition Act of 1918. **_Dennis v. U.S._**, 341 U.S. 494 (1951) was concerned with the imposition of the clear and present danger test and **_Brandenburg v. Ohio_**, 395 U.S. 444 (1969) struck down laws that prohibited speech, arguing that unless it advocated immediate violence, the government could not restrict it.

Under current judicial standards, there are virtually no situations in which the government can prohibit or punish free speech. The various tests designed to protect free speech as developed by case law include the following:

- **Prior Restraint Test.** The state must have a *compelling interest* to restrain speech prior to it being expressed. Such a test must be applied under the strictest of scrutiny. This is also known as the strict scrutiny test.

- **No Vagueness Test.** No state may pass any law that restricts free speech if the law is vague in its interpretation or in its application.

- **Content Neutral Test.** No state may enact laws that restrict free speech, whether it is content neutral or not. In other words, no state may favor one set of beliefs or positions over another.

- **Political Speech Centrality Test.** Political speech is always protected unless it can be clearly shown—under the strictest of scrutiny—that it is designed to incite violence. If it can be demonstrated that a speaker incited violence with his or her radical speech, then the speaker may be subject to punishment.

The law is clear on the subject. Speech, even if it expresses abhorrent or unpopular ideas, is protected; using abhorrent speech and unpopular ideas to incite violence, however, is not.

## Other Forms of Speech

In some cases, actions or behavior which express ideas or beliefs are considered **symbolic speech** and are protected under the First Amendment. In ***Tinker v. Des Moines Independent Community School District***, 393 U.S. 503 (1969), students were prohibited from wearing arm bands as symbolic opposition to the Vietnam War. After hearing evidence, the court held that symbolic speech that does not lead to any disruption of school activities or curriculum cannot be censored. From the Tinker case decision, we witnessed the Supreme Court expand protections of other forms of symbolic speech, including protecting the right to burn the American flag and to even fly it upside down in protest.

The question is, what is considered "disruptive?" In our current age of "political correctness," the definition of "disruptive" is subject to wide interpretation. What was considered a legitimate expression of political speech in the 1970s, may not be so considered in our post-9/11 era. Less and less leeway is afforded high school students expressing their political beliefs at school when administrators hold more and more authority to limit such speech under the guise of protecting against "disruptions."

In the case of ***Texas v. Johnson***, 491 U.S. 397 (1989), the court ruled that burning the Texas state flag was an instance of symbolic speech, and that any anti-burning statute was unconstitutional. In the case of ***U.S. v. Eichman***, 496 U.S. 310 (1990), the court issued a similar opinion regarding the burning of an American flag, ruling that such an action was symbolic political free speech. Flying an American flag upside down as a political protest is also protected free speech—see ***Spence v. Washington***, 418 U.S. 405 (1974).

In the case of obscenity, which is not protected by free speech, the law has taken a winding path over the years. Books like James Joyce's *Ulysses* and D.H. Lawrence's *Lady Chatterley's Lover*, for example, were initially declared obscene in most states, making their possession illegal. The difficulty is that one person's notion of what is lewd and obscene can be quite different from another's. As a result, the Supreme Court was faced with determining a definition of obscenity everyone could understand and adhere to. It finally did just that in the matter of ***Miller v. California***, 413 U.S. 15 (1973), notwithstanding Justice Potter Stewart's remark that when it came to obscenity, "I will know it when I see it." In its ruling, the Supreme Court held that *obscenity* can only be determined by using a three-pronged test:

- First, the material must pander to prurient interest— "prurient" is defined as appealing to sexual desire in an unwholesome manner.

- Second, the material must be patently offensive sexually— leaving the test wide open...what does "sexually offensive" really mean?

- Third, taken as a whole, the work must have no serious redeeming social or artistic value (what does *that* mean?).

It may seem that this test is incredibly vague and raises more questions than it answers, but in practice it has expanded the range of material *not* considered obscene immensely and has made it much more difficult for state and local governments to block movies and literature heavy in sexual content.

## Freedom of the Press

First Amendment free speech also includes **freedom of the press**. This was a direct response to the jailing of newspaper editors in England

and colonial America when they printed information unflattering to the government. Over time, freedom of the press has expanded under the rubric of "the public's right to know" to include many government acts that used to be carried out in secrecy.

Lately, there have been a number of disputes relating to access of the public and the press to meetings of governmental officials. They have been fraught with controversy, especially in communities where public officials have used e-mail and the Internet to discuss governmental business in secrecy and away from the scrutiny of the public and the press. Statutes have been passed throughout the United States to limit this behavior on the part of elected officials. These statutes, collectively known as **Sunshine Laws**, require all governmental communication at the state and local levels to be open to public examination. Nonetheless, many small municipalities routinely ignore the law and force outsiders to initiate legal action in order to gain access to information, which makes city attorneys very busy folks and expends considerable amounts of taxpayers' money.

A mechanism to obtain information relating to federal governmental affairs is known as the **Freedom of Information Act (FIA).** Under the FIA, all non-secret federal information may be formally requested in writing and all affected federal agencies must comply. The key to the FIA is that the requested information must not be considered "secret" or "classified," affecting national security and pending investigations, for example.

News organizations often receive tips and information from people who reveal misconduct and even illegal behavior inside government or large corporations. These whistle-blowers are often punished by their employers with demotions or dismissals. As a result, many states have enacted **shield laws** in an effort to protect such witnesses or to safeguard the identity of rape victims. The constitutionality of shield laws was brought into question in the case of ***Branzburg v. Hayes***, 408 U.S. 665 (1972) when the Supreme Court ruled that they pose a serious potential threat to thwart or obstruct justice, as they limit the right of a defendant in a criminal proceeding to confront his accuser.

Members of the press continue to argue that shield laws are necessary because a lack of protection for their sources would discourage future whistle-blowers from cooperating and from revealing wrongdoing or damaging information regarding those in power.

A different area in which speech may be constrained because of privacy issues is **defamation**. This can come in two forms: **slander**, which is a false, malicious or defamatory statement spoken out loud; and **libel**, which is a derogatory written or printed statement, picture or any other form of communication outside of oral words or gestures. Essentially, any spoken or written words used to destroy someone's reputation based on untrue statements, deceit and outright lies qualify as defamation and are not protected as free speech. The victim may seek legal remedy in a court of law.

In practice, what constitutes libel and slander are open to interpretation. What about routine jokes and negative commentaries about our public officials, for example? Many consider such words as humor and dismiss them as tongue in cheek comments. But the victims of the words may not see them in the same way and decide to go to court. Such is often the case when it comes to celebrities and public officials. How often have you read in the grocery checkout lines fantastic, sensational headlines that a movie star was abducted by aliens, or a politician fathered children with several women?

In a case in which *The New York Times* was sued for publishing defamatory articles about Southern state discrimination during the civil rights movement (***New York Times Co. v. Sullivan***, 376 U.S. 254 (1964)), the Supreme Court stated that there are two classes of people: those considered *private* and those considered *public*. It also created a simple test to determine if an individual claiming damages can proceed with a lawsuit based upon a claim of libel. Any person in the *public* domain, celebrities and public officials, for example, cannot claim damages due to libel unless he can prove that the person defaming him knew the statement was false when publishing it—this is known as **malice aforethought**. In this case, the offender knows that it could cause harm, yet does nothing to verify its accuracy or truth ahead of time. The court further ruled that if the victim is a *private* person, simply proving the information is false and that damages were actually suffered are enough to prevail in a lawsuit.

## PRIOR RESTRAINT

Although the First Amendment guarantees freedom of the press, there have been efforts throughout American history to silence its voice. One of these is **prior restraint**, which refers to the effort to prevent the press from publishing a story before it can do so. In the matter of **_Near v. Minnesota_**, 283 U.S. 697 (1931), the court ruled that no state may enact laws that restrict the rights of the press to publish articles questioning the integrity of public officials. In this case, a local newspaper called public officials "gangsters" and in response, the government, citing a Minnesota law, obtained an injunction against the paper. The court ruled the Minnesota government could enjoin the paper only if it could prove it suffered "irreparable" harm. This is a nearly impossible standard to meet, as it should be. Infringing on the First Amendment rights of the press should be held to the highest scrutiny.

Another important case dealing with prior restraint was the matter of **_New York Times Co. v. United States_**, 403 U.S. 713 (1971). In this case, Daniel Ellsberg, a U.S. military analyst, gave classified documents to *The Times* reporters revealing that the Nixon Administration was lying about American tactics in the Vietnam War. After verifying the validity and truth of the documents, it printed the first of a series of articles which would collectively become known as "The Pentagon Papers." The U.S. government, claiming national security concerns and arguing that published documents would put troops in Vietnam in imminent danger, sought an injunction against the publication of the remaining documents that Ellsberg provided. The court ruled that the government could not prove any harm, because to restrain free speech it must, under the strictest of scrutiny, demonstrate in exact terms the damage it would suffer in the event of full publication, and it could not do so. From this decision on, courts have routinely sided with the press in most prior restraint matters.

A different example of prior restraint occurred shortly after President Obama scheduled a nationwide address to America's schoolchildren about how patriotic education is. Florida state GOP Chairman Jim Greer objected, claiming the president should not be allowed to make the speech because he planned to indoctrinate them with his "socialist ideology" agenda, despite the fact that presidents for decades have addressed the nation's schoolchildren at the start of each school year. It was amazing to witness the conservative support for Greer's inane stance, making it an actual political issue in an effort to delegitimize the president. Many GOP pundits blanketed the airwaves demanding President Obama be kept from making the address, a classic example of prior restraint. They also encouraged Americans across the nation to contact their local school boards to demand that the address not be shown in classrooms. Many school boards, fearing backlash from parents, did just that, allowing students to skip school so they would not be subjected to any undue influence from the big bad president. Due to public outcry, Obama was forced to publish the text of his speech in advance. When it turned out to be just what the president had claimed all along—a pep talk to the students to pursue education—Greer and conservative pundits opined the speech had been altered from the original, which was filled with socialist propaganda, with no evidence whatsoever that such an act had taken place. As an aside, Jim Greer went on to be indicted on six felony counts for money laundering, fraud and theft.

There are areas where freedom of the press does not logically apply—namely schools. When student papers run articles that could be considered risqué by others, the protection of the First Amendment is not always obtained. In the case of ***Hazelwood v. Kuhlmeier, et al***, 484 U.S. 260 (1988), the Supreme Court ruled that not all press is free from prior restraint. In this instance, high school students wrote articles about teen pregnancy and divorce. In the Hazelwood school system student articles were routinely reviewed for content ahead of publication by the high school principal, and he decided the topic was too controversial for the student newspaper, effectively engaging in censorship. When the students protested and filed suit claiming an unconstitutional restraint on their free speech, the case went all the way to the Supreme Court, which ruled that high school students do not have the same rights as adults or college students, and school principals may censor material they deem improper or having no "educational purpose." In effect, the court ruled that order in schools is more important than students' expression of free speech.

## FREEDOM OF ASSEMBLY

Freedom of assembly and, by implication, the ability to express grievances, has also undergone evolution. The question at stake: Do the actions of a crowd listening to a speaker of unpopular ideas become the responsibility of the speaker or the crowd? In the matter of ***Feiner v. New York***, 340 U.S. 315 (1951), the Supreme Court ruled that the speaker of unpopular ideas can be held responsible for the actions of a crowd reacting violently to his incitement. On the other hand, in ***Edwards v. South Carolina***, 372 U.S. 229 (1963), the court precluded the government from dispersing an otherwise peaceful crowd, no matter how unpopular the words of the speaker—South Carolina law actually allowed for the arrest of anyone just listening to potentially dangerous speech in a public gathering. It further ruled that only after *unlawful actions* by the crowd can it be held responsible for its behavior and *not* the speaker who may have incited them to action.

More recently, in the matter of ***McCullen et al. v. Coakley***, #12-1168, (decided June 26, 2014), the Supreme Court ruled that Americans have a protected right of assembly and cannot be required to remain within a leg-islatively created "buffer zone" when expressing their opinions. In the case, anti-abortion proponents argued that such zones inhibited their freedom of assembly to offer "advice" to those entering abortion clinics. Without determining when such a right may impose on the freedoms of women entering a clinic, the Court ruled 9-0 that such zones are unconstitutional.

## THE ESTABLISHMENT CLAUSE

Many consider freedom of religion—the right to practice whatever religion one wishes to—a free speech issue. Yet it actually precedes the discussion of free speech in the First Amendment in what is commonly known as The Establishment Clause, which prohibits the government from making any law "respecting an establishment of religion." But while that the Constitution requires a religion-neutral government policy, we know from practical experience that this is not always the case. Gov-ernment at all levels—local, state and federal—embraces one form of religious identification or another, from opening prayers at city council meetings or daily sessions of Congress to the minting of "In God We Trust" on U.S. currency. There is a limit, however. The courts have con-sistently ruled that the Establishment Clause prohibits the government from favoring one religion over another and from hindering citizens to practice whatever religion they wish to follow.

When dealing with the use of public tax dollars in parochial or religious schools, the Supreme Court imposed a formal standard known as the **Lemon Test** (see ***Lemon v. Kurtzman***, 403 U.S. 602 (1971)). There are three parts to the test that have to be considered: The government's action must have a secular purpose; the government's action must not have the primary effect of either advancing or inhibiting religion; and the government's action must not result in an "excessive governmental entanglement" with religion. If any of these requirements is violated, then the government may not provide public funds to a private religious institution, as such an action would be deemed unconstitutional. Since interpretations of the Establishment Clause focus on what can't be done, it might be easier to understand if we think of it as the "Non-Establishment Clause."

The Establishment Clause has been reviewed by the Supreme Court in 2014 more than in any prior year. Although it has been a long-standing principal that freedom of religion is a personal right and not one to be endorsed by any government, the Supreme Court handed down two significant rulings altering the interpretation of the clause. In the matter of ***Town of Greece, NY v. Galloway***, #12-696, (decided May, 5, 2014), it ruled 5-4 (despite a long line of earlier decisions ruling otherwise), to allow denominational prayers at public hearings or meetings. The High Court also ruled in the matter of ***Burwell v. Hobby Lobby Stores***, #13-354, (decided June 30, 2014), that privately held corporations could dictate insurance coverage for their employees based solely upon the religious beliefs of their owners. In this case, the argument focused on exemptions from the Affordable Care Act mandating insurance coverage for women's contraceptives. Once again, it was a narrow 5-4 decision, with the court's three female judges opposing the ruling.

With such narrow decisions (some would argue politically and religiously motivated decsisions—all five concurring justices in the Hobby

Lobby ruling majority were Catholics), we can be sure that the issue of separation of church and state under the Establishment Clause of the First Amendment will continue to be at the forefront of political debate for the foreseeable future.

## THE EVOLUTION OF FUNDAMENTAL RIGHTS

Most of us take our fundamental rights for granted, not realizing that they were anything but guaranteed. When the Unites States was first founded, in order to be admitted into the Union, each state had to have an established constitution guaranteeing citizen rights. But because state constitutions differed in application from what the U.S. Constitution provided, it took some time for fundamental rights to be applied or "incorporated" equally to all Americans. This process, known as the **Theory of Incorporation** took many decades. Slowly, each of the fundamental rights established in the Bill of Rights were applied to the states and thereby incorporated as supreme law of the land.

Thus, our fundamental rights (including religious freedom) have evolved over time based on the "living" nature of the Constitution, and they inevitably will continue to evolve further. It is up to individual citizens, though, to understand the limits of their fundamental rights in order to ensure they are not arbitrarily violated by any ruling government or its affiliates.

# 15

# ✦ CIVIL LIBERTIES ✦
## WHERE DO OUR RIGHTS BEGIN AND END?

Most Americans when asked what the differences are between **civil liberties** and **civil rights** get very confused. They may suggest that civil rights pertain to efforts in the 1950s and 1960s to seek racial equality. They may not know that civil liberties are *fundamental rights*, whereas civil rights are those presented in the Constitution as **due process** rights. Put another way, the protected right to due process is a civil right. But what is due process? Basically, due process has to do with the rights of citizens against abuse by the government. While the Constitution offers some protection to individuals, the Fourteenth Amendment went even further by including the famous **Due Process Clause**, which specifically prohibits government from abusing our rights *and* depriving "persons of life, liberty, or property."

But who is eligible to enjoy the protections afforded by these rights? Are rights guaranteed by the Constitution only extended to citizens, or to anyone residing within the country? Should protected rights only be afforded to those who have citizenship? Are they instead universal and to be recognized as god-given, and therefore subject to protection no matter whether one is a citizen or not?

Pursuant to the Fourteenth Amendment, citizenship is guaranteed to anyone born *within* the United States, *regardless* of whether his or her parents are United States citizens. This is based upon the ancient principle of *jus soli*, or territory of one's birth: being a citizen is a *property* right and cannot be legislated away by any government. The Fourteenth Amendment also extends citizenship to any child born to a U.S. citizen, regardless where the birth occurs. The guarantee does *not* work in the reverse, though. A child born in the United States is granted citizenship, but the parents do *not* get citizenship as a result.

Being born in the United States is not the only way to become a U.S. citizen. Non-Americans or *aliens* may apply to become *naturalized* citizens. This requires complying with all of the following standards:

- Must be at least 18 years of age
- Must reside in the United States for a period of at least five years (including at least three years holding green card status)
- Must be able to read, write and speak ordinary English
- Must be of sound mind and good moral character, and
- Must pass an exam testing a fundamental knowledge of American History and government.

In addition, the applicant must also be willing to abide by the principles of the U.S. Constitution.[50]

With all the recent hysteria over illegal immigration, there are some pushing to amend the Fourteenth Amendment to make it more difficult to be born a U.S. citizen, as well as toughen the standards to become a *naturalized* citizen.

As far back as 1886, the Supreme Court ruled that the protections afforded in the Fourteenth Amendment applied to all persons equally, and not just those that were considered legal citizens—see ***Yick Wo v. Hopkins***, 118 U.S. 356 (1886). Harsher penalties, therefore, for non-citizens are unconstitutional despite the efforts of some Republican governors to subject illegal aliens to penalties three times as strict as those applied to citizens for felonies or felony charges.[51]

The Due Process Clause of the Fourteenth Amendment discusses two distinctive types. **Substantive due process** relates to the *substance* of the law itself. No law may be passed that prohibits or inhibits the freedoms guaranteed by the Constitution or abridges anyone's fundamental constitutional rights. **Procedural due process**, on the other hand, focuses on the *process* of law. While a law may be fair, the process to ensure compliance with that law may be skewed in a way that unfairly limits or prohibits the freedom of the affected party.

Some obvious historical examples of substantive due process protection include the prohibition of laws that inherently discriminate against someone's religion, race, gender, ethnicity or sexual orientation: laws which would, for example, prohibit women from driving automobiles (which happens *legally* in Saudi Arabia, for example), prevent blacks from learning to read and write (as was the case during slavery and in the post-reconstruction era with Jim Crow laws), or intern Japanese Americans during WWII without individual formal hearings or trials.

Procedural due process is somewhat murkier in its application. Simply put, although we have rights guaranteed under the Constitution, it has taken the test of time for the Supreme Court to properly extend certain procedural safeguards to protect us from governmental overreach—an overreach that erodes these rights and liberties. As a result, the court has established, through an evolution of case decisions, that a more concentrated scrutiny of governmental action is required to ensure none of our basic freedoms are taken away.

Examples of procedural due process include the guarantee that no person shall be jailed without a court hearing, that a person accused of a crime has the right to legal counsel throughout the legal process, that he not be required to incriminate himself, and that he can't be tried for the same crime twice if he was acquitted the first time (double jeopardy). It goes further, though, to ensure we all are afforded the same procedural safeguards, regardless of the level of influence we may have with the local court, governmental officials or regulatory agencies. Essentially, equality under law—the essence of our liberty—is embodied in the concepts of substantive and procedural due process in the Fourteenth Amendment.

Once again, these two concepts underwent considerable evolution in our legal system. The laws which expand on them according to the Bill of Rights and later in the Fourteenth Amendment did not immediately apply to all states and citizens, but were developed gradually and enforced through case law. This is another example of **incorporation**.

For a considerable period of time, court cases had outcomes that we would now consider blatant injustice. In the matter of ***Barron v. Baltimore***, 32 U.S. 243 (1833), the Supreme Court ruled that states did not have to abide by federal due process rights and could take someone's property if the right of eminent domain was not protected under Maryland's constitution.

## DOUBLE JEOPARDY

Although the Constitution protects individuals against double jeopardy in all criminal matters, in ***Palko v. Connecticut***, 302 U.S. 319 (1937), the Supreme Court held that federal law did overrule state laws allowing for a criminal defendant to be tried for the same offense twice. In this case, the defendant was initially charged with first degree murder and was sentenced to life in prison. When the prosecutor objected to the sentence, preferring the death penalty, he simply appealed. Palko took the matter to the Supreme Court claiming his right against double jeopardy was violated when the state courts ruled he could be retried and then ultimately resentenced. The Supreme Court ruled that the protection against double jeopardy only applied to federal offenses, and since murder was not a federal offense, Palko could not assert a Fourteenth Amendment due process claim. He was retried, convicted and executed in the gas chamber. The Supreme Court did not fully incorporate the protection against double jeopardy until 1969 in the matter of ***Benton v. Maryland***, 395 U.S. 784 (1969).

The road towards full incorporation of all protected rights was long and arduous. It took decades for the courts to acknowledge the right to counsel in criminal cases, which we consider to be sacrosanct. In the matter of ***Powell v. Alabama***, 287 U.S. 45 (1932), the Supreme Court ruled that a defendant is not entitled to legal counsel *except* in capital (murder) cases. An all-white jury in Alabama had convicted nine black defendants, none of whom had legal counsel, for raping two white women (even though one of the women retracted her accusation). The case became known as the **Scottsboro Boys Trial**. The Supreme Court overruled the Alabama Supreme Court by deciding *procedural due process* had in fact been denied in a capital case and sent the case back for a new trial.

It was a step forward, but it took 30 years for the Supreme Court to extend the right of legal counsel to all defendants in criminal cases in ***Gideon v. Wainwright***, 372 U.S. 335 (1963). Because Gideon had not been charged with a capital crime, the Florida Supreme Court maintained federal requirements did not apply simply because he could not afford an attorney. The Supreme Court overruled that verdict, holding procedural due process guaranteed under the Fourteenth Amendment was to be incorporated in all state criminal cases and that legal counsel must be afforded to criminal defendant, regardless whether they can afford one or not. This is now settled law.

Finally, in ***Argersinger v. Hamlin***, 407 U.S. 25 (1972), the Supreme Court ruled that in all cases involving *any* criminal charge (felony or misdemeanor), the accused had the fundamental right to legal counsel. By so ruling, the court once and for all fully incorporated both substantive and procedural due process afforded *all persons* under the Fourteenth Amendment.

## ILLEGAL SEARCH AND SEIZURE

Incorporation also took its time in the protection against illegal search and seizure. Since the time of British rule, Americans have always been suspect of government searches, surveillance and control of their private lives and residences. According to the Constitution, no search or seizure may be made without a warrant issued by a judge based on probable cause and limited in scope to a specific area of inquiry. No all-inclusive, across-the-board warrants are allowed. But with the advent of technology, our basic rights against illegal governmental intrusion have been steadily eroding.

We all can appreciate how easy it is to eavesdrop on our cell phone conversations, but when the telephone was still relatively new, a debate raged whether conversations carried out on it were subject to government monitoring. The issue first arose in the matter of ***Olmstead v. United States***, 277 U.S. 438 (1928), which concerned the defendant's involvement in the distribution of alcohol in violation of the prohibition laws. The only way Olmstead could have been caught was through the use of wiretapping over an extended period of time. When Olmstead's attorney challenged the trial testimony of federal agents, the extensive wiretapped conversations came to light. Despite repeated efforts to have the evidence excluded based upon the theory of illegal search and seizures, Chief Justice William Howard Taft and the Supreme Court ruled that wiretapping was not a direct seizure of personal and private effects, just Olmstead's conversations, and that the Fourth Amendment did not preclude such a "search or seizure" of his spoken words.

It wasn't until 1961 in the matter ***Mapp v. Ohio***, 367 U.S. 643 (1961), that the Supreme Court established the **exclusionary rule,** also known as the **"Fruit of the Poison Tree Rule,"** applying it to both federal and state criminal prosecutions. This exclusionary rule has become fundamental to our criminal process by forbidding evidence to be used in trial against a defendant if it was initially obtained without following proper legal procedures.

Dollree Mapp was confronted by police demanding entry into her home, claiming she was harboring a fugitive from the law. Mapp contacted her attorney while police waited and was advised to demand a warrant before letting anyone inside. When she did so, a police officer flashed a piece of paper claiming it was a warrant and again demanded entry. Mapp, figuring the paper was not, in fact, an actual warrant, grabbed and put it inside her blouse. The police then struggled with her, regained possession of the paper, handcuffed and shackled her, and proceeded with a search of the entire premises. Although they did not locate the fugitive, they did find a suspicious trunk in her basement. When asked about its contents, Mapp asserted it did not belong to her but had been left by a previous tenant. When the police in turn opened the trunk, they found an array of pornography. Mapp was charged with possession of "lewd and lascivious" materials in violation of Ohio law.

At the trial, evidence of her possession of obscene material was presented, but it was also determined that the police did not have a warrant to enter her home and that the paper they shoved in her face was just that, a piece of paper. Mapp's attorney then argued that the search of her home was illegal, as no warrant was issued and therefore, under the exclusionary rule, any evidence obtained should also be excluded. The Supreme Court agreed and threw all evidence of pornography out as it was obtained following an illegal entry and therefore was "the fruit of the poisoned tree." Since the Mapp case, the exclusionary rule has become fundamental protection against police and prosecutorial abuse.

In 1967, the court extended these same Fourth and Ninth Amendment protections to private conversations in the case of ***Katz v. United States***, 389 U.S. 347 (1967). It ruled that individuals held a "reasonable expectation of privacy" when on the telephone. The search and seizure of personal conversations was, in fact, "an invasion" of one's privacy, requiring that a proper warrant be obtained before any wiretap may be allowed.

However, the extension of Mapp to personal DNA was recently curtailed. In ***Maryland v. King***, 12-207 SCOTUS (2013), the Supreme Court in a split 5-4 decision ruled that all criminals suspected of "serious" crimes, may have DNA samples collected from them by policing authorities (typically via a mouth swab). According to the majority opinion, written by Justice Anthony Kennedy,

> *When officers make an arrest supported by probable cause to hold for a serious offense and they bring the suspect to the station to be detained in custody, taking and analyzing a cheek swab of the arrestee's DNA is, like fingerprinting and photographing, a legitimate police booking procedure that is reasonable under the Fourth Amendment.*

Those favoring the decision, believe the widespread use of DNA evidence can lead to more exonerations of those wrongfully accused of crimes; however, advocates for civil liberties argue the decision is a further erosion of our rightful expectations of privacy against warrantless searches and seizures.

Although the exclusionary rule is still the standard in criminal cases today, with the advent of more modern forms of electronic communication, we have begun to see a dilution of the protections it affords as courts have begun to carve out exceptions. The Internet and social media such as Twitter and Facebook connect us with others around the globe as never before. They make communicating easy, but they also make eavesdropping easier than ever. Since September 11, 2001, general concern—real and imagined—about our nation's security has given rise to demands that frequently conflict with our desire for personal liberty.

The "Uniting and Strengthening of America by Providing Appropriate Tools Required to Intercept and Obstruct Terrorism Act of 2001," commonly known as the **Patriot Act,** dramatically changed the way authorities may eavesdrop on and search the private conversations and communications of Americans. It extended government's authority to search communications and documents relating to e-mails, telephone (land and cellular), banking and medical records. It also loosened restrictions on domestic intelligence gathering previously reserved exclusively for foreign intelligence.

The Patriot Act has raised a number of legal issues that have not been resolved by the Supreme Court. One of its main applications is the use of the Foreign Intelligence Surveillance Court (FISA Court).[51] Created in 1978 to provide search warrants in secret cases involving national security, it was to be used to help protect Americans against terrorism. Under President George W. Bush, the established requirements for the FISA Court to issue such warrants regarding U.S. citizens were completely ignored. In fact, the Bush Administration routinely ordered the National Security Agency (NSA) to conduct blanket wiretaps of anyone, American citizen or not, if thought to be engaging in "suspicious" activity. It also demanded access to all telecommunication servers in an effort to surveil all cell phone and Internet activity. The idea was to "capture" certain communications using familiar catchphrases or words in order to create leads for further investigations; and the big telecom corporations were happy to perform their patriotic duty.

But when this arrangement became public along with the possible ramifications of the resulting activities, the telecoms demanded Congress pass legislation indemnifying them from any lawsuits that may be filed by U.S. citizens for illegal search and seizure. Late in President Bush's second term of office, Congress obliged and passed legislation granting them blanket immunity for their participation in the surveillance. As a result, U.S. citizens who have had their private telecommunications under surveillance may not be able to sue their service providers, for such investigations fall under the banner of "national security." None of these issues have been addressed by the Supreme Court so far, and despite the wishes of civil libertarians, President Obama has obtained an extension of the right to conduct such surveillance with impunity.

Just how quickly the federal government can react to a perceived threat on the Internet became clear in 2011 when a student kiddingly wrote on her Facebook page "Don't Shoot Drugs, Shoot Obama Instead." Representatives of Homeland Security and Secret Service agents were on her doorstep within 24 hours. It appears the phrase "shoot" with reference to any president is something automatically flagged on the Internet and is always cause for concern and further investigation. Although the student thought her comment was cute and a joke, she learned a harsh lesson that the government is watching and monitoring anything we say using electronic means of communication.

## MIRANDA RIGHTS

When it comes to self-incrimination, the fundamental right to remain silent has also evolved to the point of today's standard, which follows the legal mandate set forth in ***Miranda v. Arizona***, 384 U.S. 436 (1966). In this case, the Supreme Court ruled that any statement made by a criminal suspect to investigators can only be admitted into evidence at trial if a suspect was properly warned verbally that he or she had the right to remain silent and could ask for legal counsel in advance of any questioning. The ruling went further to allow questioning of suspects only if they have been apprised of their legal rights to remain silent and to legal counsel, and they waive those rights. This requirement has become known as the **Miranda warning** and the issuing of it is called **mirandizing** a suspect.

Police or law dramas on television have been slow to catch up to reality, regularly showing criminals breaking down with or without the appearance of an attorney during police interrogation. In real life, virtually all criminal suspects demand an attorney right away and remain silent. In fact, once a criminal suspect has requested an attorney, or in common television speak "lawyered up," no questioning can continue according to his Miranda rights.

There is an exception, which occurred in the aftermath of the 2013 Boston Marathon bombing. The surviving suspect, DzhokarTsarnarev, was not read his Miranda rights before he was questioned because of a little known public safety exception, which allows police to interrogatie a suspect when they objectively and reasonably believe there to be an existing or "imminent" threat to the public's safety. Once that threat has passed, the suspect must be read his Miranda rights (see **_New York v. Quarles_**, 467 U.S. 649 (1984)).

There is a general exception, too, pertaining to the gathering of physical evidence. In the event a criminal suspect demands an attorney, investigators may still obtain a court order to require the suspect to provide DNA samples, including hair, saliva, blood and fingerprints. Suspects may object to the collection of physical evidence, but cannot prevent it from occurring if it is ordered by a court of law. Consider state laws requiring breathalyzer testing for drivers suspected of drunk driving. The suspect may refuse to take the test, but the refusal itself is punishable, and may include a suspension of his driver's license. The Fifth Amendment protection against self-incrimination therefore does not extend to the collection of physical evidence.

Also in 2014, The Supreme Court ruled 9-0 in the case of **_Riley v. California_**, #13-132, (decided June 25, 2014) that authorities must obtain a search warrant before accessing an arrested suspect's cell or smart phone. The Court reasoned that although "privacy has its costs," proper procedures must be followed before searching the inherently personal data from an individual's smart phone is permitted. Nothing in the *Riley* decision, however, will lead to the curtailing of data collection from cell phone, email or any other electronic communication by the National Security Agency under the guise of protecting national security.

## RIGHT OF PRIVACY

Another critical area is the right of privacy guaranteed under the Fourth and Ninth Amendments, where different levels of incorporation have taken place. In the case of **_Griswold v. Connecticut_**, 381 U.S. 479 (1965), the Court finally ruled full incorporation required that rights of privacy were in fact guaranteed in every state. Griswold was the executive director of the state's Planned Parenthood office. In her capacity as director, Griswold and her medical director offered birth control counsel to married couples. At the time, Connecticut prohibited anyone from giving any advice relating to birth control. Griswold and the director were arrested, charged and in turn convicted for doing so. On appeal, the Supreme Court ruled that although the right of privacy was not explicitly stated in the Constitution, the overall implication of the Bill of Rights included such an intended right. As a result, the dissemination of birth control advice between a doctor and a patient is to be considered inherently within the scope of personal autonomy or privacy and outside the scope of any state interest. The right to privacy was now protected under the due process clause of the Fourteenth Amendment.

But where did that leave other issues considered "private" and outside the scope of a state interest? Not surprisingly, other state laws, including the right to an abortion, were scrutinized under the banner of privacy. That issue came to a head in the landmark case of **_Roe v. Wade_**, 410 U.S. 113 (1973). Jane Roe, the name given to the defendant to protect her privacy, wanted to terminate her pregnancy in violation of Texas law, which prohibited abortions except in cases where the life of the mother was in danger. The case presented the question of whether the Constitution considered the rights of a woman to decide herself whether to abort a pregnancy was a private or public matter. The Supreme Court ruled that such a decision is protected under the right of privacy, but limited absolute decision power on the part of the woman only if the abortion is performed in the first trimester. The court acknowledged that states had a valid interest in protecting the unborn and listed exceptions for abortions that may be performed *after* the first trimester.

*Roe v. Wade* has been the law of the land since 1973, but the issue of abortion rights continues to be a hot topic, especially during national and/or state political campaigns. By 1989, the ruling had been diluted to allow states an interest even in prohibiting abortions in the first trimester by permitting them to pass legislation affecting the operations of clinics where women would routinely seek to terminate a pregnancy. In the case of ***Webster v. Reproductive Health Services***, *492 U.S. 490 (1989)*, the state of Missouri enacted legislation claiming a child was "born" at conception and that it had a protected interest if it could prove when a child's life could be viable outside the womb. The court allowed the states the right to determine when a child *may* be viable, instead of allowing the decision to be exclusively determined by a woman's physician.

In recent years, claiming religious grounds, some state legislatures have tried to make abortion more difficult to obtain by passing laws requiring women to undergo extensive mandatory counseling or have a sonogram taken and be required to view the images of the fetus before pursuing an abortion (see ***Planned Parenthood v. Casey***, 505 U.S. 833 (1992)). Pro-choice advocates are worried any challenge to the constitutionality of these new laws at a time when the Supreme Court has a majority of conservative justices may lead to a modification or complete reversal of the Roe doctrine. As a result, laws making it more difficult to obtain an abortion will remain unchallenged until a solid majority of justices that share a more pro-choice ideology prevails.

These situations raise an important and related question: Is it the role of government to intrude on private lives? Is privacy a fundamental right? How, for example, does the right of privacy protect the rights of same-sex partners—the politically correct terminology for homosexuals?

Although public opinion has taken a 180-degree turn on the last question—a majority of Americans now support same-sex marriage—many states still have laws prohibiting same-sex behavior and civil unions. The ideological tide prohibiting such activity is slowly turning in favor of individual rights. Recently, the state of New York recognized the right of same-sex "civil unions," which led to the same rights being extended as if the couples were married. Such legislation is significant, as it affects property rights, taxation, wills and other financial matters, but the fundamental question remains: What right does the state have to interfere with the free choices of its citizens?

The question and its ramifications will not go away. As of this writing, the courts are hearing cases involving the use of GPS tracking devices on suspects' motor vehicles without a warrant. Authorities justify the use of such warrantless searches by claiming they are simply identifying driving patterns on public streets. But what about the collection of information that leads to an arrest based upon the "pattern" created from the use of the vehicle? Should the police obtain a warrant before they attach a device to someone's vehicle that will create a log of every trip taken by the unsuspecting driver? How important or expedient would it be to avoid a call to a judge to justify the use of such a device? How long will it be before Congress passes laws requiring *all* cars be tracked by law enforcement officials simply for the sake of "justice?" How far are we as Americans willing to go to give up our freedoms for some sense of "security?"

# 16

# ❧ EQUAL PROTECTION ❧
## For All or Just a Few?

Although the founders and framers of the Constitution were deeply concerned with human freedom and liberty, they did not extend these rights to everyone at the birth of our nation. Most African Americans remained enslaved and were not counted as full human beings. Women had limited rights and were treated as second class citizens. This is not the place to explore all the reasons for such injustices. Suffice it to say that the notion of freedom for all evolved gradually over time in all parts of the world, and continues to do so. In the United States, following the initial constitutional protections of the Bill of Rights, a second round of amendments enacted after the Civil War led to the extension of fundamental rights to ever larger segments of the American population.

In an effort to protect the rights of newly freed slaves, the Equal Protection Clause of the Fourteenth Amendment establishes, without mentioning slaves, that fundamental civil rights and liberties shall be equally protected on both federal and State levels. Although its provisions did not originally apply to private individuals or institutions, it has over time been incorporated to protect everyone, citizens and non-citizens alike. Although many of the rights protected by the Fourteenth Amendment affect every one of us, the main purpose is to protect the rights of minorities, be they religious, cultural or ethnic, or based on race, gender or sexual orientation.

Even after its passage, there have been many efforts to interfere with the rights that are to be protected under the Fourteenth Amendment. Since Reconstruction after the Civil War, African Americans have faced various forms of discrimination, but the most obvious type has been racial segregation. It is important to realize that although a state may not legislate segregation and discrimination, it may implicitly allow it to happen within its society. Passing discriminatory laws is known as *de jure* **segregation** ("de jure" meaning "by law"). If discriminatory laws leading to segregation exist in society without legal encouragement, it is known as *de facto* **segregation** ("de facto" meaning "by fact" or "by practice").

In the event a state enacts a law that classifies a group of people to be subject to its provisions, the state must establish a **compelling interest** in doing so; otherwise, the law will be suspect, considered discriminatory and overturned based on established constitutional law. The compelling interest test is applied to any state legislation that interferes with an otherwise constitutionally protected right or liberty, and requires **strict scrutiny** (the highest of standards) before it can survive a constitutional challenge.

Equal protection in the area of race has undergone significant change throughout our history. From the enforcement of Fugitive Slave Laws to the desegregation cases of the 1950s courts have followed a steady and determined path towards protecting the rights of all persons. In the area of education alone, the Supreme Court has taken a 180-degree turn from the 1896 ruling allowing "separate but equal" school accommodations in ***Plessy v. Ferguson***, 163 U.S. 537 to ***Brown v. Board of Education of Topeka***, 347 U.S. 483 in 1954. The latter decision specifically overturned the former by ruling that "separate educational facilities are inherently unequal," which led to the desegregation of all public schools and institutions in the United States. When some states dragged their feet in implementing the ruling in the Brown case, the court heard another case demanding they use "deliberate speed" in all efforts to desegregate schools (***Brown v. Board of Education of Topeka II***, 349 U.S. 294 (1955), also known as "***Brown II***").

By 1964, Congress passed **Title VII of the Civil Rights Act**, the mission of which was to protect the rights of all minorities against discriminatory actions of public and private officials (de jure vs. de facto discrimination). In an effort to end discrimination in the workplace, the act established the Equal Employment Opportunity Commission (EEOC). Although the EEOC was originally mandated to deal with cases involving racial discrimination, it expanded its range over time to hear discrimination cases of all sorts.

For a while, the U.S. government pursued legal ways to redress the ramifications of slavery and years of discrimination against African Americans through **Affirmative Action**. The idea was to favor minorities in admissions to universities and to steer local, state and federal government business contracts their way. Such race-based quotas have fallen into disfavor in recent years. In the matter of ***Regents of the University of California v. Bakke***, 438 U.S. 265 (1978), a student's application to medical school was rejected, and he sued claiming that his exam scores and grades were significantly higher than those of minority applicants who were admitted in his place. The Supreme Court ruled that racial quotas are *not* permitted but that schools may use race as a plus *factor*. Race cannot be the *sole* determining point when considering qualifications for admission to schools.

By reaffirming the Bakke decision, the Supreme Court has further ruled that race as an admission factor must be narrowly tailored as an element for university admission, ***Fisher v. The University of Texas at Austin***,11-345 (June 24, 2013). Affirmative Action was once again in the legal spotlight as challenges to its application in States led directly to the Supreme Court. In the case of ***Schuette v. Coalition to Defend***

*__Affirmative Action__*, #12-682, (decided April 22, 2014), the High Court ruled 6-2 that citizens of a state may vote to enact a State Constitutional Amendment barring race, religion, ethnicity and country of origin to be factors in university admission processes. According to the Court, voters of a State have the right to restrict public universities from using Affirmative Action as criteria for admissions. Somehow, the Court reasoned that voters, after full political debate can decide "through the political process" what standards, if any, may be used in admission processes. As we have seen through recent rulings, the impact of Affirmative Action has been diluted.

Equal protection when dealing with racial discrimination is not the only issue attracting the attention of the courts. Since the 1970s and the second wave of the women's liberation movement—the first won women the right to vote in the early part of the 20th century—gender bias has become a prominent matter. Equality of access to college sports has been extended to men and women. In the case of ***Grove City College v. Bell***, 465 U.S. 555 (1984), for example, the Supreme Court ruled that any college or university receiving federal funds must provide equal access to all men *and* women for sports competition under Title IX of the federal code, which prohibits sexual discrimination in athletics.

Sexual discrimination was prohibited in private institutions accepting federal financial aid as well. Virginia Military Institute (VMI), an all-male college, was forced to admit women when the Supreme Court heard the matter of ***U.S. v. Virginia Military Institute***, 518 U.S. 515 (1996). In light of the fact that women have been inducted into the military for years, the court reasoned that VMI cannot discriminate and refuse them admission without presenting "an exceedingly persuasive justification" for doing so. By setting such a high standard, it has become impossible for any state to protect institutions that seek to limit their admissions to men only.

Relatively recently, Congress has enacted laws protecting the rights of the disabled. The 1990 **Americans with Disability Act** gave them status as a "protected minority or class" and, as a result, guaranteed them access to all public areas and facilities. At the same time, employers are required to establish all reasonable accommodations to the disabled to allow them to work. Claims of discrimination in the workplace are now prosecuted by the Equal Employment Opportunity Commission (EEOC).

We have come a long way from the days when only white men had the right to own property and to vote. We now have an inclusive society that grants rights to every citizen, non-citizen and even corporations. Some would argue that we have gone too far—especially in the case of non-living, non-breathing entities—and much of our "progress" has come with considerable struggle, pain and discomfort. As the 19th-century German politician Otto von Bismarck said, "Making laws is like making sausage; you like it better when you do not know how it is made." But if you ask questions like, "Are we as a society more egalitarian than in the past?" or "Is it better and fairer for everyone to have equal rights under the law?" most Americans would answer with a resounding, "Yes."

To the degree that we are allowing some of our freedoms to be eroded, putting our sense of safety above all else, we must take a long, hard look at ourselves and the people we have installed to represent and govern us. We should always remember when we complain that our leaders in Washington and in our state house have begun to take us as Americans for granted, that no one has taken our government away from us. Instead, we have given it away, at great peril to all of us.

# ❊ AFTERWORD ❊

Abraham Lincoln wrote: "We the people are the rightful masters of both Congress and the courts, not to overthrow the Constitution but to overthrow the men who pervert the Constitution." Lincoln's words still ring true today.

Throughout our history, we have witnessed a cycle of important issues being fiercely and passionately debated at the highest levels of our government. Americans have always been determined to allow all sides to any argument to be thoroughly heard and, once heard, to reach a compromise that would best serve the interests of our great nation as a whole.

Recognition of the need for a new central government was in response to the obvious shortcomings of the post-revolutionary period under the Articles of Confederation. Creating a new form of federal government—guided by principles of checks and balances, separation of powers and a Bill of Rights guaranteed to limit the new government's ability to infringe on citizens' civil liberties—was a universally accepted alternative to the mechanism that failed under the Articles where some states were more powerful than others.

Amendments to the Constitution were added to safeguard the freedoms and liberties of all Americans. Congress has debated myriad issues over the past two plus centuries, and citizens have routinely relied upon it to do its best for the nation. The Supreme Court, from the earliest days of the republic, carved out its role under the Constitution and established a new American system of justice. The executive branch continues to evolve, utilizing the phrase "Custom and Usage" in Article Two of the

Constitution in ways George Washington could only have dreamed of when he first ventured to expand the role of the presidency. And the expansion of the role of the media would leave the framers dumbfounded with the use of the Internet and cell phone technologies. They would be surprised that we have not even begun to challenge the power given to the government to override our civil liberties in the guise of fighting terrorism under the Patriot Act.

But the one area that would leave our founders and framers deeply concerned would be the obvious failure of the American public to recognize and respect both the rich history of our nation and the role our federal government was designed to play. Instead of maintaining an educated electorate capable of using critical thinking skills necessary to discern facts from political narratives, we have become a nation of followers, following the lead of media pundits and talking heads. Unfortunately, the media are far too complicit in setting political agendas alongside existing political party lines. All too often our national debates are divisive and framed on what is best for a particular political party rather than what is best for our nation.

It disturbs me when ideologues portray our government as ineffective, inefficient and archaic. It troubles me that folks routinely hear disparaging remarks about the institutions of Congress, the presidency and the Supreme Court. Constant barrages of vitriolic rants have a corrosive effect on how citizens view our amazing form of government. Delegitimizing our president, members of Congress and justices of the Supreme Court to gain a political edge is abhorrent. If a politician deserves scorn, pundits in both political parties and the media should cast such scorn on the deserving individual, not the institution in which he serves. If you dislike the president's policies, dislike the person holding the office, not the presidency. All patriotic Americans should respect the offices our elected leaders hold. Only when we start educating ourselves with historical and constitutional facts will we again be able to build respect for our government. We need a call for true patriotism with an aim towards doing what is best for our nation, and not what is best for political parties or their ideologies.

Every day, citizens watch in amazement how politicians operate and then criticize them for their actions, all without full comprehension that their political actions are both expected and predictable. With this book, I am launching an effort I call "*Educate to Activate.*" It is time for our nation to become familiar again with our rich history and with the Constitution. It is time to ensure our political leaders establish policy agendas that suit *all* of us, not just interest groups who curry their favor or fulfill the mission of one particular political party. Now it is up to you to stay diligent, alert and informed. Be empowered and take charge. If you witness someone misstating facts about our real history, misapplying an ideology or being just plain wrong about the roles Congress and the president play, step forward and correct them. In doing so you have done your small part in protecting our great nation and our democratic-republic. The wisdom of "Don't complain if you don't vote" still rings true today.

Protecting liberty requires work. Educate yourself. Educate others around you. Engage your neighbors. Engage your community. Democracy and liberty are worth the effort. Discern true facts from rhetoric. Be part of the process. Get involved. Run for public office. Take charge. Be a leader, not a follower. Liberty demands it. Our Founding Fathers and framers expected it. Pass the word in the effort to educate the electorate.

# ❈ Appendix I ❈

## THE DECLARATION OF INDEPENDENCE

IN CONGRESS, July 4, 1776.

The unanimous Declaration of the thirteen United States of America:

When in the Course of human events, it becomes necessary for one people to dissolve the political bands which have connected them with another, and to assume among the powers of the earth, the separate and equal station to which the Laws of Nature and of Nature's God entitle them, a decent respect to the opinions of mankind requires that they should declare the causes which impel them to the separation.

We hold these truths to be self-evident, that all men are created equal, that they are endowed by their Creator with certain unalienable Rights, that among these are Life, Liberty and the pursuit of Happiness.—That to secure these rights, Governments are instituted among Men, deriving their just powers from the consent of the governed, —That whenever any Form of Government becomes destructive of these ends, it is the Right of the People to alter or to abolish it, and to institute new Government, laying its foundation on such principles and organizing its powers in such form, as to them shall seem most likely to effect their Safety and Happiness. Prudence, indeed, will dictate that Governments long established should not be changed for light and transient causes; and accordingly all experience hath shewn, that mankind are more disposed to suffer, while evils are sufferable, than to right themselves by abolishing the forms to which they are accustomed. But when a long train of abuses and usurpations, pursuing invariably the same Object evinces a design to reduce them under absolute Despotism, it is their right, it is their duty, to throw off such Government, and to provide new Guards for their future security.-- Such has been the patient sufferance of these Colonies; and such is now the necessity which constrains them to alter their former Systems of Government. The history of the present King of Great Britain is a history of repeated injuries and usurpations, all having in direct object the establishment of an absolute Tyranny over these States. To prove this, let Facts be submitted to a candid world.

He has refused his Assent to Laws, the most wholesome and necessary for the public good.

He has forbidden his Governors to pass Laws of immediate and pressing importance, unless suspended in their operation till his Assent should be obtained; and when so suspended, he has utterly neglected to attend to them.

He has refused to pass other Laws for the accommodation of large districts of people, unless those people would relinquish the right of Representation in the Legislature, a right inestimable to them and formidable to tyrants only.

He has called together legislative bodies at places unusual, uncomfortable, and distant from the depository of their public Records, for the sole purpose of fatiguing them into compliance with his measures.

He has dissolved Representative Houses repeatedly, for opposing with manly firmness his invasions on the rights of the people.

He has refused for a long time, after such dissolutions, to cause others to be elected; whereby the Legislative powers, incapable of Annihilation, have returned to the People at large for their exercise; the State remaining in the mean time exposed to all the dangers of invasion from without, and convulsions within.

He has endeavoured to prevent the population of these States; for that purpose obstructing the Laws for Naturalization of Foreigners; refusing to pass others to encourage their migrations hither, and raising the conditions of new Appropriations of Lands.

He has obstructed the Administration of Justice, by refusing his Assent to Laws for establishing Judiciary powers.

He has made Judges dependent on his Will alone, for the tenure of their offices, and the amount and payment of their salaries.

He has erected a multitude of New Offices, and sent hither swarms of Officers to harrass our people, and eat out their substance.

He has kept among us, in times of peace, Standing Armies without the Consent of our legislatures.

He has affected to render the Military independent of and superior to the Civil power.

He has combined with others to subject us to a jurisdiction foreign to our constitution, and unacknowledged by our laws; giving his Assent to their Acts of pretended Legislation:

For Quartering large bodies of armed troops among us:

For protecting them, by a mock Trial, from punishment for any Murders which they should commit on the Inhabitants of these States:

For cutting off our Trade with all parts of the world:

For imposing Taxes on us without our Consent:

For depriving us in many cases, of the benefits of Trial by Jury:

For transporting us beyond Seas to be tried for pretended offences.

For abolishing the free System of English Laws in a neighbouring Province, establishing therein an Arbitrary government, and enlarging its Boundaries so as to render it at once an example and fit instrument for introducing the same absolute rule into these Colonies:

For taking away our Charters, abolishing our most valuable Laws, and altering fundamentally the Forms of our Governments:

For suspending our own Legislatures, and declaring themselves invested with power to legislate for us in all cases whatsoever.

He has abdicated Government here, by declaring us out of his Protection and waging War against us.

He has plundered our seas, ravaged our Coasts, burnt our towns, and destroyed the lives of our people.

He is at this time transporting large Armies of foreign Mercenaries to compleat the works of death, desolation and tyranny, already begun with circumstances of Cruelty & perfidy scarcely paralleled in the most barbarous ages, and totally unworthy the Head of a civilized nation.

He has constrained our fellow Citizens taken Captive on the high Seas to bear Arms against their Country, to become the executioners of their friends and Brethren, or to fall themselves by their Hands.

He has excited domestic insurrections amongst us, and has endeavoured to bring on the inhabitants of our frontiers, the merciless Indian Savages, whose known rule of warfare, is an undistinguished destruction of all ages, sexes and conditions.

In every stage of these Oppressions We have Petitioned for Redress in the most humble terms: Our repeated Petitions have been answered only by repeated injury. A Prince whose character is thus marked by every act which may define a Tyrant, is unfit to be the ruler of a free people.

Nor have We been wanting in attentions to our Brittish brethren. We have warned them from time to time of attempts by their legislature to extend an unwarrantable jurisdiction over us. We have reminded them of the circumstances of our emigration and settlement here. We have appealed to their native justice and magnanimity, and we have conjured them by the ties of our common kindred to disavow these usurpations, which, would inevitably interrupt our connections and correspondence. They too have been deaf to the voice of justice and of consanguinity. We must, therefore, acquiesce in the necessity, which denounces our Separation, and hold them, as we hold the rest of mankind, Enemies in War, in Peace Friends.

We, therefore, the Representatives of the united States of America, in General Congress, Assembled, appealing to the Supreme Judge of the world for the rectitude of our intentions, do, in the Name, and by Authority of the good People of these Colonies, solemnly publish and declare, That these United Colonies are, and of Right ought to be Free and Independent States; that they are Absolved from all Allegiance to the British Crown, and that all political connection between them and the State of Great Britain, is and ought to be totally dissolved; and that as Free and Independent States, they have full Power to levy War, conclude Peace, contract Alliances, establish Commerce, and to do all other Acts and Things which Independent States may of right do. And for the support of this Declaration, with a firm reliance on the protection of divine Providence, we mutually pledge to each other our Lives, our Fortunes and our sacred Honor.

The 56 signatures on the Declaration appear in the positions indicated:

Column 1:
>    Georgia: Button Gwinnett, Lyman Hall, George Walton

Column 2:
>    North Carolina: William Hooper, Joseph Hewes, John Penn
>    South Carolina: Edward Rutledge, Thomas Heyward, Jr.,
>        Thomas Lynch, Jr., Arthur Middleton

Column 3:
>    Massachusetts: John Hancock
>    Maryland: Samuel Chase, William Paca, Thomas Stone,
>        Charles Carroll of Carrollton
>    Virginia: George Wythe, Richard Henry Lee,
>        Thomas Jefferson, Benjamin Harrison,
>        Thomas Nelson, Jr., Francis Lightfoot Lee,
>        Carter Braxton

Column 4
>    Pennsylvania: Robert Morris, Benjamin Rush,
>        Benjamin Franklin, John Morton, George Clymer
>        James Smith, George Taylor, James Wilson
>        George Ross
>    Delaware: Caesar Rodney, George Read, Thomas McKean

Column 5

New York: William Floyd, Philip Livingston, Francis Lewis
Lewis Morris
New Jersey: Richard Stockton, John Witherspoon
Francis Hopkinson, John Hart, Abraham Clark

Column 6

New Hampshire: Josiah Bartlett, William Whipple
Massachusetts: Samuel Adams, John Adams
Robert Treat Paine, Elbridge Gerry
Rhode Island: Stephen Hopkins, William Ellery
Connecticut: Roger Sherman, Samuel Huntington
William Williams, Oliver Wolcott
New Hampshire: Matthew Thornton

# ❋ APPENDIX II ❋

# THE ARTICLES OF CONFEDERATION

To all to whom these presents shall come,

We, the undersigned Delegates of the States affixed to our Names send greeting:

Whereas the Delegates of the United States of America in Congress assembled did on the fifteenth day of November in the year of our Lord one thousand seven hundred and seventy seven, and in the second year of the Independence of America agree to certain articles of Confederation and perpetual Union between the States of Newhampshire, Massachusetts-bay, Rhodeisland and Providence Plantations, Connecticut, New York, New Jersey, Pennsylvania, Delaware, Maryland, Virginia, North Carolina, South Carolina, and Georgia in the Words following, viz.

ARTICLES OF CONFEDERATION AND PERPETUAL UNION,

between the States of Newhampshire, Massachusetts-bay, Rhodeisland and Providence Plantations, Connecticut, New York, New Jersey, Pennsylvania, Delaware, Maryland, Virginia, North Carolina, South Carolina, and Georgia.

**Article I.** The style of this confederacy shall be, "THE UNITED STATES OF AMERICA."

**Article II.** Each state retains its sovereignty, freedom and independence, and every Power, Jurisdiction and right, which is not by this confederation expressly delegated to the United States, in Congress assembled.

**Article III.** The said States hereby severally enter into a firm league of friendship with each other, for their common defence, the security of their liberties, and their mutual and general welfare, binding themselves to assist each other, against all force offered to, or attacks made upon them, or any of them, on account of religion, sovereignty, trade, or any other pretence whatever.

**Article IV. §1.** The better to secure and perpetuate mutual friendship and intercourse among the people of the different States in this Union, the free inhabitants of each of these States, paupers, vagabonds and fugitives from Justice excepted, shall be entitled to all privileges and immunities of free citizens in the several States; and the people of each state shall have free ingress and regress to and from any other State, and shall enjoy therein all the privileges of trade and commerce, subject to the same duties, impositions and restrictions as the inhabitants thereof respectively, provided that such restrictions shall not extend so far as to prevent the removal of property imported into any state, to any other State of which the Owner is an inhabitant; provided also that no imposition, duties or restriction shall be laid by any State, on the property of the United States, or either of them.

**§2.** If any person guilty of, or charged with, treason, felony, or other high misdemeanor in any State, shall flee from justice, and be found in any of the United States, he shall upon demand of the Governor or executive power of the State from which he fled, be delivered up, and removed to the state having jurisdiction of his offence.

**§3.** Full faith and credit shall be given in each of these States to the records, acts and judicial proceedings of the courts and magistrates of every other State.

**Article V. §1.** For the more convenient management of the general interests of the United States, delegates shall be annually appointed in such manner as the legislature of each state shall direct, to meet in Congress on the first Monday in November, in every year, with a power reserved to each state to recall its delegates, or any of them, at any time within the year, and to send others in their stead, for the remainder of the year.

**§2.** No State shall be represented in Congress by less than two, nor by more than seven members; and no person shall be capable of being delegate for more than three years, in any term of six years; nor shall any person, being a delegate, be capable of holding any office under the United States, for which he, or another for his benefit receives any salary, fees or emolument of any kind.

**§3.** Each State shall maintain its own delegates in a meeting of the states, and while they act as members of the committee of the States.

**§4.** In determining questions in the United States, in Congress assembled, each State shall have one vote.

**§5.** Freedom of speech and debate in Congress shall not be impeached or questioned in any Court, or place out of Congress, and the members of congress shall be protected in their persons from arrests and imprisonments, during the time of their going to and from, and attendance on congress, except for treason, felony, or breach of the peace.

**Article VI. §1.** No State, without the consent of the United States, in congress assembled, shall send any embassy to, or receive any embassy from, or enter into any conferrence, agreement, alliance, or treaty, with any king, prince or State; nor shall any person holding any office of profit or trust under the United States, or any of them, accept of any present, emolument, office, or title of any kind whatever, from any king, prince, or foreign State; nor shall the United States, in congress assembled, or any of them, grant any title of nobility.

**§2.** No two or more States shall enter into any treaty, confederation, or alliance whatever between them, without the consent of the United States, in congress assembled, specifying accurately the purposes for which the same is to be entered into, and how long it shall continue.

**§3.** No State shall lay any imposts or duties, which may interfere with any stipulations in treaties, entered into by the United States in Congress assembled, with any king, prince, or State, in pursuance of any treaties already proposed by congress, to the courts of France and Spain.

**§4.** No vessels of war shall be kept up in time of peace, by any State, except such number only, as shall be deemed necessary by the United States, in Congress assembled, for the defence of such State, or its trade; nor shall any body of forces be kept up, by any State, in time of peace, except such number only as, in the judgment of the united states, in Congress assembled, shall be deemed requisite to garrison the forts necessary for the defence of such state; but every state shall always keep up a well regulated and disciplined militia, sufficiently armed and accounted, and shall provide and constantly have ready for use, in public stores, a due number of field pieces and tents, and a proper quantity of arms, ammunition, and camp equipage.

**§5.** No State shall engage in any war without the consent of the United States in congress assembled, unless such State be actually invaded by enemies, or shall have received certain advice of a resolution being formed by some nation of Indians to invade such State, and the danger is so imminent as not to admit of a delay till the united states in congress assembled, can be consulted: nor shall any state grant commissions to any ships or vessels of war, nor letters of marque or reprisal, except it be after a declaration of war by the United States in Congress assembled, and then only against the kingdom or State, and the subjects thereof, against which war has been so declared, and under such regulations as shall be established by the United States in Congress assembled, unless such State be infested by pirates, in which case vessels of war may be fitted out for that occasion, and kept so long as the danger shall continue, or until the United States in Ccongress assembled shall determine otherwise.

**Article VII.** When land forces are raised by any State, for the common defence, all officers of or under the rank of colonel, shall be appointed by the legislature of each State respectively by whom such forces shall be raised, or in such manner as such state shall direct, and all vacancies shall be filled up by the State which first made appointment.

**Article VIII.** All charges of war, and all other expenses that shall be incurred for the common defence or general welfare, and allowed by the United States in Congress assembled, shall be defrayed out of a common treasury, which shall be supplied by the several States, in proportion to the value of all land within each State, granted to or surveyed for any person, as such land and the buildings and improvements thereon shall be estimated, according to such mode as the United States, in Congress assembled, shall, from time to time, direct and appoint. The taxes for paying that proportion shall be laid and levied by the authority and direction of the legislatures of the several States within the time agreed upon by the United States in congress assembled.

**Article IX. §1.** The United States, in Congress assembled, shall have the sole and exclusive right and power of determining on peace and war, except in the cases mentioned in the sixth Article, of sending and receiving ambassadors, entering into treaties and alliances, provided that no treaty of commerce shall be made, whereby the legislative power of the respective States shall be restrained from imposing such imposts and duties on foreigners, as their own people are subjected to, or from prohibiting the exportation or importation of any species of goods or commodities whatsoever; of establishing rules for deciding, in all cases, what captures on land or water shall be legal, and in what manner prizes taken by land or naval forces in the service of the United States, shall be divided or appropriated; of granting letters of marque and reprisal in times of peace; appointing courts for the trial of piracies and felonies committed on the high seas; and establishing courts; for receiving and determining finally appeals in all cases of captures; provided that no member of Congress shall be appointed a judge of any of the said courts.

**§2.** The United States, in Congress assembled, shall also be the last resort on appeal, in all disputes and differences now subsisting, or that hereafter may arise between two or more states concerning boundary, jurisdiction, or any other cause whatever; which authority shall always be exercised in the manner following. Whenever the legislative or executive authority, or lawful agent of any State in controversy with another, shall present a petition to Congress, stating the matter in question, and praying for a hearing, notice thereof shall be given, by order of Congress, to the legislative or executive authority of the other State in controversy, and a day assigned for the appearance of the parties by their lawful agents, who shall then be directed to appoint, by joint consent, commissioners or judges to constitute a court for hearing and determining the matter in question; but if they cannot agree, Congress shall name three persons out of each of the United States, and from the list of such persons each party shall alternately strike out one, the petitioners beginning, until the number shall be reduced to thirteen; and from that number not less than seven, nor more than nine names, as Congress shall direct, shall, in the presence of Congress, be drawn out by lot, and the persons whose names shall be so drawn, or any five of them, shall be commissioners or judges, to hear and finally determine the controversy, so always as a major part of the judges, who shall hear the cause, shall agree in the determination; and if either party shall neglect to attend at the day appointed, without showing reasons which Congress shall judge sufficient, or being present, shall refuse to strike, the Congress shall proceed to nominate three persons out of each State, and the secretary of congress shall strike in behalf of such party absent or refusing; and the judgment and sentence of the court, to be appointed in the manner before prescribed, shall be final and conclusive; and if any of the parties shall refuse to submit to the authority of such court, or to appear or defend their claim or cause, the court shall nevertheless proceed to pronounce sentence, or judgment, which shall in like manner be final and decisive; the judgment or sentence and other proceedings being in either case transmitted to Congress, and lodged among the acts of Congress, for the security of the parties concerned: provided that every commissioner, before he sits in judgment, shall take an oath to be administered by one of the judges of the supreme or superior court of the State where the cause shall be tried, "well and truly to hear and determine the matter in question, according to the best of his judgment, without favour, affection, or hope of reward: "provided, also, that no State shall be deprived of territory for the benefit of the united states.

**§3.** All controversies concerning the private right of soil claimed under different grants of two or more States, whose jurisdictions as they may respect such lands, and the States which passed such grants are adjusted, the said grants or either of them being at the same time claimed to have originated antecedent to such settlement of jurisdiction, shall, on the petition of either party to the congress of the United States, be finally determined, as near as may be, in the same manner as is before prescribed for deciding disputes respecting territorial jurisdiction between different States.

**§4.** The United States, in Congress assembled, shall also have the sole and exclusive right and power of regulating the alloy and value of coin struck by their own authority, or by that of the respective States; fixing the standard of weights and measures throughout the United States; regulating the trade and managing all affairs with the Indians, not members of any of the States; provided that the legislative right of any State, within its own limits, be not infringed or violated; establishing and regulating post-offices from one State to another, throughout all the United States, and exacting such postage on the papers passing through the same, as may be requisite to defray the expenses of the said office; appointing all officers of the land forces in the service of the United States, excepting regimental officers; appointing all the officers of the naval forces, and commissioning all officers whatever in the service of the United States; making rules for the government and regulation of the said land and naval forces, and directing their operations.

**§5.** The United States, in Congress assembled, shall have authority to appoint a committee, to sit in the recess of Congress, to be denominated, "*A Committee of the States*," and to consist of one delegate from each State; and to appoint such other committees and civil officers as may be necessary for managing the general affairs of the united states under their direction; to appoint one of their number to preside; provided that no person be allowed to serve in the office of president more than one year in any term of three years; to ascertain the necessary sums of money to be raised for the service of the United States, and to appropriate and apply the same for defraying the public expenses; to borrow money or emit bills on the credit of the United States, transmitting every half year to the respective States an account of the sums of money so borrowed or emitted; to build and equip a navy; to agree upon the number of land forces, and to make requisitions from each state for its quota, in proportion to the number of white inhabitants in such State, which requisition shall be binding; and thereupon the legislature of each State shall appoint the regimental officers, raise the men, and clothe, arm, and equip them, in a soldier-like manner, at the expense of the United States; and the officers and men so clothed, armed, and equipped, shall march to the place appointed, and within the time agreed on by the United States, in Congress assembled; but if the United States, in Congress assembled, shall, on consideration of circumstances, judge proper that any state should not raise men, or should raise a smaller number than its quota, and that any other State should raise a greater number of men than the quota thereof, such extra number shall be raised, officered, clothed, armed, and equipped in the same manner as the quota of such State, unless the legislature of such State shall judge that such extra number cannot be safely spared out of the same, in which case they shall raise, officer, clothe, arm, and equip, as many of such extra number as they judge can be safely spared. And the officers and men so clothed, armed, and equipped, shall march to the place appointed, and within the time agreed on by the United States in Congress assembled.

§6. The United States, in Congress assembled, shall never engage in a war, nor grant letters of marque and reprisal in time of peace, nor enter into any treaties or alliances, nor coin money, nor regulate the value thereof nor ascertain the sums and expenses necessary for the defence and welfare of the United States, or any of them, nor emit bills, nor borrow money on the credit of the United States, nor appropriate money, nor agree upon the number of vessels of war to be built or purchased, or the number of land or sea forces to be raised, nor appoint a commander in chief of the army or navy, unless nine States assent to the same, nor shall a question on any other point, except for adjourning from day to day, be determined, unless by the votes of a majority of the United States in congress assembled.

§7. The Congress of the United States shall have power to adjourn to any time within the year, and to any place within the United States, so that no period of adjournment be for a longer duration than the space of six months, and shall publish the journal of their proceedings monthly, except such parts thereof relating to treaties, alliances, or military operations, as in their judgment require secrecy; and the yeas and nays of the delegates of each State, on any question, shall be entered on the journal, when it is desired by any delegate; and the delegates of a State, or any of them, at his or their request, shall be furnished with a transcript of the said journal, except such parts as are above excepted, to lay before the legislatures of the several States.

**Article X.** The committee of the States, or any nine of them, shall be authorized to execute, in the recess of Congress, such of the powers of Congress as the United States, in Congress assembled, by the consent of nine States, shall, from time to time, think expedient to vest them with; provided that no power be delegated to the said committee, for the exercise of which, by the Articles of Confederation, the voice of nine states, in the Congress of the United States assembled, is requisite.

**Article XI.** Canada acceding to this confederation, and joining in the measures of the United States, shall be admitted into, and entitled to all the advantages of this Union: but no other colony shall be admitted into the same, unless such admission be agreed to by nine States.

**Article XII.** All bills of credit emitted, monies borrowed, and debts contracted by or under the authority of Congress, before the assembling of the united states, in pursuance of the present confederation, shall be deemed and considered as a charge against the United States, for payment and satisfaction whereof the said United States and the public faith are hereby solemnly pledged.

**Article XIII.** Every State shall abide by the determinations of the United States, in Congress assembled, on all questions which by this confederation are submitted to them. And the Articles of this confederation shall be inviolably observed by every State, and the union shall be perpetual; nor shall any alteration at any time hereafter be made in any of them, unless such alteration be agreed to in a congress of the United States, and be afterwards confirmed by the legislatures of every State.

And whereas it hath pleased the great Governor of the world to incline the hearts of the legislatures we respectively represent in Congress, to approve of, and to authorize us to ratify the said articles of confederation and perpetual union, Know Ye, that we, the undersigned delegates, by virtue of the power and authority to us given for that purpose, do, by these presents, in the name and in behalf of our respective constituents, fully and entirely ratify and confirm each and every of the said Articles of Confederation and perpetual union, and all and singular the matters and things therein contained. And we do further solemnly plight and engage the faith of our respective constituents, that they shall abide by the determinations of the United States in congress assembled, on all questions, which by the said confederation are submitted to them. And that the articles thereof shall be inviolably observed by the States we respectively represent, and that the union shall be perpetual. In Witness whereof, we have hereunto set our hands, in Congress.

*Done at Philadelphia, in the State of Pennsylvania, the 15th day of November, in the year of our Lord 1777, and in the third year of the Independence of America.*

# ❀ APPENDIX III ❀

## THE CONSTITUTION OF THE UNITED STATES

We the People of the United States, in Order to form a more perfect Union, establish Justice, insure domestic Tranquility, provide for the common defence, promote the general Welfare, and secure the Blessings of Liberty to ourselves and our Posterity, do ordain and establish this Constitution for the United States of America.

### Article I

**Section 1**

All legislative Powers herein granted shall be vested in a Congress of the United States, which shall consist of a Senate and House of Representatives.

**Section 2**

The House of Representatives shall be composed of Members chosen every second Year by the People of the several States, and the Electors in each State shall have the Qualifications requisite for Electors of the most numerous Branch of the State Legislature.

No Person shall be a Representative who shall not have attained to the Age of twenty five Years, and been seven Years a Citizen of the United States, and who shall not, when elected, be an Inhabitant of that State in which he shall be chosen.

Representatives and direct Taxes shall be apportioned among the several States which may be included within this Union, according to their respective Numbers, which shall be determined by adding to the whole Number of free Persons, including those bound to Service for a Term of Years, and excluding Indians not taxed, three fifths of all other Persons. The actual Enumeration shall be made within three Years after the first Meeting of the Congress of the United States, and within every subsequent Term of ten Years, in such Manner as they shall by Law direct. The Number of Representatives shall not exceed one for every thirty Thousand, but each State shall have at Least one Representative; and until such enumeration shall be made, the State of New Hampshire shall be entitled to chuse three, Massachusetts eight, Rhode-Island and Providence Plantations one, Connecticut five, New-York six, New Jersey four, Pennsylvania eight, Delaware one, Maryland six, Virginia ten, North Carolina five, South Carolina five, and Georgia three.

When vacancies happen in the Representation from any State, the Executive Authority thereof shall issue Writs of Election to fill such Vacancies.

The House of Representatives shall chuse their Speaker and other Officers; and shall have the sole Power of Impeachment.

## Section 3

The Senate of the United States shall be composed of two Senators from each State, chosen by the Legislature thereof, for six Years; and each Senator shall have one Vote.

Immediately after they shall be assembled in Consequence of the first Election, they shall be divided as equally as may be into three Classes. The Seats of the Senators of the first Class shall be vacated at the Expiration of the second Year, of the second Class at the Expiration of the fourth Year, and of the third Class at the Expiration of the sixth Year, so that one third may be chosen every second Year; and if

Vacancies happen by Resignation, or otherwise, during the Recess of the Legislature of any State, the Executive thereof may make temporary Appointments until the next Meeting of the Legislature, which shall then fill such Vacancies.4

No Person shall be a Senator who shall not have attained to the Age of thirty Years, and been nine Years a Citizen of the United States, and who shall not, when elected, be an Inhabitant of that State for which he shall be chosen.

The Vice President of the United States shall be President of the Senate, but shall have no Vote, unless they be equally divided.

The Senate shall chuse their other Officers, and also a President pro tempore, in the Absence of the Vice President, or when he shall exercise the Office of President of the United States.

The Senate shall have the sole Power to try all Impeachments. When sitting for that Purpose, they shall be on Oath or Affirmation. When the President of the United States is tried, the Chief Justice shall preside: And no Person shall be convicted without the Concurrence of two thirds of the Members present.

Judgment in Cases of impeachment shall not extend further than to removal from Office, and disqualification to hold and enjoy any Office of honor, Trust or Profit under the United States: but the Party convicted shall nevertheless be liable and subject to Indictment, Trial, Judgment and Punishment, according to Law.

## Section 4

The Times, Places and Manner of holding Elections for Senators and Representatives, shall be prescribed in each State by the Legislature thereof; but the Congress may at any time by Law make or alter such Regulations, except as to the Places of chusing Senators.

The Congress shall assemble at least once in every Year, and such Meeting shall be on the first Monday in December, unless they shall by Law appoint a different Day.

## Section 5

Each House shall be the Judge of the Elections, Returns and Quali-fications of its own Members, and a Majority of each shall constitute a Quorum to do Business; but a smaller Number may adjourn from day to day, and may be authorized to compel the Attendance of absent Members, in such Manner, and under such Penalties as each House may provide.

Each House may determine the Rules of its Proceedings, punish its Members for disorderly Behaviour, and, with the Concurrence of two thirds, expel a Member.

Each House shall keep a Journal of its Proceedings, and from time to time publish the same, excepting such Parts as may in their Judg-ment require Secrecy; and the Yeas and Nays of the Members of either House on any question shall, at the Desire of one fifth of those Present, be entered on the Journal.

Neither House, during the Session of Congress, shall, without the Consent of the other, adjourn for more than three days, nor to any other Place than that in which the two Houses shall be sitting.

## Section 6

The Senators and Representatives shall receive a Compensation for their Services, to be ascertained by Law, and paid out of the Trea-sury of the United States. They shall in all Cases, except Treason, Fel-ony and Breach of the Peace, be privileged from Arrest during their Attendance at the Session of their respective Houses, and in going to and returning from the same; and for any Speech or Debate in either House, they shall not be questioned in any other Place.

No Senator or Representative shall, during the Time for which he was elected, be appointed to any civil Office under the Authority of the United States, which shall have been created, or the Emoluments whereof shall have been encreased during such time; and no Person holding any Office under the United States, shall be a Member of ei-ther House during his Continuance in Office.

## Section 7

All Bills for raising Revenue shall originate in the House of Representatives; but the Senate may propose or concur with Amendments as on other Bills.

Every Bill which shall have passed the House of Representatives and the Senate, shall, before it become a Law, be presented to the President of the United States; If he approve he shall sign it, but if not he shall return it, with his Objections to that House in which it shall have originated, who shall enter the Objections at large on their Journal, and proceed to reconsider it. If after such Reconsideration two thirds of that House shall agree to pass the Bill, it shall be sent, together with the Objections, to the other House, by which it shall likewise be reconsidered, and if approved by two thirds of that House, it shall become a Law. But in all such Cases the Votes of both Houses shall be determined by yeas and Nays, and the Names of the Persons voting for and against the Bill shall be entered on the Journal of each House respectively. If any Bill shall not be returned by the President within ten Days (Sundays excepted) after it shall have been presented to him, the Same shall be a Law, in like Manner as if he had signed it, unless the Congress by their Adjournment prevent its Return, in which Case it shall not be a Law.

Every Order, Resolution, or Vote to which the Concurrence of the Senate and House of Representatives may be necessary (except on a question of Adjournment) shall be presented to the President of the United States; and before the Same shall take Effect, shall be approved by him, or being disapproved by him, shall be repassed by two thirds of the Senate and House of Representatives, according to the Rules and Limitations prescribed in the Case of a Bill.

## Section 8

The Congress shall have Power To lay and collect Taxes, Duties, Imposts and Excises, to pay the Debts and provide for the common Defence and general Welfare of the United States; but all Duties, Imposts and Excises shall be uniform throughout the United States;

To borrow Money on the credit of the United States;

To regulate Commerce with foreign Nations, and among the several States, and with the Indian Tribes;

To establish an uniform Rule of Naturalization, and uniform Laws on the subject of Bankruptcies throughout the United States;

To coin Money, regulate the Value thereof, and of foreign Coin, and fix the Standard of Weights and Measures;

To provide for the Punishment of counterfeiting the Securities and current Coin of the United States;

To establish Post Offices and post Roads;

To promote the Progress of Science and useful Arts, by securing for limited Times to Authors and Inventors the exclusive Right to their respective Writings and Discoveries;

To constitute Tribunals inferior to the supreme Court;

To define and punish Piracies and Felonies committed on the high Seas, and Offences against the Law of Nations;

To declare War, grant Letters of Marque and Reprisal, and make Rules concerning Captures on Land and Water;

To raise and support Armies, but no Appropriation of Money to that Use shall be for a longer Term than two Years;

To provide and maintain a Navy;

To make Rules for the Government and Regulation of the land and naval Forces;

To provide for calling forth the Militia to execute the Laws of the Union, suppress Insurrections and repel Invasions;

To provide for organizing, arming, and disciplining, the Militia, and for governing such Part of them as may be employed in the Service of the United States, reserving to the States respectively, the Appointment of the Officers, and the Authority of training the Militia according to the discipline prescribed by Congress;

To exercise exclusive Legislation in all Cases whatsoever, over such District (not exceeding ten Miles square) as may, by Cession of particular States, and the Acceptance of Congress, become the Seat of the Government of the United States, and to exercise like Authority over all Places purchased by the Consent of the Legislature of the State in which the Same shall be, for the Erection of Forts, Magazines, Arsenals, dock-Yards, and other needful Buildings;--And

To make all Laws which shall be necessary and proper for carrying into Execution the foregoing Powers, and all other Powers vested by this Constitution in the Government of the United States, or in any Department or Officer thereof.

## Section 9

The Migration or Importation of such Persons as any of the States now existing shall think proper to admit, shall not be prohibited by the Congress prior to the Year one thousand eight hundred and eight, but a Tax or duty may be imposed on such Importation, not exceeding ten dollars for each Person.

The Privilege of the Writ of Habeas Corpus shall not be suspended, unless when in Cases of Rebellion or Invasion the public Safety may require it.

No Bill of Attainder or ex post facto Law shall be passed.

No Capitation, or other direct, Tax shall be laid, unless in Proportion to the Census or Enumeration herein before directed to be taken.

No Tax or Duty shall be laid on Articles exported from any State.

No Preference shall be given by any Regulation of Commerce or Revenue to the Ports of one State over those of another: nor shall Vessels bound to, or from, one State, be obliged to enter, clear, or pay Duties in another.

No Money shall be drawn from the Treasury, but in Consequence of Appropriations made by Law; and a regular Statement and Account of the Receipts and Expenditures of all public Money shall be published from time to time.

No Title of Nobility shall be granted by the United States: And no Person holding any Office of Profit or Trust under them, shall, without the Consent of the Congress, accept of any present, Emolument,

Office, or Title, of any kind whatever, from any King, Prince, or foreign State.

## Section 10

No State shall enter into any Treaty, Alliance, or Confederation; grant Letters of Marque and Reprisal; coin Money; emit Bills of Credit; make any Thing but gold and silver Coin a Tender in Payment of Debts; pass any Bill of Attainder, ex post facto Law, or Law impairing the Obligation of Contracts, or grant any Title of Nobility.

No State shall, without the Consent of the Congress, lay any Imposts or Duties on Imports or Exports, except what may be absolutely necessary for executing it's inspection Laws: and the net Produce of all Duties and Imposts, laid by any State on Imports or Exports, shall be for the Use of the Treasury of the United States; and all such Laws shall be subject to the Revision and Controul of the Congress.

No State shall, without the Consent of Congress, lay any Duty of Tonnage, keep Troops, or Ships of War in time of Peace, enter into any Agreement or Compact with another State, or with a foreign Power, or engage in War, unless actually invaded, or in such imminent Danger as will not admit of delay.

## Article II

### Section 1

The executive Power shall be vested in a President of the United States of America. He shall hold his Office during the Term of four Years, and, together with the Vice President, chosen for the same Term, be elected, as follows

Each State shall appoint, in such Manner as the Legislature thereof may direct, a Number of Electors, equal to the whole Number of Senators and Representatives to which the State may be entitled in the Congress: but no Senator or Representative, or Person holding an

Office of Trust or Profit under the United States, shall be appointed an Elector.

The Electors shall meet in their respective States, and vote by Ballot for two Persons, of whom one at least shall not be an Inhabitant of the same State with themselves. And they shall make a List of all the Persons voted for, and of the Number of Votes for each; which List they shall sign and certify, and transmit sealed to the Seat of the Government of the United States, directed to the President of the Senate. The President of the Senate shall, in the Presence of the Senate and House of Representatives, open all the Certificates, and the Votes shall then be counted. The Person having the greatest Number of Votes shall be the President, if such Number be a Majority of the whole Number of Electors appointed; and if there be more than one who have such Majority, and have an equal Number of Votes, then the House of Representatives shall immediately chuse by Ballot one of them for President; and if no Person have a Majority, then from the five highest on the List the said House shall in like Manner chuse the President. But in chusing the President, the Votes shall be taken by States, the Representation from each State having one Vote; A quorum for this Purpose shall consist of a Member or Members from two thirds of the States, and a Majority of all the States shall be necessary to a Choice. In every Case, after the Choice of the President, the Person having the greatest Number of Votes of the Electors shall be the Vice President. But if there should remain two or more who have equal Votes, the Senate shall chuse from them by Ballot the Vice President.

The Congress may determine the Time of chusing the Electors, and the Day on which they shall give their Votes; which Day shall be the same throughout the United States.

No Person except a natural born Citizen, or a Citizen of the United States, at the time of the Adoption of this Constitution, shall be eligible to the Office of President; neither shall any Person be eligible to that Office who shall not have attained to the Age of thirty five Years, and been fourteen Years a Resident within the United States.

In Case of the Removal of the President from Office, or of his Death, Resignation, or Inability to discharge the Powers and Duties of the said Office, the Same shall devolve on the VicePresident, and the Congress may by Law provide for the Case of Removal, Death, Resignation or Inability, both of the President and Vice President, declaring what Officer shall then act as President, and such Officer shall act accordingly, until the Disability be removed, or a President shall be elected.

The President shall, at stated Times, receive for his Services, a Compensation, which shall neither be encreased nor diminished during the Period for which he shall have been elected, and he shall not receive within that Period any other Emolument from the United States, or any of them.

Before he enter on the Execution of his Office, he shall take the following Oath or Affirmation—"I do solemnly swear (or affirm) that I will faithfully execute the Office of President of the United States, and will to the best of my Ability, preserve, protect and defend the Constitution of the United States."

**Section 2**

The President shall be Commander in Chief of the Army and Navy of the United States, and of the Militia of the several States, when called into the actual Service of the United States; he may require the Opinion, in writing, of the principal Officer in each of the executive Departments, upon any Subject relating to the Duties of their respective Offices, and he shall have Power to grant Reprieves and Pardons for Offences against the United States, except in Cases of Impeachment.

He shall have Power, by and with the Advice and Consent of the Senate, to make Treaties, provided two thirds of the Senators present concur; and he shall nominate, and by and with the Advice and Consent of the Senate, shall appoint Ambassadors, other public Ministers and Consuls, Judges of the supreme Court, and all other Officers of the

United States, whose Appointments are not herein otherwise provided for, and which shall be established by Law: but the Congress may by Law vest the Appointment of such inferior Officers, as they think proper, in the President alone, in the Courts of Law, or in the Heads of Departments.

The President shall have Power to fill up all Vacancies that may happen during the Recess of the Senate, by granting Commissions which shall expire at the End of their next Session.

## Section 3

He shall from time to time give to the Congress Information of the State of the Union, and recommend to their Consideration such Measures as he shall judge necessary and expedient; he may, on extraordinary Occasions, convene both Houses, or either of them, and in Case of Disagreement between them, with Respect to the Time of Adjournment, he may adjourn them to such Time as he shall think proper; he shall receive Ambassadors and other public Ministers; he shall take Care that the Laws be faithfully executed, and shall Commission all the Officers of the United States.

## Section 4

The President, Vice President and all civil Officers of the United States, shall be removed from Office on Impeachment for, and Conviction of, Treason, Bribery, or other high Crimes and Misdemeanors.

## Article III

### Section 1

The judicial Power of the United States, shall be vested in one supreme Court, and in such inferior Courts as the Congress may from time to time ordain and establish. The Judges, both of the supreme and inferior Courts, shall hold their Offices during good Behaviour, and shall, at stated Times, receive for their Services, a Compensation, which shall not be diminished during their Continuance in Office.

## Section 2

The judicial Power shall extend to all Cases, in Law and Equity, arising under this Constitution, the Laws of the United States, and Treaties made, or which shall be made, under their Authority;–to all Cases affecting Ambassadors, other public Ministers and Consuls;–to all Cases of admiralty and maritime Jurisdiction;–to Controversies to which the United States shall be a Party;–to Controversies between two or more States;–between a State and Citizens of another State; –between Citizens of different States, –between Citizens of the same State claiming Lands under Grants of different States, and between a State, or the Citizens thereof, and foreign States, Citizens or Subjects.

In all Cases affecting Ambassadors, other public Ministers and Consuls, and those in which a State shall be Party, the supreme Court shall have original Jurisdiction. In all the other Cases before mentioned, the supreme Court shall have appellate Jurisdiction, both as to Law and Fact, with such Exceptions, and under such Regulations as the Congress shall make.

The Trial of all Crimes, except in Cases of Impeachment, shall be by Jury; and such Trial shall be held in the State where the said Crimes shall have been committed; but when not committed within any State, the Trial shall be at such Place or Places as the Congress may by Law have directed.

## Section 3

Treason against the United States, shall consist only in levying War against them, or in adhering to their Enemies, giving them Aid and Comfort. No Person shall be convicted of Treason unless on the Testimony of two Witnesses to the same overt Act, or on Confession in open Court.

The Congress shall have Power to declare the Punishment of Treason, but no Attainder of Treason shall work Corruption of Blood, or Forfeiture except during the Life of the Person attainted.

## Article IV

### Section 1

Full Faith and Credit shall be given in each State to the public Acts, Records, and judicial Proceedings of every other State. And the Congress may by general Laws prescribe the Manner in which such Acts, Records and Proceedings shall be proved, and the Effect thereof.

### Section 2

The Citizens of each State shall be entitled to all Privileges and Immunities of Citizens in the several States.

A Person charged in any State with Treason, Felony, or other Crime, who shall flee from Justice, and be found in another State, shall on Demand of the executive Authority of the State from which he fled, be delivered up, to be removed to the State having Jurisdiction of the Crime.

No Person held to Service or Labour in one State, under the Laws thereof, escaping into another, shall, in Consequence of any Law or Regulation therein, be discharged from such Service or Labour, but shall be delivered up on Claim of the Party to whom such Service or Labour may be due.

### Section 3

New States may be admitted by the Congress into this Union; but no new State shall be formed or erected within the Jurisdiction of any other State; nor any State be formed by the Junction of two or more States, or Parts of States, without the Consent of the Legislatures of the States concerned as well as of the Congress.

The Congress shall have Power to dispose of and make all needful Rules and Regulations respecting the Territory or other Property belonging to the United States; and nothing in this Constitution shall be so construed as to Prejudice any Claims of the United States, or of any particular State.

**Section 4**

The United States shall guarantee to every State in this Union a Republican Form of Government, and shall protect each of them against Invasion; and on Application of the Legislature, or of the Executive (when the Legislature cannot be convened) against domestic Violence.

**Article V**

The Congress, whenever two thirds of both Houses shall deem it necessary, shall propose Amendments to this Constitution, or, on the Application of the Legislatures of two thirds of the several States, shall call a Convention for proposing Amendments, which, in either Case, shall be valid to all Intents and Purposes, as Part of this Constitution, when ratified by the Legislatures of three fourths of the several States, or by Conventions in three fourths thereof, as the one or the other Mode of Ratification may be proposed by the Congress; Provided that no Amendment which may be made prior to the Year One thousand eight hundred and eight shall in any Manner affect the first and fourth Clauses in the Ninth Section of the first Article; and that no State, without its Consent, shall be deprived of its equal Suffrage in the Senate.

**Article VI**

All Debts contracted and Engagements entered into, before the Adoption of this Constitution, shall be as valid against the United States under this Constitution, as under the Confederation.

This Constitution, and the Laws of the United States which shall be made in Pursuance thereof; and all Treaties made, or which shall be made, under the Authority of the United States, shall be the supreme Law of the Land; and the Judges in every State shall be bound thereby, any Thing in the Constitution or Laws of any State to the Contrary notwithstanding.

The Senators and Representatives before mentioned, and the Members of the several State Legislatures, and all executive and judicial Officers, both of the United States and of the several States, shall be bound by Oath or Affirmation, to support this Constitution; but no religious Test shall ever be required as a Qualification to any Office or public Trust under the United States.

### Article VII

The Ratification of the Conventions of nine States, shall be sufficient for the Establishment of this Constitution between the States so ratifying the Same.

The Word "the," being interlined between the seventh and eight Lines of the first Page, The Word "Thirty" being partly written on an Erazure in the fifteenth Line of the first Page. The Words "is tried" being interlined between the thirty second and thirty third Lines of the first Page and the Word "the" being interlined between the forty third and forty fourth Lines of the second Page.

done in Convention by the Unanimous Consent of the States present the Seventeenth Day of September in the Year of our Lord one thousand seven hundred and Eighty seven and of the Independence of the United States of America the Twelfth In witness whereof We have hereunto subscribed our Names,

Attest William Jackson Secretary

Go: Washington -Presidt. and deputy from Virginia

Delaware:

    Geo: Read, Gunning Bedford jun, John Dickinson

    Richard Bassett, Jaco: Broom

Maryland:

    James McHenry, Dan of St, Thos. Jenifer, Danl Carroll.

Virginia:

    John Blair, James Madison Jr.

North Carolina:

    Wm Blount, Richd. Dobbs Spaight, Hu Williamson

South Carolina:

    J. Rutledge, Charles Cotesworth Pinckney, Charles Pinckney

    Pierce Butler.

Georgia:

    William Few, Abr Baldwin

New Hampshire:

    John Langdon, Nicholas Gilman

Massachusetts:

    Nathaniel Gorham, Rufus King

Connecticut:

    Wm. Saml. Johnson, Roger Sherman

New York:

    Alexander Hamilton

New Jersey:

    Wil. Livingston, David Brearley, Wm. Paterson, Jona: Dayton

Pennsylvania

    B Franklin, Thomas Mifflin, Robt Morris, Geo. Clymer

    Thos. FitzSimons, Jared Ingersoll, James Wilson.

    Gouv Morris

# Preamble

Congress of the United States begun and held at the City of New-York, on Wednesday the fourth of March, one thousand seven hundred and eighty nine.

THE Conventions of a number of the States, having at the time of their adopting the Constitution, expressed a desire, in order to prevent misconstruction or abuse of its powers, that further declaratory and restrictive clauses should be added: And as extending the ground of public confidence in the Government, will best ensure the beneficent ends of its institution.

RESOLVED by the Senate and House of Representatives of the United States of America, in Congress assembled, two thirds of both Houses concurring, that the following Articles be proposed to the Legislatures of the several States, as amendments to the Constitution of the United States, all, or any of which Articles, when ratified by three fourths of the said Legislatures, to be valid to all intents and purposes, as part of the said Constitution; viz.

ARTICLES in addition to, and Amendment of the Constitution of the United States of America, proposed by Congress, and ratified by the Legislatures of the several States, pursuant to the fifth Article of the original Constitution.

(Articles I through X are known as the Bill of Rights)

## AMENDMENT I

Congress shall make no law respecting an establishment of religion, or prohibiting the free exercise thereof; or abridging the freedom of speech, or of the press, or the right of the people peaceably to assemble, and to petitition the Government for a redress of grievances.

## AMENDMENT II

A well regulated Militia, being necessary to the security of a free State, the right of the people to keep and bear Arms, shall not be infringed.

## AMENDMENT III

No Soldier shall, in time of peace be quartered in any house, without the consent of the Owner; nor in time of war, but in a manner to be prescribed by law.

## AMENDMENT IV

The right of the people to be secure in their persons, houses, papers, and effects, against unreasonable searches and seizures, shall not be violated, and no Warrants shall issue, but upon probable cause, supported by Oath or affirmation, and particularly describing the place to be searched, and the persons or things to be seized.

## AMENDMENT V

No person shall be held to answer for a capital, or otherwise infamous crime, unless on a presentment or indictment of a Grand Jury, except in cases arising in the land or naval forces, or in the Militia, when in actual service in time of War or public danger; nor shall any person be subject for the same offence to be twice put in jeopardy of life or limb; nor shall be compelled in any criminal case to be a witness against himself; nor be deprived of life, liberty, or property, without due process of law; nor shall private property be taken for public use without just compensation.

## AMENDMENT VI

In all criminal prosecutions, the accused shall enjoy the right to a speedy and public trial, by an impartial jury of the State and district wherein the crime shall have been committed; which district shall have been previously ascertained by law, and to be informed of the nature and cause of the accusation; to be confronted with the witnesses against him; to have compulsory process for obtaining witnesses in his favor; and to have the assistance of counsel for his defence.

## AMENDMENT VII

In Suits at common law, where the value in controversy shall exceed twenty dollars, the right of trial by jury shall be preserved, and no fact tried by a jury shall be otherwise reexamined in any Court of the United States, than according to the rules of common law.

## AMENDMENT VIII

Excessive bail shall not be required, nor excessive fines imposed, nor cruel and unusual punishments inflicted.

## AMENDMENT IX

The enumeration in the Constitution of certain rights shall not be construed to deny or disparage others retained by the people.

## AMENDMENT X

The powers not delegated to the United States by the Constitution, nor prohibited by it to the States, are reserved to the States respectively, or to the people.

## AMENDMENT XI
Passed by Congress March 4, 1794. Ratified February 7, 1795.

The Judicial power of the United States shall not be construed to extend to any suit in law or equity, commenced or prosecuted against one of the United States by Citizens of another State, or by Citizens or Subjects of any Foreign State.

## AMENDMENT XII
Passed by Congress December 9, 1803. Ratified June 15, 1804.

The Electors shall meet in their respective states and vote by ballot for President and Vice-President, one of whom, at least, shall not be an inhabitant of the same state with themselves; they shall name in their ballots the person voted for as President, and in distinct ballots the person voted for as Vice-President, and they shall make distinct lists of all persons voted for as President, and of all persons voted for as Vice-President, and of the number of votes for each, which lists they shall sign and certify, and transmit sealed to the seat of the government of the United States, directed to the President of the Senate; -- the President of the Senate shall, in the presence of the Senate and House of Representatives, open all the certificates and the votes shall then be counted; -- The person having the greatest number of votes for President, shall be the President, if such number be a majority of the whole number of Electors appointed; and if no person have such majority, then from the persons having the highest numbers not exceeding three on the list of those voted for as President, the House of Representatives shall choose immediately, by ballot, the President. But in choosing the President, the votes shall be taken by states, the representation from each state having one vote; a quorum for this purpose shall consist of a member or members from two-thirds of the states, and a majority of all the states shall be necessary to a choice. And if the House of Representatives shall not choose a President whenever the right of choice shall devolve upon them, before the fourth day of March next following, then the Vice-President shall act as President, as in case of the death or other constitutional disability of the President. The person having the greatest number of votes as Vice-President, shall be the Vice-President, if such number be a majority of the whole number of Electors appointed, and if no person have a majority, then from the two highest numbers on the list, the Senate shall choose the Vice-President; a quorum for the purpose shall consist of two-thirds of the whole number of Senators, and a majority of the whole number shall be necessary to a choice. But no person constitutionally ineligible to the office of President shall be eligible to that of Vice-President of the United States.

## AMENDMENT XIII
Passed by Congress January 31, 1865. Ratified December 6, 1865.

Section 1. Neither slavery nor involuntary servitude, except as a punishment for crime whereof the party shall have been duly convicted, shall exist within the United States, or any place subject to their jurisdiction.
Section 2. Congress shall have power to enforce this article by appropriate legislation.

## AMENDMENT XIV
Passed by Congress June 13, 1866. Ratified July 9, 1868.

Section 1. All persons born or naturalized in the United States, and subject to the jurisdiction thereof, are citizens of the United States and of the State wherein they reside. No State shall make or enforce any law which shall abridge the privileges or immunities of citizens of the United States; nor shall any State deprive any person of life, liberty, or property, without due process of law; nor deny to any person within its jurisdiction the equal protection of the laws.
Section 2. Representatives shall be apportioned among the several States according to their respective numbers, counting the whole

number of persons in each State, excluding Indians not taxed. But when the right to vote at any election for the choice of electors for President and Vice-President of the United States, Representatives in Congress, the Executive and Judicial officers of a State, or the members of the Legislature thereof, is denied to any of the male inhabitants of such State, being twenty-one years of age, and citizens of the United States, or in any way abridged, except for participation in rebellion, or other crime, the basis of representation therein shall be reduced in the proportion which the number of such male citizens shall bear to the whole number of male citizens twenty-one years of age in such State.

Section 3. No person shall be a Senator or Representative in Congress, or elector of President and Vice-President, or hold any office, civil or military, under the United States, or under any State, who, having previously taken an oath, as a member of Congress, or as an officer of the United States, or as a member of any State legislature, or as an executive or judicial officer of any State, to support the Constitution of the United States, shall have engaged in insurrection or rebellion against the same, or given aid or comfort to the enemies thereof. But Congress may by a vote of two-thirds of each House, remove such disability.

Section 4. The validity of the public debt of the United States, authorized by law, including debts incurred for payment of pensions and bounties for services in suppressing insurrection or rebellion, shall not be questioned. But neither the United States nor any State shall assume or pay any debt or obligation incurred in aid of insurrection or rebellion against the United States, or any claim for the loss or emancipation of any slave; but all such debts, obligations and claims shall be held illegal and void.

Section 5. The Congress shall have the power to enforce, by appropriate legislation, the provisions of this article.

**AMENDMENT XV**
Passed by Congress February 26, 1869. Ratified February 3, 1870.

Section 1. The right of citizens of the United States to vote shall not be denied or abridged by the United States or by any State on account of race, color, or previous condition of servitude--
Section 2. The Congress shall have the power to enforce this article by appropriate legislation.

**AMENDMENT XVI**
Passed by Congress July 2, 1909. Ratified February 3, 1913.

The Congress shall have power to lay and collect taxes on incomes, from whatever source derived, without apportionment among the several States, and without regard to any census or enumeration.

**AMENDMENT XVII**
Passed by Congress May 13, 1912. Ratified April 8, 1913.

The Senate of the United States shall be composed of two Senators from each State, elected by the people thereof, for six years; and each Senator shall have one vote. The electors in each State shall have the qualifications requisite for electors of the most numerous branch of the State legislatures.

When vacancies happen in the representation of any State in the Senate, the executive authority of such State shall issue writs of election to fill such vacancies: Provided, That the legislature of any State may empower the executive thereof to make temporary appointments until the people fill the vacancies by election as the legislature may direct.

This amendment shall not be so construed as to affect the election or term of any Senator chosen before it becomes valid as part of the Constitution.

## AMENDMENT XVIII
Passed by Congress December 18, 1917. Ratified January 16, 1919. Repealed by amendment 21.

Section 1. After one year from the ratification of this article the manufacture, sale, or transportation of intoxicating liquors within, the importation thereof into, or the exportation thereof from the United States and all territory subject to the jurisdiction thereof for beverage purposes is hereby prohibited.

Section 2. The Congress and the several States shall have concurrent power to enforce this article by appropriate legislation.

Section 3. This article shall be inoperative unless it shall have been ratified as an amendment to the Constitution by the legislatures of the several States, as provided in the Constitution, within seven years from the date of the submission hereof to the States by the Congress.

## AMENDMENT XIX
Passed by Congress June 4, 1919. Ratified August 18, 1920.

The right of citizens of the United States to vote shall not be denied or abridged by the United States or by any State on account of sex.

Congress shall have power to enforce this article by appropriate legislation.

## AMENDMENT XX
Passed by Congress March 2, 1932. Ratified January 23, 1933.

Section 1. The terms of the President and the Vice President shall end at noon on the 20th day of January, and the terms of Senators and Representatives at noon on the 3rd day of January, of the years in which such terms would have ended if this article had not been ratified; and the terms of their successors shall then begin.

Section 2. The Congress shall assemble at least once in every year, and such meeting shall begin at noon on the 3d day of January, unless they shall by law appoint a different day.

Section 3. If, at the time fixed for the beginning of the term of the President, the President elect shall have died, the Vice President elect shall become President. If a President shall not have been chosen before the time fixed for the beginning of his term, or if the President elect shall have failed to qualify, then the Vice President elect shall act as President until a President shall have qualified; and the Congress may by law provide for the case wherein neither a President elect nor a Vice President shall have qualified, declaring who shall then act as President, or the manner in which one who is to act shall be selected, and such person shall act accordingly until a President or Vice President shall have qualified.

Section 4. The Congress may by law provide for the case of the death of any of the persons from whom the House of Representatives may choose a President whenever the right of choice shall have devolved upon them, and for the case of the death of any of the persons from whom the Senate may choose a Vice President whenever the right of choice shall have devolved upon them.

Section 5. Sections 1 and 2 shall take effect on the 15th day of October following the ratification of this article.

Section 6. This article shall be inoperative unless it shall have been ratified as an amendment to the Constitution by the legislatures of three-fourths of the several States within seven years from the date of its submission.

## AMENDMENT XXI

Passed by Congress February 20, 1933. Ratified December 5, 1933.

Section 1. The eighteenth article of amendment to the Constitution of the United States is hereby repealed.

Section 2. The transportation or importation into any State, Territory, or Possession of the United States for delivery or use therein of intoxicating liquors, in violation of the laws thereof, is hereby prohibited.

Section 3. This article shall be inoperative unless it shall have been ratified as an amendment to the Constitution by conventions in the several States, as provided in the Constitution, within seven years from the date of the submission hereof to the States by the Congress.

### AMENDMENT XXII
Passed by Congress March 21, 1947. Ratified February 27, 1951.

Section 1. No person shall be elected to the office of the President more than twice, and no person who has held the office of President, or acted as President, for more than two years of a term to which some other person was elected President shall be elected to the office of President more than once. But this Article shall not apply to any person holding the office of President when this Article was proposed by Congress, and shall not prevent any person who may be holding the office of President, or acting as President, during the term within which this Article becomes operative from holding the office of President or acting as President during the remainder of such term.

Section 2. This article shall be inoperative unless it shall have been ratified as an amendment to the Constitution by the legislatures of three-fourths of the several States within seven years from the date of its submission to the States by the Congress.

### AMENDMENT XXIII
Passed by Congress June 16, 1960. Ratified March 29, 1961.

Section 1. The District constituting the seat of Government of the United States shall appoint in such manner as Congress may direct:

A number of electors of President and Vice President equal to the whole number of Senators and Representatives in Congress to which the District would be entitled if it were a State, but in no event more than the least populous State; they shall be in addition to those appointed by the States, but they shall be considered, for the purposes of the election of President and Vice President, to be electors appointed by a State; and they shall meet in the District and perform such duties as provided by the twelfth article of amendment.

Section 2. The Congress shall have power to enforce this article by appropriate legislation.

## AMENDMENT XXIV
Passed by Congress August 27, 1962. Ratified January 23, 1964.

Section 1. The right of citizens of the United States to vote in any primary or other election for President or Vice President, for electors for President or Vice President, or for Senator or Representative in Congress, shall not be denied or abridged by the United States or any State by reason of failure to pay any poll tax or other tax.

Section 2. The Congress shall have power to enforce this article by appropriate legislation.

## AMENDMENT XXV
Passed by Congress July 6, 1965. Ratified February 10, 1967.

Section 1. In case of the removal of the President from office or of his death or resignation, the Vice President shall become President.

Section 2. Whenever there is a vacancy in the office of the Vice President, the President shall nominate a Vice President who shall take office upon confirmation by a majority vote of both Houses of Congress.

Section 3. Whenever the President transmits to the President pro tempore of the Senate and the Speaker of the House of Representatives his written declaration that he is unable to discharge the powers and duties of his office, and until he transmits to them a written declaration to the contrary, such powers and duties shall be discharged by the Vice President as Acting President.

Section 4. Whenever the Vice President and a majority of either the principal officers of the executive departments or of such other body as Congress may by law provide, transmit to the President pro tempore of the Senate and the Speaker of the House of Representatives their written declaration that the President is unable to discharge the powers and duties of his office, the Vice President shall immediately assume the powers and duties of the office as Acting President.

Thereafter, when the President transmits to the President pro tempore of the Senate and the Speaker of the House of Representatives his written declaration that no inability exists, he shall resume the powers and duties of his office unless the Vice President and a majority of either the principal officers of the executive department or of such other body as Congress may by law provide, transmit within four days to the President pro tempore of the Senate and the Speaker of the House of Representatives their written declaration that the President is unable to discharge the powers and duties of his office. Thereupon Congress shall decide the issue, assembling within forty-eight hours for that purpose if not in session. If the Congress, within twenty-one days after receipt of the latter written declaration, or, if Congress is not in session, within twenty-one days after Congress is required to assemble, determines by two-thirds vote of both Houses that the President is unable to discharge the powers and duties of his office, the Vice President shall continue to discharge the same as Acting President; otherwise, the President shall resume the powers and duties of his office.

## AMENDMENT XXVI
Passed by Congress March 23, 1971. Ratified July 1, 1971.

Section 1. The right of citizens of the United States, who are eighteen years of age or older, to vote shall not be denied or abridged by the United States or by any State on account of age.

Section 2. The Congress shall have power to enforce this article by appropriate legislation.

**AMENDMENT XXVII**
Originally proposed Sept. 25, 1789. Ratified May 7, 1992.

No law, varying the compensation for the services of the Senators and Representatives, shall take effect, until an election of representatives shall have intervened.

# ❧ End Notes ❧

1. *www.rethinkingschools.org/special.../v_seed184.shtml*

2. *thepoliticalenvironment.blogspot.com/.../when-republicans-run-against-epa-they.html*

3. *www.thecuttingedgenews.com/index.php?article=21692*

4. *http://thinkprogress.org/politics/2009/07/21/51962/jindal-stimulus-check*

5. *www.washingtonpost.com?...doma-unconsitutional/.../gJQAnufp4U*

6. *www.redstate.com/.../republicans-should-ride-the-keystone-pipeline*

7. *www.nytimes.com/.../senate-blocks-obama-choice-for-consumer-pan*

8. *www.reuters.com/article/idUSBRE84M13G20120513?irps+932*

9. *www.articles.cnn.com/.../brown.fema.emails_1_international-arabian-horse*

10. *www.newsandsentinel.com/page/mboard.detail/fNav/28.htm*

11. *http://www.politico.com/news/stories/0611/570114.html#ixzz1PNPO5hpa*

12. *http://thinkprogress.org/jsutice/2012/01/04/397589*

13. *http:/www.politico.com/news/stories/0611/57028.html#ixzz1PNgJgl4M*

14. *http://www.cbo.gove*

15. *http:/mediamatters.org/mobile/research/201112200003*

16. *www.justice.gov.osg*

17. *http:/legalblogwatch.typepad.com/legal_blog_watch/2006/12/gerald_fords_su.html*

18. *ww.bls.gove/oco/cg/cgs041.htm*

19. source: 2007 US Military Average Annual Salary Chart

20. *www.usa.gov/Agencies/Federal/Independent.shtm*

21. *The Washington Post*, January 25, 2011 and *The New York Times*, January, 20, 2011

22. *www.nytimes.com?...?l-bureaucrat-bashing-can-lead-to-tragedy-333295*

23. *www.popularmechanics.com/.../obama-annoucnes-54-6-mpg-cafe-st*

24. *www.project.propublica.org/bailout/*

25. *online.wsj.com/.../SB10001424052970204368104577138891310 89)*

26. source: Pioneer Press, August 12, 2011

27. www.nytimes.com/2008/11/03/books/03infl.html

28. http://www.princeton.edu/~bartels/economic.pdf

29. http://geocommons.com/overlays/6806

30. source: *The New York Times* OpEd, August 15, 2011

31. http://multiamerican.scpr.org/2012/05/while-illegal-immigration-from mexico-is-down-legal-immigration-isnt/

32. http://online.wsj.com/article/SB100014240527023035924045773608 33838004406.html

33. www.opensecrets.org

34. www.gop.com/images/legal/2008_RULES_Adopted.pdf

35. source: *The New York Times/CBS* poll, August 4, 2011

36. Center for Responsive Politics

37. www.sfexaminer.com

38. source: *TheWashington Post,* August 9, 2011

39. www.huffingtonpost.com/.../montana-citizens-united-campaign-finance-law_n_1530771.html

40. source: *LA Times*

41. source: Audit Bureau of Circulations, 11/2/2011

42. www.usnews.com

43. source: *MediaBistro.com*, August 9, 2011

44. source: *Sarasota Herald Tribune,* June 7, 2011

45. source: *The Wall Street Journal*, April 26, 2011

46. www.nytimes.com/.../house-passes-ryan-budget-blueprint-along-party-lines.html

47. source: Institute for Democratic Electoral Assistance, 2005

48. http:/computerworld.com/s/article/9217359/Sarah_Palin_fans_tryp_ to_rewrite_history_on_Wikipedia

49. http://www.nationalreview.com

50. see: US Bureau of Citizenship and Immigration Services, www.uscis.gov

51. source: FISA Intelligence Surveillance Act of 1978 as amended in 2008

# ✿ Index ✿

For more information,
checkout the author's blog
at
*www.howourgovernmentworks.com*

CPSIA information can be obtained at www.ICGtesting.com
Printed in the USA
BVOW03s1846080915

417095BV00001B/68/P